China and America

A companion volume by
Foster Rhea Dulles
THE ROAD TO TEHERAN
The Story of Russia and America,
1781-1943

China
and America

The Story of
Their Relations since 1784

FOSTER RHEA DULLES

GREENWOOD PRESS, PUBLISHERS
WESTPORT, CONNECTICUT

Library of Congress Cataloging in Publication Data

Dulles, Foster Rhea, 1900-1970.
  China and America.

    Reprint of the ed. published by Princeton
University Press, Princeton, N.J.
    Bibliography: p.
    Includes index.
    1. United States--Foreign relations--China.
  2. China--Foreign relations--United States.
  3. Eastern question (Far East) I. Title.
  [E183.8.C5D8 1981]   327.51073   81-16
  ISBN 0-313-22146-4 (lib. bdg.)

Reprinted in 1981 by Greenwood Press
A division of Congressional Information Service, Inc.
88 Post Road West, Westport, Connecticut 06881

Printed in the United States of America

10 9 8 7 6 5 4 3 2 1

PREFACE

THE purpose of this book is to tell the story of the relations between the United States and China over a period of more than one hundred and fifty years—from the opening of their trade at the close of the eighteenth century to the conclusion of their common war against Japan in 1945.

Throughout this whole period the two great nations have in general been in friendly accord, yet there have been occasions when the United States has been charged with not fully living up to its professed friendship for China. The American people cannot evade their share of responsibility for the semicolonial status which until very recent times was imposed upon China by the western world. Since the beginning of the present century, we have nevertheless stood committed to the two closely interrelated principles, clearly foreshadowed in all our early dealings with China, of the Open Door to trade and of Chinese territorial integrity. Directly reflecting what has been believed to be our own interests in eastern Asia, these commitments were largely responsible for our entry into the Pacific war.

Now we have once again asserted our determination to uphold a fully independent and sovereign China, and to assist her in every possible way in attaining her goal of becoming a strong, united, democratic nation. Upon our present-day efforts to maintain a friendship more than ever necessary for the peace and stability of eastern Asia and the whole Pacific world, the historic course of Chinese-American relations has a direct and important bearing.

There is an almost overwhelming mass of literature on the Far Eastern policy of the United States. But no attempt has been made to treat as a separate subject our relations with China from the origins of our trade at Canton in 1784 to the present day. It is in many ways a difficult undertaking because our Chinese policy cannot be dissociated from our Far Eastern policy in general. Nevertheless it has appeared to be worth while to center major attention upon China in this book because our attitude toward her has always been the key to our relations with the other countries of eastern Asia, and Chinese-American relations throw a revealing light on the entire history of international developments in that part of the world.

In so far as possible the author has gone to official documents, contemporary records, the personal accounts of actors on the Far Eastern stage and contemporary newspapers for the source materials of this book. His debt to earlier writers, however, remains very great. Some indication of this may be found in the appended bibliography, and he would especially single out the books of such Far Eastern experts as Tyler Dennett, A. W. Griswold, Owen Lattimore, Nathaniel Peffer, T. A. Bisson and Lawrence K. Rosinger in appreciative recognition of their contribution to his own understanding of American-Chinese relations. He would also like to acknowledge an even more direct debt to Jean MacLachlan of Princeton University Press, upon whose suggestion the book was written, and to Marion Dulles for invaluable help throughout the process of writing it.

FOSTER RHEA DULLES

Ohio State University

CONTENTS

I

PIONEERS OF TRADE

ON August 28, 1784, a former privateersman of Revolutionary days, renamed the *Empress of China*, reached the Canton anchorage at Whampoa. She had been sent out on this distant voyage "in the adventurous pursuit of commerce," and from this early period, when America looked to China for teas and silks, until our present-day interest in the immense potential market represented by her more than four hundred million people, trade has been a basic factor in the close ties between the two countries. Our traditional friendship for China grew out of the desire of our pioneering merchants in Canton to promote the commerce inaugurated by the *Empress of China*, and so too did our insistence upon the right to share whatever special privileges other nations exacted from China either by guile or force.

The little 360-ton vessel which first hoisted the American ensign in Chinese waters had made a long and tedious voyage of six months around the Cape of Good Hope and through the Indian Ocean. Her master, Captain John Green, had every reason for proud satisfaction when he gave the foreign shipping already crowded in the Canton anchorage a thirteen-gun salute. Set against the background of the restrictions which Great Britain had imposed on all colonial trade, and the general hazards of navigation in the eighteenth century, his 13,000-mile voyage was a spectacularly daring enterprise in what was for Americans a wholly strange and unknown part of the world.

It had been undertaken with the backing of Robert Morris, financier of the Revolution, and the New York firm of Daniel Parker & Company. Its sponsors hoped not only to make good profits for themselves, but to open up an entirely new trade with the Orient. The *Empress of China* was to point the way to economic independence for the young republic which had so recently won political independence. Recognizing the importance of the venture for the entire country, Congress had given the expedition its blessing and armed Captain Green with an official sea letter. It duly informed the "most Serene, Serene, most puissant, puissant, high illustrious, noble, honorable, venerable, wise and prudent, Emperors, Kings, Republicks, Princes, Dukes, Earls, Barons, Lords, Burgomasters, Councillors . . . who shall see these patents or hear them read," of Captain Green's status as a citizen of the United States of America and requested them "to receive him with goodness and to treat him in a becoming manner."

The cargo of this pioneering vessel was carefully selected to meet the demands of the Canton market. Fur, raw cotton and lead made up part of the goods laden in the ship's hold, but more important were some thirty tons of the curious drug ginseng, collected in the New England woods, which Chinese mandarins fondly believed would restore virility. It was to be exchanged for tea, greatly in demand among all Americans, and also for Chinese cotton goods, silks and chinaware. The total investment in the voyage was $120,000.

Aboard ship as supercargo was a young Bostonian, Samuel Shaw, who had served during the Revolution as aide-de-camp to General Knox. "The terms on which I go," he wrote his brother on the eve of sailing, "promise something clever, and I hope to shake you by the hand in two years." When the *Empress of China* returned to New York fifteen months rather than two years after her departure, this "something clever" had been realized. Shaw had succeeded in trading his cargo for 3,000 piculs* of Hyson and Bohea tea, 962 piculs of chinaware, 24 piculs of nankeens and 490 pieces of silk at an over-all profit of $30,000, or some 25 per cent of the original investment. Even though the financial reward for the owners did not

* A picul is the Chinese "hundredweight," generally equal to 133 1/3 ℔s. avoirdupois.

altogether come up to expectations, the voyage was enthusiastically hailed by New York's *Independent Journal* as "a judicious, eminently distinguished, and very prosperous achievement." The monopoly heretofore enjoyed by the East India Company in supplying America with tea had been broken, and the new commerce of which Robert Morris had dreamed was successfully established.

Within a year of the return of this first vessel in the China trade, five ships sailed for Canton. The *Empress of China* was promptly dispatched on a second voyage; from New York also sailed the *Hope* and the *Experiment*; the *Canton* put out from Philadelphia, and the fifth vessel was the *Grand Turk*, a Salem ship that had already made a voyage as far as the Cape of Good Hope. By 1789, there were fifteen American vessels trading with China, and it was estimated the next year that something like one-seventh of the country's imports was derived from this thriving commerce.

The China trade had been established and developed wholly on the initiative of the merchants involved, but Congress further recognized its importance after the return of the *Empress of China*. Postponements were allowed in paying customs duties on all tea imports, and Samuel Shaw, making a second voyage aboard the *Hope*, was officially designated as our consul in Canton. "Neither salary nor perquisites are annexed to it," wrote John Jay, then Secretary for Foreign Affairs, "yet so distinguished a mark of the confidence and esteem of the United States will naturally give you a degree of weight and respectability which the highest personal merit cannot very soon obtain for a stranger in a foreign land." There was no attempt to open diplomatic relations with the Chinese government, however, and Shaw's consular rank was designed merely to establish his status among the other foreign merchants in Canton.

The early American trade with China was centered upon this southern port for the very good reason that it was the only one to which foreigners were admitted. Even this concession to the insistent pressure of the West had been made reluctantly by the Imperial Government. While the Canton anchorage was crowded with British, French, Dutch and Danish vessels when the first Americans arrived, the activities of "foreign devils" were carefully restricted by the suspicious mandarins. Through the haughty condescension of the Son of Heaven, they were permitted to trade with a selected group of so-called hong merchants, paying heavy tribute for the privilege, and they could maintain residences and warehouses, known as factories, in one closely segregated district along the river bank. They were not allowed, however, to enter Canton itself or to wander about the countryside. Their ships were forbidden "to rove about the bays at pleasure." On only four days of each moon, and then in "droves" of no more than ten at a time, could they visit certain nearby resorts for "refreshment." And neatly grouping arms and females as elements equally likely to disturb the calm of the Celestial Empire, a further regulation stated that "neither women, guns, spears nor arms of any kind can be brought to the Factories."

The Americans were naturally compelled to submit to these confining regulations along with all other foreigners. They were to find them, and especially those relating to trade, increasingly irksome as time went on. Samuel Shaw nevertheless thought the commerce of Canton "to be as little embarrassed, and is perhaps, as simple as any in the known world." However supercilious the attitude of the silk-gowned mandarins, the hong merchants were quite aware of the profitable nature of the trade in which they were engaged, and they were willing to meet the Westerners more than halfway in combating the petty annoyances imposed by officialdom. "As respectable a set of men as are commonly found in other parts of the world . . ." was Shaw's testimony. "They are intelligent, exact accountants, punctual to their engagements, and, though none the worse for being well looked after, value themselves much upon maintaining a fair character."

These American and Chinese merchants got along well from

the very first. Trade was their common interest and it drew them together in spite of all differences in race, background and outlook upon the world. The attitude of the Americans seems to have been singularly free of the racial prejudice which already marked British dealings with the peoples of the Orient. In many instances real bonds of friendship were formed. Just as the Americans considered the hong merchants to be honest and reliable, so did the latter apparently find the Americans fair-dealing and trustworthy. However, an interesting and perhaps highly significant sidelight upon conditions in Canton is revealed in Shaw's account of a conversation with one Chinese merchant:

" 'You are not Englishmen?' said he. 'No.' 'But you speak English word, and when you first come, I no can tell difference; but now I understand very well. When I speak Englishman his price, he say "So much—take it—let alone." I tell him, "No, my friend, I give you so much." He look at me—"Go to hell, you *damned* rascal; what! you come here—set a price my goods?" Truly, Massa Typan, I see very well you no hap Englishman. All Chinaman very much love your country.' "

"Thus far it may be supposed," continues Shaw, "the fellow's remarks pleased me. Justice obliges me to add his conclusion: 'All men come first time China very good gentlemen, all same you. I think two three time more you come Canton, you make all same Englishman too.' "

This was a shrewd reflection. Many Americans undoubtedly swung over to a more superior attitude toward the Chinese as time went on. Moreover, the later policy of demanding for the United States whatever privileges Great Britain could wring from the Imperial Government gave even greater point to the comment that Americans "make all same Englishman too."

The small size of the vessels that pioneered in the China trade became a characteristic feature of our Far Eastern commerce. The brigs and brigantines, sloops and schooners, that were found rounding Java Head and beating their way up the China coast during the fall monsoon seldom displaced more than one or two hundred tons. They were adventure craft, sailing by dead reckoning or the crudest of nautical instruments, and in every instance they were heavily armed against attack by pirates or unfriendly natives. Their crews were young men and boys whose average age was in the early twenties.

The *Experiment,* second vessel to sail for Canton, under command of Stewart Dean, was an 80-ton sloop originally built for trade on the Hudson, and she carried a crew of eight men and two boys; the brigantine *Hope,* which Joseph Ingraham brought into the Whampoa anchorage in 1792, was described as "being only seventy tons and slightly built"; the *Betsy,* commanded by Edmund Fanning, was 93 tons and, among her crew of thirty, not one was over twenty-eight years old; and the *Union,* a sloop-rigged vessel of 89 tons, anchored at Canton in 1795 in the course of an around-the-world voyage under command of twenty-year-old John Boit, Jr. The English sailors aboard the great thousand-ton East Indiamen were constantly amazed at the size and seaworthiness of these tiny craft, and English merchants were no less astounded at the skill with which their youthful masters carried on their trade.

Immense profits were made in the cargoes carried back to the United States. It was nothing unusual for an owner to recover the total cost of his investment in a single voyage. New York, Philadelphia, Baltimore, Boston and especially Salem were the ports principally engaged in the commerce, and imports from China had no little to do with their reviving prosperity in the years after the Revolution. Many a New England fortune, which was later to be invested in cotton mills, was founded upon tea.

Take the voyage of the *Experiment.* Her cargo, assembled at a total cost of £8,860, consisted of 18 boxes of silver dollars, 50 boxes and 15 casks of ginseng, a considerable quantity of furs and several small shipments of tar, turpentine, tobacco, snuff and Madeira. At Canton these goods were exchanged for a return cargo of 308 chests of Hyson tea, 100 chests of Souchong, 80 bales of nankeens and 31 chests of chinaware which sold at New York for £37,000. That same year the *Grand Turk*, from Salem, took out a more varied cargo of goods: kegs of pork, beef and hams; 483 iron bars and 50 cases of oil; boxes of prunes, chocolates, cheese and spermaceti candles, barrels of flour and casks of brandy, and many hogsheads of tobacco, sugar and good New England rum. The total cost was £7,183, but the return cargo of Hyson, Souchong and Bohea teas was valued at £23,218.

Tea, nankeens and chinaware were not the only products brought back from China. Cassia bark and rhubarb were imported, and on private account of owner, captain, members of crew or other individual venturers, a vast miscellany of other goods was packed into the bulging holds of the returning China vessels. Paper hangings, lacquer tea trays, silk handkerchiefs, bundles of hair, boxes of pictures, tubs of candy, china dishes, Canton shawls, floor mats, ivory boxes, satin scrolls—these and many other such articles had their place. As an introduction to Americans of the products of Chinese handicraft, they were an important link between the two countries. Few were the well-to-do households in the Atlantic ports that did not have some such direct evidence of China's existence.

The chief difficulty which American merchants faced in their trade was in finding products for which there was any real demand in Canton. Eventually the problem was solved by the shipment of cotton manufactures, and Lowell sheetings and drillings were exchanged for tea and chinaware. But until the development of the New England textile industry, the China traders were driven to scour the entire world for goods that could be profitably sold to the hong merchants. On the voyage about the Cape of Good Hope, they called at the island of Mauritius, dropped anchor in Indian ports, traded at Batavia in trying to collect a suitable cargo for Canton. Sailing westward about Cape Horn, they exchanged home manufactures all along the South American coast for silver specie.

Far more profitable, however, were the consequences of discovering on the Northwest Coast of America the easy availability of sea otter furs. For these rich and glossy pelts could be cheaply obtained in trade from the Indians, and then sold to the hong merchants at Canton for fabulous prices. Blankets, iron chisels, muskets and rum were the staples in this commerce. On one occasion, however, the Indians were found ready to exchange the fur of a sea otter for a handful of green glass beads, and on another they "instantly stripped themselves, and for a moderate quantity of large spike nails, we received sixty fine skins." Here were profits of which even the tight-fisted Yankee traders had never dreamed.

The voyage of the ship *Columbia*, Captain Robert Gray, opened up this branch of the old China trade at the close of the 1780's. She had been sent out by a group of Boston merchants who had heard of the potentialities of the fur trade and it was quickly found that they had not been exaggerated. After a voyage which first carried the American flag around the world, the *Columbia* and four other vessels then returned to the Northwest Coast in 1790. The discovery of the river to which Captain Gray gave his vessel's name was the most important result of the *Columbia's* second voyage, but the new impetus given to the China trade was a more immediate consequence. Between 1790 and 1818, no fewer than one hundred and eight American vessels visited the Northwest Coast to load their holds with sea otter skins for the Canton market.

Trading along this bleak, rocky and fog-bound shore was highly dangerous. There was not only the constant risk of shipwreck as the little vessels threaded their way through innumerable bays and inlets. The Indians were often even more treacherous than hidden rifts and swift currents. Every ship carried cannon mounted on her deck, and the crew kept close at hand their muskets and pistols, cutlasses and pikes. When the Indians came out to trade in their long canoes, boarding nets were swung out and only a few were allowed to come aboard ship at a time. The treatment accorded the Indians by the whites was in part responsible for the former's hostility, but wherever the responsibility lay, the Nor'westmen learned that eternal vigilance was the price of safety.

Captain Gray of the *Columbia* lost one of his men at Murderer's Harbor on his first expedition, and three of his crew were killed during the second voyage. When Captain John Salter, cruising along the coast in the *Boston* with a cargo of English cloth, beads, looking glasses and rum, made the fatal error of letting too many Indians come aboard, he met even worse misfortune. Only two of his crew survived an attack so sudden that the seamen had no time to seize their weapons. In 1811 the ship *Tonquin* had a similar experience, after a quarrel between her captain and one of the native chiefs had stirred up bad blood. A group of apparently peaceful Indians all at once drew knives from their bundles of furs and cut down the crew almost to the last man in a swift and bloody massacre.

There were other occasions when ships and seamen effected miraculous escapes. Captain Richard Cleveland, trading along the Coast in a 50-ton cutter, was once surrounded by twenty-six canoes, with perhaps five hundred heavily armed savages, as his little vessel lay helplessly becalmed. He loaded his four cannon with bags of musket balls, served out two muskets and two pistols to each of his crew, and fearfully awaited the attack he could hardly hope to repel. The Indians held off until evening, apparently awaiting reinforcements, and when a slight breeze sprang up Captain Cleveland quietly got his vessel under way and somehow succeeded in slipping off in the darkness. His good luck also held another time when the cutter was dangerously impaled on a sunken reef and an attack would have been wholly disastrous. Fortunately no Indians put in an appearance and after spending ten agonizing hours with the vessel canted at a 45-degree angle, "at half past twelve in the night we had the indescribable pleasure of seeing her afloat again."

In spite of all such hazards, there was no daunting the Boston seamen who largely monopolized this trade. They came to know the rocky shoreline of the Northwest Coast as well as they knew their own native New England shores; they explored every inlet and bay from Alaska to California. Their insatiable hunger for the furs which fetched such high prices in Canton was proof against all risks. On the eve of the War of 1812, John Jacob Astor, at this time one of the foremost fur traders in the country, founded Astoria to develop the trade still more intensively. Together with Captain Gray's discovery of the Columbia River, Astor's settlement became a basis for our later claims to the Oregon country. In part a consequence of the demands of the China trade, a new American empire was carved out in the Northwest.

Off the coast lay Hawaii. Its friendly and hospitable climate, and no less friendly and hospitable natives, were tremendous attractions and the Nor'westmen soon began to winter at the islands in the course of their voyages. Moreover, they discovered in Hawaii another product that could be sold in Canton. Special contracts, payable in rum and muskets, were made with King Tamaamaah for collecting sandalwood, and while the Yankee sailors idled on the beaches with the beguiling Hawaiian girls, the natives stored the vessels' holds with this fragrant commodity. It was as a way station on the route between the Northwest Coast and China that Hawaii first became of interest to the United States, starting a train of events that a century later was to lead to annexation.

The hunt for still other products that might appeal to Chinese tastes soon led these pioneers of trade to explore the length and breadth of the whole Pacific. If it were not furs or sandalwood, it might be tortoise shell and mother of pearl, the edible birds' nests that tickled mandarin palates, or *bêche de mer*, a sea slug the Chinese prized for making soups. Again natives would be persuaded to collect these exotic commodities in exchange for so many gross of iron chisels, knives or needles, so many bolts of calico. It all meant just so many more chests of Hyson and Souchong, bales of nankeens, and boxes of chinaware to be brought back to American markets.

There was hardly a South Sea island that the China traders

did not eventually visit. They knew the Marquesas and Tahiti, the Fiji Islands and the Society Islands. Every one of the future Pacific possessions of the United States was a port of call. The Philippines became an important entrepôt for the China market, twenty-three vessels stopping at Manila in the single year 1819; there was frequent trade with the natives of Samoa; Guam was visited on several occasions, and at least one Yankee vessel called at Wake Island. All that distant world which was to be rediscovered by Americans under such dramatic circumstances well over a century later—New Guinea and the Solomon Islands, the Carolines, the Marianas and the Bonin Islands— was familiar to the seamen who trafficked with the hong merchants of Canton. Only Japan, still cut off by her self-imposed barriers of isolation, lay beyond their adventurous province.

Some among the traders sailed farther south, into the frozen waters that washed Antarctica, in still another phase of their restless search for something that could be exchanged for China tea. On many of the islands in these distant regions there were great herds of fur seals whose skins, rivaling those of the sea otter in the Canton market, were to be had for the taking. Every year dozens of little vessels, generally hailing from Connecticut just as the Northwest traders hailed from Massachusetts, anchored off the bleak shores of the Falkland Islands, South Georgia or the Aucklands while their crews went ashore to collect seal skins by the thousands. One ship alone obtained some 80,000, worth $3.00 apiece at Canton, on a single voyage. The cargo of tea for which these skins were traded later netted the vessel's owners $280,000.

The Northwest Coast, the islands of the South Sea, and the seal fisheries played an important part in building up our trade with China, but before too long these resources were exhausted. Avid for the articles to be obtained in exchange for the furs, the Northwest Indians exterminated the sea otters, and the indiscriminate slaughter of the seal herds in the South Pacific was little less disastrous. By this time, however, the products of New England mills were finding a larger place on ships' manifests. The Yankee vessels no longer made the long, circuitous voyages of the eighteenth century but sailed with cargoes of cotton goods directly for China. And just as these more prosaic articles of commerce replaced the specie, furs, sandalwood and sharks' fins of an earlier day, so did tea largely supplant other products in the vessels' homeward-bound cargoes. Cassia bark, rhubarb, crapes and shawls, lacquer and chinaware were still imported, but only in very small quantities.

The annual totals of this commerce fluctuated greatly, but they did not show any notable increase under these new conditions. The number of American vessels calling every year at Canton was somewhere between thirty and forty in the period between 1821 and 1841, and the average annual value of their trade was about $10,000,000. It was no longer handled by ships' captains and supercargoes. Four firms with resident merchants in Canton accounted for the great bulk of the business, and while they still could deal only with the Chinese hong merchants, they otherwise carried on their commercial activities much as they would have in any other part of the world.

The actual living conditions in Canton, and also relations between foreigners and Chinese, nevertheless changed very little. They remained much as Samuel Shaw had found them on his first visit to the port in 1784. The resident merchants had a busy time when the teas were in the market, and the Whampoa anchorage filled with shipping. But for the greater part of the year they lived the monotonous life of exiles barred from any normal association with the people among whom they had been cast. The original restrictions imposed upon the foreign community were only slightly modified. Excursions into the country were occasionally permitted; boat club regattas on the river were allowed. Yet there was really little to do, and when in the summer months the foreigners withdrew to the nearby Portuguese colony of Macao, life was hardly more exciting. One American revealed the continual boredom of living in Canton by recalling somewhat ruefully the endless hours spent in pacing up and down the square in front of the factories for want of any other occupation or amusement. The dreariness of such an existence was somewhat mitigated by its comforts and luxuries, and there was much good fellowship among the exiles, but residents in China made a heavy sacrifice for the material gains they drew from trade.

The rule against bringing foreign women to China was never relaxed during these years. William A. Low, a partner of the well-known Canton house of Russell & Company, tried to evade this restriction upon one occasion and arrived at the American factory with his family. It was a futile gesture. The Chinese authorities declared that all trade with Russell & Company would be stopped "if one Low did not immediately remove his family to Macao." His sprightly twenty-year-old niece was especially chagrined, confiding her opinion of the Chinese to her diary—"good-for-nothing creatures that they are!"

There was apparently no way to remedy these conditions or to break down the haughty indifference of the Chinese officials in refusing to recognize formally the existence of western nations. British embassies sent to the Imperial Court at Peking at the close of the eighteenth century, and again in 1816, returned to Canton without having made any impression upon the mandarinate. The Son of Heaven acknowledged no sovereign with whom he would deal on terms of equality and the foreign missions were casually dismissed as tribute bearers. Trade was allowed only as a generous gesture to peoples so dependent upon the products of China that the Emperor felt moved to compassion in their behalf. Any further concessions were out of the question. "As the dispositions of these said foreigners are depraved by the education and customs of countries beyond the bounds of civilization," read one imperial edict, "they are incapable of following right reason; their characters are formed; their perverse obstinacy is untameable; and they are dead to the influence of our renovating laws and manners."

The attitude of the Chinese officials toward the Americans was further revealed in their original refusal to allow them to raise the American flag over their factory. Permission to do so was eventually obtained through the friendly aid of the East India Company, which had succeeded in winning such a privilege for the English, but the rule was laid down that all future favors sought by the Americans should be requested through the Chinese hong merchants. There were to be none but verbal communications between the United States consul and the Canton government itself.

As a consequence of such regulations, the duties of the consul were limited to administering the estate of any American who might die in Canton, disciplining mutinous sailors, caring for the improvident and reporting to Washington upon trade matters. The latter task was found to be extremely difficult. The independent and mutually jealous merchants had little more idea of cooperating with the official American envoy than had the Chinese themselves. "The secret manner of transacting business at Canton," Consul Samuel Snow reported in 1800, "makes it almost impossible to obtain accurate knowledge of the cargoes in the common way." This was perhaps hardly surprising. The consul was himself engaged in trade and was a business rival.

The first serious controversy involving Americans and Chinese took place in 1821. Under somewhat obscure circumstances, a Chinese woman peddling fruit in a small boat alongside the ship *Emily*, Captain Howland, fell overboard and was drowned. The Americans claimed it was wholly an accident. The Chinese insisted that the death had been caused when a sailor, one Francis Terranova, hurled a jar at the woman. They demanded his surrender on the basis of Chinese law demanding a life for a life. Under threat that if the sailor were not handed over, the authorities would stop all trade, the American community was faced with the important question of whether it should submit to Chinese legal jurisdiction.

Settlement of the question was not left to the consul. A committee of five sea captains, five supercargoes and five resident merchants was appointed to decide it. The policy adopted was one of nonresistance. The Americans refused to surrender Terranova, but they agreed to allow him to be tried by the Chinese, aboard the *Emily*, on a murder charge. The trial was a farce. Terranova was arbitrarily found guilty. The Americans were now more than ever reluctant to give him up for certain execution, but when additional threats of stopping their trade were made, they took a highly equivocal position. If the Chinese attempted to take Terranova by force, they would make no resistance so long as he was assured of another trial in Canton. Within a few days the accused man was consequently seized, and after another farcical trial sentenced to death by strangulation.

"We are bound to submit to your laws while we are in your waters, be they ever so unjust," the American committee had told the Chinese officials after the first trial. "We will not resist them. You have, following upon your ideas of justice, condemned the man unheard. But the flag of our country has never been disgraced. It now waves over you. It is no disgrace to submit to your power, surrounded as we are by an overwhelming force, backed by that of a great empire. You have the power to compel us. We believe the man innocent, when he is taken from the ship we leave her; and the commander strikes his colors."

Such an attitude was bitterly condemned by the English at Canton. The Select Committee of the East India Company, declaring that it should be held "in eternal execration by every moral, honorable and feeling mind," reported that the Americans had "barbarously abandoned a man serving under their flag to the sanguinary laws of this Empire without an endeavor to obtain common justice for him." Yet what could the Americans have done? It was a question of either submitting to Chinese law or losing the right to trade. There was no hope whatsoever of effective support from their own government had they tried to make a more determined stand against

Chinese demands. They were in Canton on sufferance, as individual traders. There was as yet no idea in Washington of formulating, let alone enforcing, a policy that would meet the unusual conditions of our trade in China. This incident was nevertheless to have far-reaching consequences. It dramatically demonstrated an apparently unbridgeable gulf between western and Chinese ideas of justice, and emphasized the necessity of discovering some formula to safeguard the interests of American merchants and seamen. When some twenty years later the first treaty was concluded between China and the United States, the Terranova incident played an important part in our insistence upon the establishment of consular jurisdiction as a means of avoiding any further miscarriages of justice as interpreted by American laws and American judicial principles.

At the time, however, the Americans in Canton were entirely correct in assuming that their government would ignore their predicament. For while the consul made a full report on the Terranova case, no official comment was ever forthcoming. Canton was still too far away for events there to arouse very much concern at home—so long, that is, as the Americans continued to enjoy the advantages of trade.

A hesitant beginning of a broader interest in the Far East could nevertheless be observed as the years went by. An American man-of-war, the frigate *Congress*, briefly visited Canton in 1819. Eleven years later the *Vincennes*, on an around-the-world voyage, paid a more extended call. Significant of the prudent policy being followed by Americans resident in China as a result of the Terranova incident was their warning to the commander of the latter vessel against any infringement of native customs. Only if the greatest care was observed, they declared, could the visits of American naval vessels prove of any benefit in allaying "the petty delays and impositions peculiar to our flag." There was always the risk that if too bold a course were followed, the Chinese would retaliate by cutting off all trade.

Some time after the visit of the *Vincennes*, the frigate *Potomac* and sloop-of-war *Peacock* reached Canton, the latter having as passenger Edmund Roberts, a special agent commissioned by President Jackson to negotiate commercial treaties with Cochin China, Siam and Muscat. As might well be expected, the Chinese had no idea whatsoever of recognizing Roberts' official status or affording him diplomatic privileges. On the contrary, orders were quickly issued that the American warships should "unfurl their sails and return home; they will not be permitted to delay and loiter about, and the day of their departure must be made known. Hasten, hasten!"

Throughout the early years of our trade at Canton, American policy toward China was the policy of the Americans on the ground. And their only concern was that nothing should be allowed to interfere with the trade that actually existed. They were willing to make almost any concession to remain in the good graces of Chinese officialdom, and their caution made them look with serious misgivings upon these visits of United States naval vessels to Chinese waters. Fearful of losing what they had, rather than anxious to gain further privileges, they were always ready to let well enough alone.

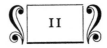

II

EARLY TREATY RELATIONS

WHILE the Americans in Canton were content to accept things as they were during the first sixty years of their trade, a situation of increasing tension had developed between the English and the Chinese by the close of the 1830's. It was to lead to open conflict, to the extortion of new privileges from the Imperial Government and to an entirely new era in the relations between China and the western world. These developments at long last awoke the United States to an official concern over its own policy, and to the conclusion of our first treaty with China securing the right to participate on equal terms in all privileges granted to Great Britain or any other country.

It has already been noted that two British embassies to the Imperial Court at Peking had returned without having won any recognition of their official status. China was more than satisfied with her isolation of the eighteenth century, and saw no reason to admit closer ties with foreign nations seeking to promote their own economic interests at her expense. Moreover, the complacent sense of superiority prevailing not only in court circles but throughout the entire mandarinate made it seem only natural to counter the requests for imperial audiences by simply ignoring them. For so long had the Chinese thought of their country as the Middle Kingdom, and all peoples not of their own race as "outside barbarians," that they blinded themselves completely to any possible values—or strength—in western civilization. Foreign ambassadors would be received only if they acknowledged, through the ceremony of the kowtow—that is, prostration before the Dragon Throne of the Son of Heaven—that the countries they represented were tribute-bearing nations.

Great Britain was unwilling to accept the check to her expanding commercial interests which acknowledgment of Chinese isolation would have meant, and in 1834 once again tried to open up official relations. She did not this time send an embassy to Peking but, seizing the occasion of the abolition of the East India Company's monopolistic privileges, dispatched Lord Napier to Canton as Chief Superintendent of Trade, with instructions to announce his arrival by formal letter to the resident Viceroy. Such procedure directly violated the Chinese regulation that all communications from foreigners should be made through the hong merchants. When Lord Napier, upon reaching Macao, followed his official instructions, the Viceroy refused to accept his letter and peremptorily ordered the English envoy to remain in Macao until the Emperor had been memorialized.

Lord Napier nevertheless went on to Canton. This act of defiance against the laws of the Celestial Empire outraged the Viceroy, and he ordered all trade with the English to be completely stopped. "Considering that the said nation's King has hitherto been in the highest degree reverently obedient," read his flamboyant proclamation, "he cannot in sending Lord Napier at this time have desired him thus obstinately to resist." Hostilities between England and China might well have developed then and there, but Lord Napier found himself in the impossible situation, despite urgent pleas to his government, of lacking all force to maintain his stand. Somewhat as the Americans had surrendered to Chinese threats against their trade at the time of the Terranova incident, he gave up the struggle to secure recognition of his official position and returned in discomfiture to Macao.

Following this affair the old conditions of trade were maintained for five years. In 1839, however, a new conflict developed. Underlying it was the basic controversy over China's refusal to deal with foreigners on terms of equality, but the thoroughly unsavory issue that precipitated the crisis was the opium trade. Almost all the foreign merchants in Canton had been engaged in it, but the Imperial Government, at last aroused to its harmful consequences, suddenly took the drastic step of categorically prohibiting further opium imports and demanded the immediate surrender of all stocks on hand in Canton. The English decided to accept the challenge of such arbitrary interference with their commerce. Captain Charles Elliot, the new Superintendent of Trade, refused to acknowledge the right of the Chinese to confiscate the opium, broke off all trade relations and ordered the English merchants in Canton to withdraw to Macao. In this policy he was supported by his government, in spite of its failure to stand by Lord Napier on a much more justified grievance, and a powerful force of British naval vessels and troop transports soon reached Canton, prepared to obtain "satisfaction and reparation for the late injurious proceedings."

There was no formal declaration of war between England and China, but hostilities continued throughout 1840 and 1841. British military and naval forces destroyed the Chinese forts guarding Canton, the city saving itself from attack only by paying a heavy ransom. The British then moved north and ·captured the ports of Amoy, Tinghai, Chinhai, Ningpo and eventually Shanghai. Fighting with old-fashioned muskets and spears, the Chinese put up a desperate although ineffective resistance against troops far superior in arms and equipment. Only when Nanking was threatened with attack did the Imperial Government finally capitulate and sue for peace. Western arms had breached the ramparts of Chinese self-sufficiency and humbled the arrogance of the Son of Heaven.

The Treaty of Nanking, imposed upon China on August 29, 1842, marked an important triumph for the political and commercial interests of Great Britain in eastern Asia. The occasion presented by the dispute over opium had been seized upon to advance British imperial policies all along the line, and to create a wholly new relationship between China and the western world. The treaty compelled the Imperial Government to recognize the equality of Great Britain; to allow its merchants full privileges of trade not only in Canton but in four additional cities that were to be opened up to commerce—Amoy, Ningpo, Foochow and Shanghai, and to accept in each of these so-called treaty ports the appointment of consuls for the protection of British interests. Moreover, England exacted from China a heavy indemnity and the cession of the island of Hongkong. Whatever illusions the Chinese might still have harbored as to their ability to withstand the pressure of the West, a first step had been taken in the restriction of their independence through superior force.

During the critical period leading up to the outbreak of the Anglo-Chinese hostilities, and also during the course of the war itself, the Americans in Canton observed a careful neutrality. While it could hardly be maintained that the quarrel was none of their concern, for their own interests in China closely corresponded to those of the British, they hoped to ride out the storm without becoming involved in any conflict of their own with the Chinese. As individuals they also were anxious to make the most of the opportunities for trade opened up to them while British commerce was interrupted. Not until the end of the war drew near did they become concerned over the effect upon their own interests of the cessions Great Britain was prepared to demand from the defeated Chinese.

In so far as the immediate cause of the war was concerned— that is, the quarrel over opium—the Americans were only slightly involved. This did not mean that they felt any moral scruples over traffic in this drug. With the exception of Olyphant & Company, whose attitude toward the opium trade and missionary affiliations caused its factory to be known as "Zion's Corner," all other American firms in Canton had made the most of their opportunities to import opium. But the fact was that England exercised a monopoly over all opium grown in India, and with only the limited sources of such Turkish ports as Smyrna available to them, the Americans had been unable to develop an important trade. The East India Company itself reported that the American share in the traffic amounted to only approximately 3 per cent of the total. Under such circumstances, the Americans had little hesitation in complying with the Chinese demand that all opium imports should cease, and they agreed to sign a bond wherein they definitely undertook to have nothing further to do with the proscribed trade.

Our consul during these critical days, Peter W. Snow, made some effort to persuade his countrymen to support the stand taken by the British and to withdraw from Canton in protest against the arbitrary confiscation of existing opium stocks. The American merchants, who were "under no control, subject to no law, except that of self interest," as one of them pointed out, refused to endanger their own position by associating themselves so closely with the British. Robert B. Forbes, of Russell & Company, emphatically told Captain Elliot that he intended to remain on the job in Canton as long as he could "sell a yard of goods or buy a pound of tea."

There was no interruption of normal activity even when war broke out. Except for a brief period while Canton was under blockade, business went on as usual. Indeed, the Americans took over much of the trade normally handled by the British and reaped immense profits while their rivals were standing on the sidelines.

In the meantime, news of these developments reaching the United States had for the first time aroused a real interest in Congress over the status of the Americans in Canton. On the eve of the Anglo-Chinese hostilities, various memorials were submitted, both from the resident China merchants and their home offices, urging that some action be taken to protect our trade. It was first suggested that measures be adopted in co-operation with Great Britain and other nations to compel the Chinese to establish relations on a formal basis, but as tension in the Far East mounted Congress was warned against any policy that might lead the Chinese to associate the Americans with the British in the impending war. In March 1840 the whole question came up for lively debate and Caleb Cushing, a lawyer from Newburyport, Massachusetts, who had close associations with the China trade, introduced a resolution calling for a full inquiry.

Cushing made it clear that while he thought the time might have arrived to attempt to regularize our relations with China, he had no more idea than the Americans in Canton that we should engage in hostilities. "God forbid," he exclaimed, "that I should entertain the idea of cooperating with the British government in the purpose, if purpose it has, of upholding the base cupidity and violence and high-handed infraction of all law, human and divine, which have characterized the operations of the British, individually and collectively, in the seas of China."

His intemperate attitude was inspired both by the widespread belief in the United States that there was no further cause for the Anglo-Chinese war than the determination of England to force opium upon China, and by a general feeling of Anglophobia growing out of boundary disputes over Maine and Oregon. Cushing completely ignored the issue of international equality underlying the dispute in China. He passed over in significant silence the fact that the Americans also had been engaged, even though to a more limited degree, in the nefarious opium trade. What was implicit in his attitude was the fear that unless the United States closely safeguarded its interests, Great Britain might as a result of military victory over the Chinese obtain new and exclusive trading privileges that would seriously hamper our commerce.

There was only one important voice raised to question the general condemnation of British policy in China. John Quincy Adams, whose views may well have been influenced by the fact that he had been Secretary of State at the time of the Terranova incident, looked beyond the immediate controversy over opium to the more fundamental question of China's international relations. In an address before the Massachusetts Historical Society, which the *North American Review* refused to publish, and in subsequent speeches before Congress, he emphatically declared that the real issue at stake in the Far East was China's boasted superiority as seen in the Emperor's ridiculous claim that he was entitled to tribute from all other countries. What was the purpose of the struggle Great Britain was waging in China? In root and substance, Adams stated categorically, it was to obtain the "equal rights of independent nations, against the insolent and absurd assumption of despotic supremacy."

In spite of Adams' stand, our neutrality was sustained and no definite action was taken to implement our Far Eastern policy until hostilities drew to a close. It was then realized that, whatever the rights and wrongs of the war, conditions of trade had materially changed. The United States would have to uphold the interests of its merchants in China if their British trade rivals were not to steal a march on them. The obvious need was to obtain assurances from the Imperial Government that special privileges granted to the British should also be extended on like terms to the citizens of the United States. This principle of most-favored-nation treatment was already embodied in a number of American commercial treaties. Sentiment grew in Congress in favor of seeking its adoption by China in a formal pact that would place the Americans there on an equal footing with the nationals of any other country.

Caleb Cushing took the lead, in the autumn of 1842, in suggesting to President Tyler that a special mission should be dispatched to China to negotiate such a treaty. He reported that he had information, which he must have received from his associates in the Canton trade, that the Chinese would welcome it in a friendly spirit. "The more so," he further stated, "as we can only, by the extent of our commerce, act in counterpoise to that of England, and thus save the Chinese from that which would be extremely inconvenient for them, viz., the condition of being an exclusive monopoly in the hands of England." Responding to such suggestions, the President proposed in a special message to Congress the appointment of a commissioner to the Chinese government, charged with opening up diplomatic relations.

John Quincy Adams gave his support to this proposal and

introduced a resolution in the House for carrying it out. There was some spirited debate before it won Congressional approval. It was maintained, on the one hand, that it would be impossible to overcome the Chinese aversion to entering upon diplomatic relations, and, on the other, that a treaty was unnecessary. Senator Benton waxed sarcastic over the spectacle of an American minister creeping in behind the British minister to claim the protection of Queen Victoria's petticoats, while he bumped "his head nineteen times against the ground in order to purchase the privilege of standing up before his Celestial Majesty." Supporters of the measure declared that our trade with China was of incalculable importance and that every effort should be made to secure its further development. "How much of our tobacco," exclaimed one optimistic congressman, "might be there chewed, in place of opium!"

After final passage of the measure, Caleb Cushing was appointed to be the first American commissioner to the Chinese Empire, with instructions to negotiate a treaty that would make accessible for American trade those ports that had been newly opened up for the British. He was further to impress upon the Imperial Government, "in decided terms and a positive manner," that the United States could not remain in friendly relations with China if greater privileges were granted to any other nationals than to the citizens of the United States.

In addition to Cushing, the mission was to include three secretaries, a surgeon, and four unpaid attachés "to add dignity and importance to the occasion." No presents were to be taken to the Emperor for fear that they would be considered tribute, but a varied collection of scientific objects was assembled to impress upon Chinese officials the wonders of western civilization. There were, among other things, a pair of six-shooters, models of a steam excavator and a steam vessel, a daguerreotype apparatus, a telescope and barometer, several articles made of India rubber, and the *Encyclopedia Americana*. A further impressive touch to the arrangements was the provision of the uniform of a major general for the commissioner. The usual blue coat and gilt buttons, gold-striped pantaloons, and *chapeau* with white plume were to be further enlivened with "some slight additions in the way of embroideries."

Finally, Cushing was to convey to the Emperor a letter from President Tyler which would appear to have been designed to rebuke the high pretensions of the Son of Heaven by lecturing him in the simple language customarily used in notes to petty Indian chiefs. Addressed to our "Great and Good Friend," it carefully listed the names of the twenty-six states of which the Union was composed and then launched forth:

"I hope your health is good. China is a great empire, extending over a great part of the world. The Chinese are numerous. You have millions and millions of subjects. The twenty-six United States are as large as China, though our people are not so numerous. The rising sun looks upon the great mountains and great rivers of China. When he sets, he looks upon rivers and mountains equally large in the United States. Our territories extend from one great ocean to the other; and on the west we are divided from your dominions only by the sea. Leaving the mouth of one of our great rivers, and going constantly toward the setting sun, we sail to Japan and the Yellow Sea.

"Now, my words are, that the Governments of two such great countries should be at peace. It is proper, and according to the will of Heaven, that they should respect each other, and act wisely. I therefore send to your Court Caleb Cushing, one of the wise and learned men of this country. On his first arrival in China, he will inquire for your health. He has then strict orders to go to your great city of Pekin, and there to deliver this letter. He will have with him secretaries and interpreters.

"The Chinese love to trade with our people, and sell them tea and silk, for which our people pay silver, and sometimes other articles. But if the Chinese and the Americans will trade, there should be rules, so that they shall not break your laws nor our laws. . . ."

It was a curious document to be sent to the ruler of an empire whose civilization was old when most of Europe was sunk in barbarism, but the young republic of the West was determined that the Chinese should have no illusions as to its attitude in seeking treaty relations. The letter closed: "Let the treaty be signed by your own imperial hand. It shall be signed by mine, by the high authority of our great council, the Senate."

Armed with this letter, his samples of modern science, and the uniform of a major general with slight embroideries, Caleb Cushing embarked on his mission at the end of July, 1843. A naval squadron of four vessels: the steam frigate *Missouri*, the frigate *Brandywine*, the brig *Perry* and the sloop-of-war *St. Louis*, was to convey him, his secretaries and aides, to China.

Even before the mission had finally been decided upon, a highly significant development had taken place in Canton that paved the way for its success. In October 1842, some six weeks after the signing of the Treaty of Nanking, one of the Chinese delegates at the peace conference, Commissioner Kiying, gave the American community explicit assurances that American interests would be safeguarded under the new conditions resulting from the war. The particulars of foreign trade, he declared, were "to be regulated uniformly by one rule, without the least partiality to be manifested toward any one."

This pledge had been made to Commodore Lawrence Kearny, of the frigate *Constellation*, who had reached Canton just as peace was being concluded between Great Britain and China. Whether his presence in the Chinese port was a matter of chance, or the result of earlier requests for support from the American merchants, is not entirely clear. In any event, Commodore Kearny had quickly sized up the situation and taken it upon himself to enter into communication with Kiying. In behalf of his government, he expressed the hope that as a result of the concessions granted Great Britain, the trade and commerce of the citizens of the United States would be "placed upon the same footing as the merchants of the nation most favored." In so far as Kiying spoke officially, the principle of equality of trade had thus already been adopted by China. It was left to Cushing only to incorporate it in a formal treaty.

Conditions in Canton were almost normal when the squadron bearing the American mission reached Chinese waters in February 1844. Trade was flourishing. The resident Americans found no barriers placed in the way of their usual activities, and with assurance that they too would enjoy all privileges given to the British, they felt confident of the future. On the friendliest possible terms with the Chinese, they consequently looked upon Cushing's arrival with somewhat the same misgivings as they had viewed the earlier visits of American naval officials. Again they were inclined to let well enough alone rather than run the risk, in attempting to persuade the Chinese to sign a new treaty, of stirring up fresh sources of controversy or possible hostility.

Cushing was nevertheless determined to carry out his mission. He wished to conclude a treaty that would permanently guarantee the rights the Americans were enjoying merely on sufferance, and also secure further benefits for their commerce. He was at once conciliatory and firm in his conversations with the Chinese authorities. When he met the stiffest possible opposition to presenting his credentials in person at the Imperial Court, he wisely let that issue drop. On the other hand, he insisted that the Emperor authorize a special commissioner to take up the matter of the proposed treaty. With the backing of the powerful naval squadron at his command, these tactics succeeded in convincing the Chinese of the importance of entering into formal relations with the United States. Kiying was appointed to meet with the American commissioner and negotiate a treaty.

During these preliminaries, Cushing had remained at Macao, but the actual treaty negotiations were held at the nearby Chinese village of Wanghia. They were very brief and conducted in the most cordial atmosphere.

"In drawing up these minutes," Cushing stated in a letter accompanying the draft document he presented to Kiying, "I have not looked to the side of the United States alone. I felt that it would not be honorable, in dealing with Your Excellency, to take a partial view of the subject. I have inserted a multitude of provisions in the interest and for the benefit of China." There was much truth in this statement. Under existing circumstances, the proposed treaty was of perhaps equal benefit and advantage to both nations. Kiying quickly recognized this. After proposing some minor modifications, he accepted Cushing's draft. The final treaty establishing political and commercial relations between the United States and China was signed by the two commissioners on July 3, 1844.

So memorable an event, sealing the friendship of the two peoples, was celebrated at a formal banquet that was replete with Chinese delicacies. The two delegations feasted upon birds'-nest soup, sharks' fins and *bêche de mer*, with generous provision of native wines. Cushing admitted a feeling of "slight languor" the following day, and perhaps Kiying was not himself. He told his American colleague that upon receiving President Tyler's letter to the Emperor, he was so affected by its superlative beauty that "he could not restrain his spirit from delight and his heart from dilating with joy."

The terms of the treaty signed under such happy auspices secured for the United States all those privileges, with the exception of the cession of the island of Hongkong, that Great Britain had obtained in the Treaty of Nanking. Its citizens were given access to the newly opened ports on the same basis as British citizens. They were assured of absolute equality of treatment in the application of fixed customs duties and the enforcement of other trade regulations, together with the right to maintain their own consuls. There were further provisions in the treaty relating to the residence of Americans in the treaty ports, and they were to be allowed not only to establish homes and places of business but also hospitals and churches. On its part, the United States agreed that any of its citizens who tried to trade in ports not open by treaty, or who trafficked in opium or any other contraband, should be dealt with by the Chinese government "without being entitled to any countenance or protection from that of the United States."

In another highly important respect, Cushing obtained concessions that actually went somewhat further than anything granted the British. Amplifying the provisions written into the Anglo-Chinese accord, the Treaty of Wanghia expressly stipulated that American citizens committing any crime in China (other than trading outside the treaty ports or dealing in opium) were to be subject to trial and punishment only by the American consul, and that all disputes or controversies among themselves were to be handled by the authorities of their own government. This undertaking was the basis for all subsequent foreign consular jurisdiction in China, and the foundation for those additional extraterritorial rights that were with time to characterize more and more the relations between China and the western world.

The need for some such provision to avoid dangerous disputes between Chinese and Americans arising out of their different legal and judicial concepts had been first demonstrated when the Canton authorities had executed the sailor Terranova on a charge of murder. There had been other if less dramatic incidents of the same sort. Cushing had felt that some solution to this problem had to be found in the interest of China quite as much as that of the United States. He was convinced that his inclusion of extraterritorial rights in the Treaty of Wanghia was his most important contribution to friendly relations between the two countries. He declared that he had no idea of permanently infringing upon China's sovereignty, but that it would be time enough for China to claim jurisdiction over all foreigners when it was possible for them to travel throughout the country in freedom and safety.

The Chinese made no objection to granting extraterritorial rights in 1844. There was yet no feeling of nationalism among the people. Kiying apparently recognized the reasonableness of the position assumed by Cushing, and he accepted his solution of what had proved to be a very difficult problem. Under the conditions actually prevailing in the treaty ports, it then appeared to be very much to the advantage of the Imperial Government to empower the foreign consuls to administer justice among their own nationals and assume responsibility for their good behavior.

As the original extraterritorial rights conceded by China were expanded by additional privileges wrested through force from an increasingly impotent Imperial Government, the situation as it had existed in the 1840's completely changed. The Chinese came to resent bitterly this infringement upon their sovereignty, especially as every western nation took advantage of it under the most-favored-nation clause of its own treaty. The principles written into the Treaty of Wanghia remained a persistent barrier to China's attempts to recover full control of her own affairs. However justified extraterritoriality may have been at the time, its establishment thus had highly ironical aspects. The result of British and American efforts to compel China to recognize the equality of other nations was to impose upon her an unequal status that she was unable to alter for a full century.

The Treaty of Wanghia was promptly ratified by both China and the United States. The Emperor declared its terms to be "all perspicuous, and entirely and permanently judicious, and forever worthy of adherence." The United States Senate approved it unanimously. Political relations between the two nations, bringing to a close that memorable period when the old China trade had grown and prospered without benefit of diplomatic protection, were entered upon with high hopes that they would lead to still further expansion of our commerce and even closer ties between China and the United States.

III

AMERICAN INTEREST IN THE ORIENT

POPULAR interest in the Orient grew slowly during the days when Yankee traders trafficked in teas and silks at Canton. It was greatly stimulated by the negotiation of our first treaty with China and the opening up of new ports to trade. The lure of eastern markets quickened the imagination, and gradually the conviction was born—to be stubbornly maintained down through the years—that here was the answer to the needs of our expanding commerce. The possibilities of trade with China helped to attract settlers to our western coast. Once California and the Oregon country were acquired, moreover, Asia did not seem to be quite so distant as when it could be reached only by the endlessly long voyage about Cape Horn or the Cape of Good Hope, and the swift clipper ships of the 1850's still further narrowed the broad barrier of the Pacific.

The clippers also brought back from the new treaty ports of Amoy, Ningpo, Foochow and Shanghai something more than so many chests of Souchong, Young Hyson and Bohea; and they took out to those cities more than Lowell drillings and sheetings. There was trade in ideas as well as in commodities. Even though the vast masses of the Chinese peasantry remained wholly ignorant of the United States, and the average American may have thought of the Chinese as outlandish heathen, each nation began to learn something of the other's strangely contrasting civilization. It at least became known in this country that there were such things as Chinese art and Chinese philosophy, and American missionaries began to spread through the Orient some knowledge not only of Christianity but also of the ideas and institutions of democracy. Without overemphasizing the contemporary importance of these developments, a start was made in that attempt to understand each other in which the United States and China are still engaged.

Evidence of the interest in China may be found in the debates and discussion over American occupation of Oregon and California as early as the 1820's. Again and again proponents of our westward expansion put forward the argument that the United States should hold the Pacific Coast as a means of promoting commerce with the Orient. John Floyd of Virginia declared, in 1821, that one of the great rewards for settlement in the Northwest would be control of that trade "which the West has been seeking ever since Solomon sent out his ships in search of the gold of Ophir." A few years later, Thomas Hart Benton told the Senate that the Columbia Valley should be developed as a granary to supply the needs of Asia. He even envisaged the Oregon country, under American rule, as an outlet for Asia's "imprisoned and exuberant population," foreseeing a day when, through the establishment of American institutions on the Pacific Coast, "science, liberal principles in government, and the true religion might cast their lights across the intervening sea."

When an increasing number of pioneers began to trek westward along the Oregon Trail in the 1840's, we find Hall J. Kelly, propagandist extraordinary, repeatedly emphasizing that settlement in the Northwest would enable our China traders to conduct "the full tide of a golden traffic into the reservoir of our national finance." A Senate committee went even further in its halcyon prophecies of future commerce. American tobacco was to take the place of opium for the Chinese people, and American wheat become a substitute for rice. In return for such exports, it was enthusiastically stated, the United States would be able as no other nation to tap the incalculable riches of the East and "all this mighty laboratory whence the world has supplied itself with articles of comfort, luxury and use, will pour itself forth in exchange for the products of the Mississippi Valley."

Such dazzling dreams of oriental trade were not so important a factor in our expansion to the Pacific Coast as the irresistible urge of the American people to occupy new land. Yet these dreams played their part in the westward movement, and they helped to win support for it from the commercial interests of the Atlantic seaboard. Daniel Webster was not alone in looking covetously upon California because of the importance of San Francisco as a great commercial port.

It was then only natural that final acquisition of Oregon and California should even further emphasize our interest in Asia. The original proposals for constructing a transcontinental railroad were put forward on the ground that it would provide an essential link in the trade with China. Asa Whitney pointed out that it would enable New England to transport its products to this great market in thirty days, and "the teas and rich silks of China, in exchange come back . . . in thirty days more." Establishment of a line of mail steamers between San Francisco and Shanghai was also urged in the 1850's. The Atlantic was "a petty and petulant sea" in comparison with the broad and calm reaches of the Pacific, the proponents of this idea argued, and Asia a far greater potential market for American goods than Europe would ever be. The very conservatism of the Chinese was said to be of peculiar advantage in developing this commerce since it "renders it more easy for us to manufacture for them by machinery."

Both railroads and steamship lines were postponed until the 1860's. For in the heyday of the clipper ship it still seemed impossible that steam transportation could actually rival the incredible records the clippers were making in their fast passages from our eastern seaboard to China's distant ports. Indeed, the new links which they forged between America and Asia were at this time as important as those resulting from our expansion to the Pacific Coast. It was long before overland communications and steamships fulfilled Whitney's dream of New England merchandise reaching Chinese ports in thirty days.

The beginning of clipper ships goes back to the late 1830's.

As the tea trade gradually expanded until exports from China to the United States reached an annual total averaging some 16,000,000 pounds, the increasing competition to bring the first cargoes of each new crop to the American market placed a premium on fast transportation. Shipbuilders began to experiment with new types of vessels. Their problem was to obtain more speed from full-rigged ships without too great a sacrifice of cargo capacity. It was from these experiments in meeting the needs of the China trade that the clipper ships gradually evolved. Ploughing their swift furrows across the Pacific beneath great clouds of billowing sail, they ushered in a brief, exciting day in which America enjoyed such maritime fame as never before nor since.

One of the first vessels whose sharper lines and tall, raking masts foreshadowed the extreme clippers of a later day, was the 650-ton *Akbar*, built in 1839 for John M. Forbes. She proved her worth on her very first voyage. Sailing from New York to Canton, she made a passage of 109 days to establish a new record in Pacific sailing. Other ships were soon challenging her laurels. The *Paul Jones,* a vessel jointly owned by Forbes and Russell & Company, made Hongkong 111 days out of Boston; the *Houqua,* named after the well-known hong merchant and built for A. A. Low & Brother, on one exceptional voyage sighted Hongkong 84 days out of New York, and the *Coquette,* another vessel owned by Russell & Company, was 99 days from Boston to Canton. On the return as well, new marks were set up. The *Houqua,* for example, sailed from Canton to New York in 90 days, and the *Paul Jones* once reached New York 76 days after passing Java Head.

These craft and their average runs were in turn surpassed after the appearance, in 1845, of the *Rainbow.* This 750-ton ship built for the New York firm of Howland & Aspinwall is generally accepted as the first extreme clipper. As word got about before her launching of new and revolutionary innovations in design, a sceptical shipping world wondered whether she would be able to sail at all. She soon showed that she could not only sail but leave in her foam-streaked wake any other vessel in the China trade. On her second voyage between New York and Canton, she went out against the monsoon in 92 days, and then, having spent two weeks in taking on her cargo of tea, returned to her home port in 88 days. Making a round trip of six months and fourteen days—in comparison with the fourteen months and nine days of the *Empress of China's* first voyage sixty years earlier—the *Rainbow* brought to her owners the first news of her own arrival in Canton.

So fast were the new American clipper ships of mid-century that after the repeal of the British navigation laws they began to take over the freighting business of English merchants in China. As Shanghai gradually became the center of the tea trade, the start of every season would see a fleet of Yankee merchantmen piling on all possible canvas in a 16,000-mile race to get the first shipments of the new tea crop to London.

Even after the California run had created a still greater demand for speed, which was answered by the creation of such fabulous ships as the *Great Republic* and the *Sovereign of the Seas*, the *Lightning* and the *Flying Cloud*, many of the clippers remained in the China trade. After unloading their cargoes of eastern manufactures in San Francisco, they would cross the Pacific in ballast and take on a cargo of tea for their home ports.

As a consequence both of settlement on the western coast and the high drama of the clipper ship era, Americans looked toward Asia in the middle of the century as they would not again until its close. It was not only China that caught their imagination; but that great country remained the key to the period's expanding interest in the Pacific world. We came near to annexing the Hawaiian Islands as a way station on the road to China, and Commodore Perry's expedition to open up Japan was in part inspired by the need to obtain coaling depots for the new steam vessels on the long voyage to Chinese ports. Looking deep into the future, William H. Seward proclaimed in an often-quoted statement that the Pacific Ocean, its shores, its islands and the vast regions beyond would become the chief theater of events in the world's great hereafter. He even projected the idea that our commerce with Asia, having brought the ancient continent near to us, "created necessities for new position—perhaps connections or colonies there."

Commodore Perry shared these imperialistic views, and his epochal voyage to Japan first raised the question of possible overseas expansion. His all-important objectives, after bringing his "black ships" to anchor in the harbor of Yedo in 1853, were to secure adequate protection for American sailors shipwrecked on the Japanese coast, obtain for the United States the coaling privileges it desired, and to open up Japan for foreign trade. They were successfully achieved in the conclusion of Japan's first treaty with a foreign power. But in his dispatches to the State Department, Commodore Perry also urged American annexation of what were then called the Liuchiu Islands. In the middle of the last century these islands—the principal one now has world fame as Okinawa—were still under Chinese sovereignty. The suggestion that they be annexed was consequently rejected not only on the ground that the United States had no desire for "connections or colonies" off the Asiatic coast, but because it was no part of our policy to infringe upon China's territorial rights. To calm whatever fears Commodore Perry's ambitious imperialism might possibly have aroused in Peking, our commissioner was instructed to assure the Imperial Government that the United States did not have any intention of interfering in Chinese affairs, attacking Chinese sovereignty, or trying to gain a foothold in Chinese territory.

In the gradual growth of other than political or commercial ties between the United States and China, the introduction of Chinese manufactures into American homes was a first and important step in spreading somewhat more broadly a knowledge of oriental civilization. Many of these exotic articles became widely popular. The tremendous vogue for things Chinese that had already made itself felt in both England and

France was reflected in the America of the late eighteenth and early nineteenth centuries. There were not only increasing imports of tea, but, as we have seen, the old China traders brought back varied cargoes of embroidered silk goods, painted chinaware, carved lacquer and curiosities of all sorts. The private ventures of New England merchants on these voyages to Canton revealed how keen was the desire to furnish their houses with China imports. Many a corner cupboard in town and country had its blue and white Nanking ware, its mandarin-patterned porcelain, its dishes and vases hand-painted in Canton. Chinese Chippendale furniture, in heavy mahogany; bamboo chairs and settees; lacquered screens and silk hangings; painted wallpaper with all manner of oriental designs, carvings in ivory and jade . . . these and innumerable other objects graced the homes not only of retired merchants and sea captains, but of countless other families which had direct or indirect associations with the old China trade. Of how many Boston or Salem homes could it not be said:

> O'er our cabinets Confucius nods
> 'Midst porcelain elephants and China gods.

A more general interest in China was demonstrated by the popular enthusiasm over the remarkable Chinese collection established in Philadelphia by Nathan Dunn in 1839. The objects assembled represented every phase of Chinese civilization. There were life-size figures in native costumes, models of streets and houses, scenes of manufacturing and farming and examples of the handicraft of Chinese artisans. The collection was visited by throngs, widely discussed in the press and magazines.

Chinese visitors to the United States, although very few actually came to this country until after California gold rush days, were another link with the Orient. Cantonese who had shipped as deckhands or stewards aboard American ships, were a not altogether unfamiliar sight along the docks of New York, Philadelphia, Boston and Salem. In 1809, John Jacob Astor succeeded in slipping one of his vessels through the current trade embargo by representing a Chinese member of the crew as an important mandarin. The early return of this official to Canton, the shrewd fur merchant persuaded President Jefferson, could not be delayed without prejudicing American-Chinese relations! Some of the traders brought home Chinese servants. John P. Cushing, retiring in 1830 after many years' residence in Canton, is reputed to have had a whole retinue of them. There is also the record of a Chinese girl brought back by some sea captain and exhibited in a New York theater, where her bound feet created a sensation.

Five or more Chinese boys were enrolled as students at the school established in Cornwall, Connecticut, in 1816 for the education of Indians and other "heathen youth" as missionaries. Contemporary accounts indicate that the experiment was not highly successful. All but one of the Chinese appear to have been dismissed for misconduct of one sort or another. However, a youth named Lieaou Ah See, regarded as the first Chinese convert to Protestantism, returned as a Christian to his native land. The school was closed in 1827 after two of the Cherokee Indian students married white girls in Cornwall.

Some knowledge of China gradually reached the public through books and magazine articles. The journal of Lord Macartney's embassy to Peking in 1793, as well as another account of this mission by his valet, was published in this country. There were a number of firsthand American records of visits to China, including Samuel Shaw's journal, and many exciting narratives of Pacific voyages to the Northwest Coast and South Seas. Both *Hunt's Merchants' Magazine* and *Niles' Register* had frequent articles dealing with the Canton trade, and there were occasional descriptive essays in other periodicals. Generally speaking, however, little authentic information about China was available for the average person, and fundamental misconceptions about the nature of Chinese civilization characterized the few references to it in geographies and school texts. As late as 1867—and comparable statements may, indeed, be found in much more recent books—one geography stated that "half-civilized" people like the Mexicans and Chinese had towns and cities, cultivated the soil and exchanged products, and then concluded dogmatically that they "have few arts and little intelligence."

There is important evidence of the impact of oriental thought in intellectual and literary circles. Even aside from the new and firsthand knowledge of eastern civilizations that the China traders brought back with them from Asiatic ports, their distant voyaging in the Pacific had a stimulating and quickening effect on the New England mind. It helped to break the bonds of colonial dependence on England; it opened up new and distant horizons. Somewhat as the voyages of Elizabethan seamen stirred the imagination of all England, so did these ventures to China, the South Seas and the East Indies create a new awareness of a larger world in early nineteenth century America.

The influence of the Orient on transcendentalism is well known. The *Bhagavadgita,* the *Upanishads* and the classical writings of Confucius and Mencius were widely read in translation by the philosophers of Concord. And apart from such evidence of the spell cast by the ancient faiths of Asia, almost all the New England writers, and many from other parts of the country, had an intimate association with the new commerce that was spreading throughout the Pacific and opening up the world of China.

Melville voyaged on Pacific whalers to visit the islands of the South Seas, and the father of Nathaniel Hawthorne was an East India sea captain. Thoreau knew well the tales of returning travelers, and many phrases in *Walden* show how familiar he was with the Canton trade. When he wanted an example of commerce, it was natural that he should begin: "If your trade is with the Celestial Empire . . . ." Even before he began reading the oriental classics, we find Emerson making references to what was happening in the East, and in this early period poking fun at "the mountainous nonsense of Chinese diplomacy." Washington Irving was inspired to write of the fur trade between China and the Northwest Coast in *Astoria*, and Cooper drew upon the voyages to the South Pacific in *The Crater*.

In the cultural influences which flowed from the United States to China, the role of missionaries was far more significant than that of the traders. The latter had few personal associations except with hong merchants and factory servants. They very seldom learned Chinese. The American Protestant missionaries, however, became the medium for the transmission of western culture in all its many manifestations. As early as 1834, one of them was instructed by his home board not only to employ his medical skill in relieving the afflictions of the people, but to be ready to give them "our arts and sciences."

The first American missionaries to China, David Abeel and Elijah C. Bridgeman, reached Canton in 1830. They had been given passage in one of the ships of D. W. C. Olyphant, whose zeal for missionary enterprise, as already noted, earned for his factory the name of Zion's Corner, and they began at once upon the heroic task of converting the Chinese to Christianity. Within a few years the American Board of Commissioners for Foreign Missions, the Presbyterians, the Baptists and the Episcopalians had sent additional men to this foreign field. In close cooperation with English missionaries, they were busily engaged in translating the Bible into Chinese, distributing tracts among the natives, establishing schools and preaching the gospel. Among these pioneers were such men as Samuel Wells Williams, whose book *The Middle Kingdom* became a classic account of Chinese civilization; W. A. P. Martin, another author as well as missionary; Peter Parker, the first medical missionary and later an American diplomatic representative; and Issachar J. Roberts, a Baptist evangelist whose principal convert was later to become the leader of the Taiping Rebellion.

After 1844, this slowly growing band of missionaries extended their activities to the new treaty ports, and under the protection assured through treaty provisions they began to expand their work. There was no disposition on their part to forego any privileges obtained from the Chinese government through force of arms. As time went on, indeed, the missionaries became fully as zealous as the foreign merchants in insisting on their rights, and they continually exercised strong pressure on their home governments to secure additional concessions. Their demand for protection both for themselves and for their Christian converts, after mid-century based upon the toleration clauses of a new American-Chinese treaty, led to what became known as the "gunboat policy" of supporting missionary enterprise. It was always a great source of friction with the Chinese officials. The bitterness roused in some quarters by aggressive missionary tactics was illustrated toward the close of the century by the outburst of Prince Kung, the Minister of Foreign Affairs. "Take away your opium and your missionaries," he exclaimed, "and you will be welcome."

Some eighty-eight American Protestant workers had arrived in China by 1860, and they had established stations in all of the treaty ports. They organized a Society for the Diffusion of Christian and General Knowledge; set up printing presses with the aid of the American Bible Society to publish Bibles, religious literature and tracts; and started not only schools but also a number of colleges. Even the education of girls fell within their province, the Methodists establishing in 1859 the Baltimore Female Seminary at Foochow.

Missionary influence either in this mid-century period or in later years is difficult to evaluate. Although some few of the Chinese persuaded to accept the new faith were eventually to play an important role in their country's life, the number of converts to Christianity among the great masses of the people was negligible. More significant was the part played by missionaries in spreading other western ideas and practices, and the subsequent impetus given to secular education and reform. As the principal channel through which China gradually learned more of the West, the missionaries were preparing the ground for the revolution that was to lead to the overthrow of the Manchu dynasty and establishment of a Chinese republic. Their activities were not by any means the sole cause for these later events. China finally began to adapt herself to the modern world as a consequence of the general impact of the West upon her national life in many different forms—military, political and economic as well as cultural. Nevertheless, the influence of American missionaries helped materially to shape the course of future events.

It is interesting to note that references to the United States in Chinese histories of this period reflected a very favorable view of American institutions. This was true of the first of such accounts in the *Hai Kuo T'u Chih* of Commissioner Lin, the official who in 1839 had seized the foreign opium stocks, and also of the book by another mandarin named Sen Ki-yu. In a striking eulogy of Washington, the latter credited our first President with proposing the election of men to public office and then commented: "Where in the world can be found a mode more equitable?"

In some respects quite as important as the role of the missionaries in teaching the Chinese the ways of the West, was their part in interpreting to Westerners the ways of China. Through books, official reports and other publications, including the *Chinese Repository* which was founded as a medium for explaining Chinese culture, they added greatly to American knowledge of China. As many of the missionaries came from small towns and were supported by local church communities, new ties were also formed with China in parts of the country that had formerly had no contacts whatsoever with the Asiatic world. The curiosity over things Chinese, at first largely confined to the Atlantic seaboard, gradually spread more widely through the Middle West. A basis was established for a national interest in China quite apart from economic considerations.

Although the United States had not hesitated to compel China to grant it the commercial privileges which Great Britain had secured from the Imperial Government through war, and the missionaries themselves stubbornly insisted upon full protection for their rights however they had been obtained, an underlying American sympathy for China was progressively strengthened during those mid-century days. It led to a sense of national obligation to aid in the rejuvenation of the Chinese people. Practice all too often failed to conform to our lofty ideals, but the concept of helping China along the difficult path of adjusting herself to western civilization was never wholly forgotten.

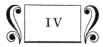

REVISING THE TREATIES

THE Treaty of Wanghia had established the permanent bases of American policy toward China. Its provisions for extraterritoriality and most-favored-nation treatment provided a framework within which it was hoped our trade would continue to grow and expand. Events in the Far East during the 1850's were to put these principles to the test against a troubled background of war and civil strife that nearly caused the collapse of the Chinese Empire. While our growing national interest in eastern Asia was being reflected in the voyages of the tea clippers, missionary enterprise in China and Commodore Perry's expedition to open up Japan, diplomacy also wrote a new chapter in American-Chinese political relations that had both important and far-reaching consequences.

Neither the Emperor nor the Imperial Court had fully accepted the implications of the concessions that China had been compelled to make to the western powers after her defeat in the Anglo-Chinese war. Basic differences in their concepts of law and treaties were a barrier to full understanding between China and the West under the best of circumstances, and circumstances were not of the best. The officials charged with the conduct of foreign relations skillfully evaded all possible treaty obligations. The foreign envoys were not allowed to go to Peking; efforts to communicate directly with the Emperor were completely blocked. The attitude of the mandarins remained one of indifference to all matters of trade and commerce. The privileges that had been granted, they felt, need not be taken too seriously. In spite of the shattering impact of England's military might, China's outlook had changed very slightly. In stubborn complacency, her rulers believed that the unwelcome importunities of the West could somehow still be ignored.

The terms of the Treaty of Wanghia definitely provided for direct diplomatic relations between the United States and China. But again and again the Imperial commissioner in Canton, who was also the Governor-General of the southern provinces, politely rejected the approaches of our diplomatic envoys. When Humphrey Marshall, the American commissioner in 1853, requested an interview upon reaching China, he received the bland reply that while the Imperial commissioner was "exceedingly desirous" for such a meeting, it was hardly possible: "I, the minister, am at present at the Shaouchow Pass, and I, the governor, having superintendance of everything, have not the slightest leisure." A year later Marshall's successor, Robert M. McLane, was put off with an equally baffling rebuff. "Just at this moment I, the Minister," read the official notice, "am superintending the affairs of the army in several provinces and day and night have no rest. Suffer me then to wait for a little leisure, when I will make selection of a propitious day, that we may have a pleasant meeting."

The propitious day never arrived. Neither Marshall nor McLane could make any impression upon what the former angrily declared to be the elusive mandarin's "ridiculous exclusiveness and arrogant pretensions of superiority." Each in turn soon realized that the Imperial commissioner's "want of leisure" was a deliberate policy, upon implicit orders from Peking, to avoid any direct contact with the foreign envoys. Marshall would have liked to counter these rebuffs by proceeding to the north and insisting upon direct communications with the Imperial Court, but he lacked the military or naval support without which such a gesture would have been completely futile.

The situation in which the foreigners found themselves grew particularly vexatious in Canton. Anti-foreign feeling remained strong in this port where the English and Chinese had first come into open conflict. Treaty guarantees of protection were of little avail when the local officials completely shut their eyes to them. Trade was hampered at every turn, access to the city of Canton was arrogantly refused, and neither Americans nor British felt their lives were safe. Increasing friction almost inevitably led to open clashes and, as a decade earlier, England was prepared to use force in protecting and expanding her interests.

The incident which brought matters to a head was the seizure by the Canton authorities of some Chinese sailors aboard a British-registered ship, the *Arrow*, in October 1856. When the Imperial Commissioner refused to make amends for this insult to the British flag, naval operations were at once commenced and Great Britain and China found themselves involved in hostilities which were to become known as the Arrow War.

The Americans in Canton, conforming in turn to their policy on earlier occasions, tried to maintain a careful neutrality. After their withdrawal from Canton, however, a boat flying the American flag was fired upon by the Chinese forts guarding the outer defenses of the city. Commodore James Armstrong, in command of our naval forces in Chinese waters, refused to let this attack pass without retaliation and returned the next day to bombard the forts. An apology by the Chinese officials for firing on the American flag prevented this collision, however, from having any further serious repercussions, and American forces did not again intervene in the continuing hostilities between the British and Chinese.

As evidence of our official policy of avoiding conflict with the Chinese, even though it might mean standing aside while England contested for what were quite as much American as British rights, Commodore Armstrong was mildly rebuked for his forceful action. Secretary of State Marcy wrote our commissioner in China that President Pierce was not happy over the situation. "I think he is inclined to regret," Marcy said, "that there had not been more caution on the part of our naval force in the beginning and more forbearance in the subsequent steps."

The Americans on the ground felt quite otherwise. The incident was interpreted as conclusively proving that only a display of military power could persuade China to acknowledge her international commitments. It was believed that the time had long since arrived when the United States should make it clear to the Chinese that for Americans, as well as for the British, injury added to insult in the treatment of foreigners would not be tolerated. "Diplomatic intercourse can only be had with this government," McLane forcefully declared, "at the cannon's mouth."

As for conditions farther north, they were marked on the one hand by the spectacular growth of Shanghai as the principal center for foreign trade, and on the other by increasing difficulties, not alone the fault of the Chinese authorities, in administering commercial regulations. When Marshall arrived at this thriving port in 1853, he found a community of 271 foreign residents who already had their own hotel, bank, hospital, church and newspaper. With some seventy-one American vessels visiting it in a single year, he was convinced that Shanghai was "destined to become the greatest city of Eastern Asia, and most intimately of all connected with America." Yet conditions were in many ways chaotic. In spite of the fact that our treaty with China had outlawed the traffic in opium, a smuggling trade had arisen with the connivance of Chinese officials; there were widespread graft and corruption in the collection of duties on legitimate imports, and no adequate provision had been made for maintaining order among American sailors. The last-named problem was a responsibility of the United States Government under the extraterritoriality terms of the treaty, but the disgraceful brawls and drunken rioting in the Shanghai foreign community had become notorious. It was true that the Chinese were either unable or unwilling to carry out their obligations under the treaties, but the attitude of the Americans, as well as other foreigners, revealed little of the spirit of cooperation that could alone have made the new treaty arrangements workable.

The immediate situation in either Canton or Shanghai was overshadowed in the early 1850's, however, by far more important developments that for a time cast in doubt the whole basis of our relationship with China. It was in these mid-century years that China was swept by the bloody scourge of the Taiping Rebellion.

This great revolt, breaking out in the general vicinity of Canton in 1849, reflected the underlying discontent of the Chinese masses with Manchu rule. It was inspired in part by the failure of the imperial authorities to protect China from the western barbarians and foreshadowed later upsurges of nationalistic feeling directed against both the Manchus and other foreigners. Thousands of peasants were attracted to the banner of its visionary leader, Hung Hsui-chuan, and they had gradually swept northward in a victorious march to the Yangtze Valley. There they had set up, in 1853, a new government, in sharp defiance of the Son of Heaven. The movement had a pseudo-religious as well as political character. Hung Hsui-chuan had come under the influence of the Baptist missionary, Issachar J. Roberts. Interpreting as revelations from Heaven the visions that came to him during the epileptic fits to which he was periodically subject, Hung became convinced that he was himself a second Son of God, a divine younger brother of Jesus Christ. The rule which he established at his capital in Nanking, where twenty thousand Manchus were slaughtered in consolidating his authority, was to revive the ancient glories of China through establishment of the Taiping Tienkuo, or Heavenly Kingdom of Great Peace.

The Manchu bannermen and other imperial forces had been unable to halt the advance of these fanatical rebels who laid waste villages, massacred the peasants and cut down all forces sent against them. Dominating the Yangtze Valley, they menaced Shanghai and attempted to march farther north to Peking itself. "Any day may bring forth the fruits of successful revolution, in the utter overthrow of the existing dynasty," Commissioner Marshall reported home in April 1853. But the attitude of the foreigners was for a time one of hope rather than fear. Disregarding the excesses that had marked the rebels' northward march and the tyrannical nature of Hung Hsui-chuan's government, they believed that the Taipings had truly adopted Christianity and that their triumph might mean a new day for China and the breaking-down of her hostility to the West. These optimistic views, crossing the Pacific, were reflected in President Pierce's annual message to Congress. "The condition of China at this time," he declared, "renders it probable that some important changes will occur in that vast empire which will lead to a more unrestricted intercourse with it."

Missionary circles both in China and at home showed even more sympathy for the Taipings. The professions of religious faith made by Hung Hsui-chuan were taken very seriously. He had summoned Issachar J. Roberts to Nanking "to assist in establishing the truth." While his missionary mentor was not to reach the capital until several years later, when disillusionment had already set in as to the nature of the Taiping movement, this invitation was regarded as proof of the rebel chieftain's sincerity.

Among Americans whose interest was trade and commerce, the conversion of the Chinese to Christianity did not seem so important, but what appeared to be the impossibility of working with the Imperial Government made them welcome the prospect of any other regime replacing it. There was also the belief in some quarters that the Taipings might overthrow the Manchu dynasty, but would then prove incapable of maintaining their own nationwide control. And the expected result was the break-up of China, and new opportunities for the foreigner. "It will not be many years," a writer who held this point of view wrote in the *North American Review*, "ere we find European influence, hitherto so powerless in the high exclusive walls of Peking, operating with wonderful force at the courts of a score of kingdoms, petty in comparison with the great aggregate of which they once formed a part . . . ."

Although Marshall had himself predicted the overthrow of the Manchus, he soon reached the conclusion that such an event would be wholly inimical to American interests. He was prepared to run counter to general foreign opinion in China, and also to American opinion at home, in urging support of the Imperial Government. It was not that he had any love for the mandarinate at Peking. He believed it to be impotent, ignorant and conceited. But the Taipings were no better, in his opinion, and they had no real idea whatsoever of the functions of government. The consequence of their triumph would be internal chaos, Marshall believed, inspiring the other powers, notably Great Britain or Russia, to try to win control over a prostrate country lying "like a lamb before the shearers, as easy a conquest as were the provinces of India." What would then happen to American rights and privileges, he asked; how could the United States safeguard its interests?

"Whenever the avarice or the ambitions of Russia or Great Britain shall tempt them to take the prizes," Marshall reported, "the fate of Asia will be sealed, and the future Chinese relations of the United States may be considered as closed for the ages, unless *now* the United States shall foil the untoward result by adopting a sound policy. It is my opinion that the highest interests of the United States are involved in sustaining China—maintaining order here and engrafting on this worn-out stock the healthy principles which give life and health to governments, rather than to see China become the theater of widespread anarchy, and ultimately the prey of European ambitions."

Since the United States had been promised most-favored-nation treatment in the development of its trade, it appeared logical to Marshall to seek to support the government that had made this pledge. His stand in the 1850's was exactly that which Secretary Hay was to take at the close of the century. The Open Door doctrine, and its corollary of sustaining China's political and territorial integrity, could not have been more clearly forecast. Ironically enough, considerations involving that nation whose attack on China almost a century later was to draw us into war in defense of our traditional policy, served somewhat to tie Marshall's hands. He was unable to secure the cooperation of the commander of our naval forces in the Far East in upholding his policy because Commodore Perry wished to keep clear of all possible entanglements in China while trying to open up Japan.

At the same time, Marshall did not wish to bolster up the Manchu regime without a guarantee of additional commercial privileges. This did not mean any sort of territorial concessions. "An interference by the United States in Chinese affairs," he wrote, "would have no object but to preserve the nationality of China; to revivify her, to elevate her people, and to stimulate them to win augmented happiness by a proper and peaceful, but scientific, employment of their natural energies." Yet the conditions for such development, in his opinion, were that the entire Yangtze Valley should be thrown open to trade, full freedom accorded for religious worship and international relations placed upon a practical basis with establishment of a ministry of foreign affairs at Peking.

Only in one highly limited respect did Marshall find an opportunity to support the imperial authorities. In September 1853 a band of rebels, formerly associated with the Taipings but at this point acting independently of them, attacked Shanghai. They made no attempt to invade the foreign settlement, where hastily enrolled volunteer troops stood on guard, but they easily won full control of the Chinese city. With the complete collapse of all authority, the question arose as to whether the foreigners, zealously pursuing their trade in spite of war and turmoil, were under any obligation to make their usual customs payments or otherwise observe their treaty obligations. In the face of the wavering attitude of the British, who still regarded the Taipings with considerable sympathy, Marshall took the unequivocal stand that the United States would in so far as possible act to uphold the authority of the Imperial

Government and protect its rights in so important a source of revenue as customs collections.

"It is my purpose," he stated, "to perform, punctiliously, every obligation assumed by the United States under the treaty, and to refrain from embarrassing the public administration of Chinese affairs by throwing unnecessary obstacles in the way. No precedent, no example furnished by other powers, will induce me to forego the faithful and honest execution of our plain international obligations."

His stand compelled the British to modify their attitude and eventually swing over wholly to the American position. They could not afford to do otherwise in the light of possible reestablishment of imperial authority. Also, they were gradually beginning to feel that British interests, quite as much as American interests, would in the long run be best served by the maintenance of Manchu rule rather than by any further extension of that of the Taipings. After a period during which Marshall had collected in behalf of the Chinese government all tariff duties owed by Americans, the issue appeared to be solved with reestablishment of imperial control over the local custom houses.

This was the measure of Marshall's intervention in Chinese affairs and soon afterwards he returned to the United States. The customs house business had, however, an important sequel. When the new American commissioner, Robert M. McLane, reached China in April 1854, the imperial authorities had once again been forced to abandon revenue collections, and as far as the foreigners were concerned, Shanghai had become virtually a free port. The British were now fully prepared, however, to cooperate with the Americans in maintaining the stand Marshall had originally taken. A system was consequently worked out, perhaps on British suggestion but pressed most vigorously by McLane, whereby a foreign board of customs inspectors was established. The duties this board collected were to be handed over to the agents of the Imperial Government, thus assuring Peking of the revenue of which it was being deprived by the inability of local officials to handle the situation.

If the immediate importance of this move was the proof it afforded of the desire of the Anglo-American powers to uphold the Manchu regime, its long-range significance lay in what was to prove to be the permanent establishment of foreign control over the collection of duties in the Chinese treaty ports. As in the case of the grant of extraterritoriality itself, the creation of this Inspectorate of Maritime Customs was at the time designed to safeguard Chinese quite as much as foreign interests. It had the full approval of the Imperial Government. But also like extraterritoriality, control over customs collections was to become a deeply resented infringement of Chinese sovereignty. For despite the mounting insistence of the Chinese in later years that they were capable of handling their own affairs, the powers refused to relinquish what had proved to be a highly advantageous privilege. It was not until 1930 that China finally succeeded in recovering her right both to determine her own tariffs and to collect her own customs duties.

Marshall and McLane were also involved in these years in the complicated negotiations which provided a basis for establishment of Shanghai's International Settlement. Although set against a background of civil war and constant threats to the security of the foreign community, this issue did not actually involve either the Taipings or the Imperials. The Chinese government had already set aside an area in Shanghai where foreigners could settle, with enjoyment of the extraterritorial rights to which their treaties entitled them, and the real question at stake appeared to be whether it was to be wholly controlled by the British. Questions of land titles and consular jurisdiction created continual conflict, and the Americans felt that their rights were being ignored. The solution finally worked out provided for joint control over the area ceded by the Chinese through establishment of a foreign municipal government, deriving its authority from the Chinese government but wholly independent of it under authority of the several powers' extraterritorial rights.

It was first proposed that all Chinese be expressly forbidden to live in what became the International Settlement, and one of the provisional regulations of its municipal code laid down such a ban. Marshall stubbornly opposed this plan. Such a regulation, he declared, was "wholly objectionable as creating invidious distinctions against the Chinese, and exercising exactly the spirit of exclusiveness towards them which we now complain of when exercised towards ourselves." Once again he won his point. Marshall's sometimes angry resentment of the haughty pretensions of the Manchu mandarinate did not lead him to ignore the rights of the Chinese people. He ably defended American interests during his brief stay in Shanghai, but on broad grounds that sought also to promote what he believed to be the well-being of China.

The problems involved in establishing the International Settlement had, in any event, been so reasonably handled that McLane was able to report in 1854 that the new system of government was working out to the mutual benefit of both foreigners and Chinese. "The concurrent and joint action of the consuls and the local authorities of China," he wrote, ". . . [have] established a fundamental basis on which the rights and privileges of all are firmly planted."

In dispatching McLane to China, the State Department had instructed him to investigate the Taiping regime at Nanking with the possible view of granting it *de facto* recognition. This policy accorded with the general sympathy for the rebels in the United States, but McLane was quickly convinced that Marshall's attitude was the far sounder one. For all its efforts to maintain order and institute reforms, the Taiping government appeared to be losing control of the situation at Nanking. Internal rivalries that were later to lead to a reign of bloody lawlessness had already become a weakening influence, and debauchery was widely prevalent in court circles. Moreover, when McLane sought to get in touch with the minister of foreign affairs, to arrange a visit to Nanking, he was treated with little respect. "If you do indeed respect Heaven and recognize the Sovereign," the American commissioner was told, "then our celestial court . . . will most assuredly regard your faithful purpose and permit you year by year to bring tribute. . . ."

Any idea of dealing with the Taipings was now completely dismissed, but the Imperial Government's continued disregard of its treaty obligations led to renewed insistence that Peking somehow be compelled to provide more protection for foreign trade. McLane consequently soon received instructions from Washington to demand a revision of the Treaty of Wanghia in accordance with its own provisions for review after twelve years. He was directed to proceed north, in company with the British envoy, to the mouth of the Peiho River, leading to Peking, and there enter into negotiations with the imperial authorities. This mission was not one whit more successful than previous attempts to deal directly with the court. The Imperial Government was dangerously threatened by the Taipings. Its very existence appeared to be at stake. But the mandarins saw no reason to make further concessions to "foreign devils" for whom they had no more love than they had for "the long-haired robbers" of the Yangtze Valley. The demand for treaty revision was abruptly refused. The inhospitable treatment meted out to the two envoys graphically demonstrated the unchanging attitude of the court in spite of its misfortunes at the hands of domestic rebels.

McLane was incensed. The reward for the measures which both he and Marshall had initiated to sustain the imperial authority at Shanghai was a humiliating and ignominious rebuff. Should the Emperor persist in his obdurate refusal to consider revision of the treaties, he now recommended that all the principal rivers of China should be placed under naval blockade "until the commercial privileges of buying from and selling to persons in China, without limitation or restraint, is respected, and all the other treaty stipulations recognized and enforced. . . ."

Compelled to resign because of ill-health soon after this un-lucky northern expedition, McLane gave over his post to Dr. Peter Parker, the former medical missionary in Canton. The new commissioner was even more aggressive in his demand for bringing pressure upon the Imperial Government. An imperialist of the Seward and Perry school, he was anything but averse to the idea of taking advantage of China's recalcitrance for obtaining an American territorial foothold in eastern Asia. In December 1856, he specifically proposed that the United States take over Formosa (England and France being urged at the same time to occupy other territory) and hold the island until full satisfaction was obtained for injuries done Americans or the American flag.

The State Department disapproved of all suggestions for forceful action or for seeking to gain a territorial stake in China. It might prove necessary to increase our naval forces in Chinese waters to assure greater respect for American rights, Secretary Marcy declared, but "the President will not do it for aggressive purposes." The desirability of treaty revision was fully recognized in Washington, but it was to be obtained, if at all, by peaceful persuasion rather than any threat of force. Moreover overtures from England and France for joint action to present a united front against China were rejected. The United States, as we have seen, would take no part in the hostilities that had already broken out at this time between England and China in the so-called Arrow War, and it was determined at all costs to pursue a policy of friendly neutrality in all phases of its Chinese policy.

Nevertheless a highly anomalous situation was rapidly developing. England and France were resolved to force the Imperial Government to revise its treaties, and a highly unfortunate train of events was soon to lead to what is known as the Anglo-French war with China. President Buchanan, coming into office in 1857 in succession to President Pierce, at one and the same time declared his sympathy for Anglo-French aims and his refusal to give them any armed support.

William B. Reed was sent out to China in the new capacity of envoy extraordinary and minister plenipotentiary, to place him on a level with the other foreign envoys, with instructions to cooperate with the British and French envoys, but under no circumstances to let such cooperation involve the United States in any hostilities.

In 1858 the curious spectacle was consequently presented of the American minister, together with the Russian minister who had somewhat comparable instructions, accompanying the British and French ministers to the mouth of the Peiho, and calmly standing aside while Anglo-French naval forces battered down the Taku forts which guarded the river's approaches. As the British and French ministers then proceeded triumphantly upstream in a vessel flying both their national flags, Reed and his Russian colleague followed more sedately in a steamer flying American and Russian ensigns. Negotiations were then held at Tientsin between the chastened plenipotentiaries of the Imperial Government and the envoys of both the belligerent and neutral nations, which resulted in a complete revision of China's treaty relations with the western world.

The major interest of the United States in these negotiations, as Humphrey Marshall had first declared, was to secure more binding guarantees for the protection of American lives and property, additional opportunities for trade through the opening of the Yangtze ports, full religious toleration for both missionaries and their converts and direct access to the Imperial Court at Peking. These objectives were obtained and through application of the most-favored-nation clause, such additional privileges as Great Britain and France secured were also shared by the Americans. Trade with the interior was largely opened up, and, most important, China was restricted to levying no more than a 5 per cent duty on imports, to be wholly collected by the foreign-controlled Inspectorate of Maritime Customs. Included in the new tariff schedules was a customs duty on opium, in effect legalizing a traffic which the Americans had formerly declared to be contraband.

It is true that in negotiating the Treaty of Tientsin the United States sought to demonstrate its continued friendship for China. It was expressly stipulated that "if any other nation should act unjustly or oppressively, the United States will exert their good offices . . . to bring about an amicable arrangement of the question. . . ." Yet we made little effort to safeguard what even several members of the American mission considered China's justified rights. We not only held ourselves aloof while England and France struck a disastrous blow at Chinese sovereignty by forcefully compelling treaty revision, but after the deed was done, we claimed our share of the plunder. Whatever may be said as to China's bringing of such treatment upon herself through her own supercilious and arrogant attitude, the role of the United States had very little to commend it.

The treaty was signed on June 18, 1858, and duly ratified by the United States and Chinese governments. Normally this would have meant an end to the matter, but the formal exchange of ratifications brought up once again the bitterly disputed issue of the reception of foreign envoys at the Imperial Court. When the United States minister especially deputed to exchange ratifications, John E. Ward, reached the mouth of the Peiho in company with the other foreign envoys charged with the same mission, it quickly became apparent that Peking was not prepared even yet to receive these emissaries on terms of equality. Barriers placed across the river's mouth barred the entrance of the foreign vessels.

The situation confronting Ward closely paralleled that with which Reed had been faced just a year earlier. For while the United States was not prepared to use force in breaking down this new show of Chinese resistance, both Great Britain and France were ready to do so. So once again the Americans stood aside while the Anglo-French allies attacked the Taku forts. On this occasion, however, an unexpected incident marred the otherwise perfect picture of our magnanimous neutrality. When the Allies were unexpectedly repulsed in their assault and the English admiral wounded, Commodore Tatnall of the

U.S. Frigate *Powhatan*, the vessel which had brought Ward north, went to the rescue and American sailors briefly helped to serve the guns on a British ship. It was an occasion which gave birth to a famous phrase, Commodore Tatnall reputedly shouting "Blood is thicker than water" as his men went to the Englishmen's aid.

The risks of further hostilities caused the British and French envoys to return to Shanghai for reinforcements after this encounter, but when Ward was informed that he would be allowed to proceed to Peking by another route, he pursued his mission independently. The Chinese provided carts for his party and it reached the capital without further incident. Only then did our envoy learn, as still another ironical touch in this long battle over diplomatic usage, that these carts were the traditional conveyances for the emissaries of tribute-bearing nations.

Ward nevertheless stanchly upheld national dignity when the Emperor insisted that if he were to be received at court, he should comply with the custom of the kowtow. "I kneel only to God and woman," was his proud reply. As the Chinese refused even to accept his conciliatory undertaking "to bend the body and slightly crook the right knee," he thereupon left the capital. If the issue were so important as a matter of prestige to the Chinese, Ward felt he could make no further compromise. The treaty ratifications were exchanged, however, at the coast.

It was left to England and France, for the third time, to assume the responsibility of enforcing the demand for recognition of international equality. After another and successful attack on the Taku forts, Anglo-French troops marched overland to occupy Peking. Once in the capital they callously looted the city and, in stern retribution for alleged Chinese atrocities, burned down the Emperor's rich and splendid Summer Palace. The Imperial Government now had no alternative other than complete surrender and unreserved acknowledgment of the right of diplomatic residence in Peking.

It may well be asked what attitude was being taken toward the Taipings while this war was fought against the Imperial Government. In sharp contrast to their policy in the north, the western powers were in central China doing what they could to uphold the Manchu dynasty. Although they did not intervene officially in the civil war, which continued to rage bitterly for all the alarms and excursions on the international front, they lent their tacit support to Peking's campaign against the Taipings and allowed their nationals to enlist in the imperial armies. Once the Emperor had been forced to make the concessions they considered so essential to their own commercial interests, the powers were then all the more convinced that reestablishment of the Manchu dynasty's control over central China had become necessary for Asiatic peace.

An American played an important role in the aid given the imperial troops. Frederick Townsend Ward, soldier of fortune, was supported by both the American and British envoys in Shanghai in raising a heterogeneous force of westerners, Filipinos and Chinese to wage war against the Taipings on a contract basis. With the promise of substantial bounties for every city he recovered from the rebels, Ward led his little army to a series of spectacular victories that for the first time made serious inroads on Taiping power in the Yangtze Valley. A colorful, romantic figure, who went into battle carrying only a walking stick, as casually as if he were on an afternoon stroll, this adventurous Yankee won the devotion of his men for his unfailing courage as well as military skill. The Chinese showered him with honors. His successes, however, were not destined to continue for very long. In an attack against one of the rebel strongholds in 1862, he was fatally wounded. What had become known as the Ever Victorious Army lost its driving force and appeared about to break up.

Its work had proved so effective that the American and British envoys were not willing to let Ward's death bring this form of foreign aid to an end, and they persuaded the imperial authorities to name a new commander for the Ever Victorious

Army. Eventually Major Charles G. Gordon, of the British forces in China, took over the post and in the final suppression of the Taiping Rebellion, following a succession of imperial victories in 1864 and 1865, "Chinese" Gordon and his troops played a notable part.

Torn between the conflicting desires to maintain the friendship of the Chinese and to secure new trade privileges, the United States had followed a policy that was neither war nor peace in these complicated developments in North China. To some degree we had exercised a restraining influence upon the rapacity of the other powers. We had definitely taken the lead in supporting the Imperial Government against the Taipings. Yet we had also sought to attain the same objectives for which England and France went to war, stood aside while they brought the Chinese to terms, and then insisted upon the right to enjoy the new privileges which the Imperial Government had been compelled to concede.

"The English barbarians," the Imperial Commissioner wrote the Emperor about this time, "are . . . full of insidious schemes, uncontrollably fierce and imperious. The American nation does no more than follow in their direction."

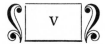

THE BURLINGAME MISSION

In the years following the negotiation of the Treaty of Tientsin, the people of the United States were far too deeply absorbed in their own civil war to pay much attention to what was happening in China. During this period, and in immediate postwar days, our minister in China nevertheless made a determined effort to re-establish the friendly relations with the Imperial Government that had been so severely strained by the events leading to the Anglo-French war and the forceful revision of the earlier treaties. The United States pioneered in promoting a cooperative policy among all the western powers which sought to substitute for the coercion of the 1850's fairer and more equitable treatment of China. Our willingness to share in the concessions obtained at the cannon's mouth was to be justified through throwing our national influence behind the movement to carry to the Chinese people "the blessings of Christian ethics, Christian science, and Christian civilization."

Secretary of State Seward was in full sympathy with these objectives in our policy toward China. His deep interest in the Pacific has already been noted. Convinced that it was the great theater of future events, he sought in every possible way, after the close of the Civil War, to extend American influence throughout its entire area. The purchase of Alaska in 1867, which he engineered almost singlehandedly, was linked with his ambition to make the United States the dominant naval power in the Pacific and the controlling force in Far Eastern trade. While his critics ridiculed "Seward's Folly" and "Seward's Ice-Box," the far-seeing Secretary of State stoutly maintained that Alaska and the Aleutian Islands were destined to become a drawbridge between America and Asia.

It was reported that his soaring imperialism looked beyond

Alaska and the Hawaiian Islands, which he also tried to annex, even to the shores of China itself. But there is no evidence that he actually contemplated trying to obtain any Chinese territory and his attitude toward China was uniformly friendly and conciliatory. In visiting that country after his retirement from the State Department, he had to meet the complaints of the "old China hands" that he had not upheld American interests in the Far East with sufficient force. "I think we are obliged to conclude from all these premises," he answered in surveying existing conditions in China, "that a policy of justice, moderation and friendship is the only one that we have had a choice to pursue, and that it has been as wise as it has been unavoidable. . . . The United States cannot be an aggressive nation . . . least of all against China."

For all Seward's support, our cooperative attitude in China still remained far more the policy of our minister in Peking than that of the State Department. For between 1861 and 1868—and it was the first time an American envoy had remained in China for more than the briefest period—the United States was represented by a man who felt the greatest sympathy for the Chinese people and who was endowed with the qualities of leadership that caused his ideals largely to dominate the diplomatic circles of the Chinese capital. Anson Burlingame became one of the key figures in the general development of our Far Eastern policy, and even more important than his actual achievements was the new spirit of cordiality that he introduced into American-Chinese relations.

He arrived in Shanghai in October 1861 as the power of the Taipings was finally waning. He gave his full support to Frederick Townsend Ward and the Ever Victorious Army, convinced as his predecessors had been that the Taipings stood only for "blasphemy, massacre and pillage." He then proceeded north and established residence in Peking, the first American minister to be accredited directly to the Imperial Court. The Emperor had but recently died, following his flight from the capital upon the approach of the Anglo-French forces in 1860, but Burlingame at once took up the problem of smoothing out Chinese-American relations with Prince Kung, who had been appointed to head the newly established Tsungli Yamen, or Ministry of Foreign Affairs. He also held frequent conversations with his diplomatic colleagues, working out the new cooperative approach which he had been instructed to adopt.

"The policy upon which we agreed," Burlingame was able to report to Secretary Seward by June 1863, "is briefly this: that while we claim our treaty right to buy and sell and hire in the treaty ports, subject, in respect to our rights of property and person, to the jurisdiction of our own governments, we will not ask for, nor take concessions of, territory in the treaty ports, or in any way interfere with the jurisdiction of the Chinese Government over its own people, nor ever menace the territorial integrity of the Chinese Empire."

The United States, for all its somewhat pusillanimous attitude in 1858, was ready to do everything possible to sustain China's independence. Burlingame was carrying another step forward the policy initiated by Caleb Cushing and reaffirmed by Humphrey Marshall. He was also pointing the way toward the policy of John Hay and Henry Stimson and Cordell Hull. Acting upon the thesis that the cause of peace in the Far East could be best served if the western powers "could agree among themselves to the neutrality of China," he hoped to establish a hands-off policy, leaving the Middle Kingdom free to work out her own adjustments to the impact of the West upon her traditional ideas and ancient customs. As in every phase of our Chinese policy, the underlying motive behind this cooperative approach was to safeguard the commercial interests of the United States. We were looking toward trade. Nevertheless Burlingame, perhaps more than any other statesman concerned with our position in eastern Asia, had also the best interests of China at heart and sincerely hoped that it would be possible to "engraft western upon eastern civilization, without a disruption of the Chinese Empire."

There were obviously many serious obstacles in the path of continued international cooperation in China. It depended in the first instance upon the willingness of the diplomatic envoys in Peking as a group to exercise a large measure of patience. Many of the Chinese officials were still unreconciled to dealing with the western powers on terms of equality, and others with more liberal views could not wholly grasp the implications of the new international situation. Fortunately for Burlingame, he found among the representatives of England, France and Russia men who were willing to follow his lead and who could work together. But there was always the danger that less enlightened statesmanship on the part of any single foreign envoy would upset the whole program—unless, and such an eventuality was remote in the 1860's, coercive pressure could be brought against the nation adopting aggressive measures. Secretary Seward recognized the somewhat precarious basis of cooperation. He told Burlingame, however, that President Lincoln fully approved of what he was doing, felt that his ideas should be given a fair trial and hoped that the sympathetic support which the other foreign envoys were giving his program would "render its continuance afterwards a cardinal fact in the policy of all the maritime powers."

There were various ways in which Burlingame was able to make his influence felt in Peking, and he succeeded in winning both the confidence of his diplomatic colleagues and the grateful appreciation of the Imperial Government. He stood out resolutely against all proposals that China should be induced to make further concessions in the treaty ports, and on several occasions served as a mediator in the controversies that inevitably arose with the Chinese authorities. He sought to help the Chinese in understanding the West by sponsoring the translation of a text on international law, and with a long view toward the future, he engaged the services of an American geologist, Ralph Pumpelly, to make the first survey of China's coal resources. In the protection of our own immediate national interests, he persuaded the Tsungli Yamen to refuse permission for Confederate cruisers, notably the *Alabama*, to take refuge in Chinese ports during their Civil War forays upon American commerce in the Pacific.

The full measure of Burlingame's services was attested when, as the time approached for a possible further revision of treaty relations in 1868, China sought his aid in presenting her case to the western world. Knowing that he was about to resign his post at Peking, the Imperial Government asked him to head a Chinese mission, in his private capacity as an American citizen, to visit the United States and then proceed around the world on a goodwill tour. With some doubts and misgivings Burlingame accepted this post as a special minister "for the management of China's diplomatic relations." Two mandarin officials were associated with him in the undertaking, and the mission further consisted of some thirty Chinese, including six student interpreters, and two foreign secretaries.

Its objective, or perhaps more accurately Burlingame's objective, was to strengthen the basis of the cooperative policy in China by securing more direct support for it from the governments concerned. Even when trying to act in good faith, the imperial authorities often found themselves unable to carry out the terms of the new treaties. Unless Washington and London, Paris and St. Petersburg, more clearly understood the difficulties under which the Chinese officials labored, they might easily be led to insist upon the impossible. As already suggested, moreover, the anti-foreign elements in China were still powerful. The Imperial Court itself had by no means altogether shed its old attitude of arrogant superiority, and there had been strong opposition in some quarters to the very idea of the Son of Heaven demeaning himself by sending a mission to foreign countries. Burlingame wished to arouse popular sympathy for China and thereby prevent any reversion to a policy of force, which on the pretext of upholding international equality would take advantage of Chinese political and military weakness to demand new concessions.

News of the dispatch of the mission was generally hailed in this country both as a sign of China's new forward-looking attitude and of the helpful role the United States was playing in the national development of the Chinese people. "Of all the great powers who have had treaties with them," the *Nation* wrote, "America stands alone as their constant friend and adviser, without territorial aspirations, without schemes of self-aggrandizement—the unpretending but firm advocate of peace and justice." If this encomium on our foreign policy happily overlooked our insistence upon all rights enjoyed in China by other nations, however derogatory of Chinese sovereignty, it was still true that the United States had been more friendly toward China than any European power, and sacrifice of the privileges claimed on a most-favored-nation basis would not necessarily have benefited China in any way. It would—at this time or in later years—have in effect forced our withdrawal from the Far East and left China even more at the mercy of western imperialism.

Burlingame and the two Chinese envoys arrived in San Francisco in April 1868 and were greeted by the residents of that city with immense enthusiasm. Curiosity naturally played its part in drawing out the crowds which welcomed these first official visitors from the Middle Kingdom, but there was no question of the general attitude of friendliness. Indeed, from the moment of its first landing, the mission's progress across the country was a series of popular ovations. Upon arriving in Washington, its members put up at Brown's Hotel on Pennsylvania Avenue and for the first time in any American city, there was flung to the breezes the huge yellow flag bearing the imperial dragon which was the standard of the Son of Heaven. The Chinese attracted public attention wherever they went and created a sensation at the entertainments offered them by Washington society. "Whether in the public assembly or the fashionable soiree or in the domestic circle," a contemporary observer wrote with unconscious condescension, "they were everywhere at ease. Their gracefulness of manner, their unpretending and cordial politeness, their ready wit and pleasantry were subjects of general remark."

They were received by President Johnson at the White House with customary ceremony and then entertained at an elaborate state dinner. Both houses of Congress held receptions for them with a welcome that was said to rival the ovations given Lafayette and Kossuth. After such impressive ceremonies at the capital, they went on to visit the cities of the Atlantic seaboard. The leading citizens of New York gave them a great banquet with the governor of the state in the chair; in Boston the City Council entertained them and Emerson was among the speakers. If Burlingame had ever had any qualms as to the mission's reception by the American public, they had long since disappeared. It had won a popular triumph.

Throughout the tour Burlingame served as the spokesman for his Chinese colleagues, and he made a series of memorable speeches calling upon the nations of the West, and particularly the United States, to continue the policy of friendly cooperation. He eloquently declared that China was ready and anxious to receive envoys of western civilization, to develop trade relations with all foreign countries and generally to adjust herself to the nineteenth century world of factories and machines, railways and steamship lines, in accordance with her own developing needs.

China wished to live at peace with the rest of the world, Burlingame told his audiences. She asked only respect for her neutrality and for the integrity of her territory; she sought merely a generous and Christian construction upon the treaties she had signed under the compulsion of war. And in return she was prepared to come forth from her centuries of seclusion and meet the West on terms of mutual goodwill.

"I aver that there is no spot on earth where there has been greater progress made within the past few years than in the Empire of China," this American spokesman for the Imperial Government declared in a notable address in New York. "She has expanded her trade, she has reformed her revenue system, she has built or established a great school where modern science and foreign languages are to be taught. . . . She finds that she must come into relations with this civilization that is pressing around her, and feeling that, she does not wait but comes out to you and extends to you her hand. . . . She tells you that she is willing to trade with you, to buy of you, to sell to you, to help you strike off the shackles from trade. She invites your merchants, she invites your missionaries. She tells the latter to plant the shining cross on every hill and in every valley."

"Let her alone; let her have independence," Burlingame pleaded; "let her develop herself in her own time. She has no hostility to you. Let her do this and she will initiate a movement which will be felt in every workshop of the civilized world. . . . The imagination kindles at the future which may be, and which will be, if you will be fair and just to China."

These were fine, brave words; and a moving appeal for international equality between the West and the East. They aroused an immediate response in the United States. "What a grand spectacle," exclaimed one congressman caught up by Burlingame's oratory, "to witness the four hundred millions of Chinamen, as it were, stopping in the long tide of centuries, resting on their oars and catching across the ocean the sounds of republican America, the hum of their machinery, the scream of their whistles, the roar of their trains, and all the multitudinous voices of progress so familiar to us."

A glowing vision, but did it in any way conform to realities? Among foreigners in the Far East, those who were actually engaged in trade and commerce in China, there was an immediate and overwhelming protest. Burlingame was drawing such a favorable and optimistic picture of conditions that it could not be recognized. He was placing the China problem before his audiences in a completely false light, wholly misrepresenting the Imperial Government's attitude both toward foreigners and toward trade. There was no recognition whatsoever in Burlingame's talks, it was said, of the feeling of superiority toward all Westerners that still held sway in court circles, of the anti-foreignism that pervaded so much of the mandarinate, and of the generally apathetic if not definitely obstructive attitude toward what the West considered progress. The old China hands declared that stay-at-home Americans were being blinded to "the imbecility of the government and the real barbarism that prevails among a large portion of the population."

The controversy that raged in the press and magazines between Burlingame's supporters and his critics generally reflected a basic difference as to the policy the United States should follow in the Far East. It was the old issue of friendly and patient cooperation on China's own terms, as opposed to forcible insistence upon the rights and privileges to which American merchants—and missionaries—felt themselves entitled. Still, there was no question that Burlingame had been carried away by his sympathy for the Chinese to overplay his hand, and to depict their country in the roseate hues of his own hopes rather than in the drab colors of reality. He overlooked or ignored every instance of reactionary opposition to foreign innovations; he magnified beyond all reason such slight evidence as there was of a more progressive spirit. The Chinese people had not yet awakened in 1868 to any true desire to adapt their ancient civilization to western ways. They felt no compelling interest to develop foreign trade. Nothing could have been more wildly distorted than the picture of China asking America "to plant the shining cross on every hill and in every valley."

The real power in China at this time was that remarkable woman, the Empress Dowager Tzu Hsi, who completely dominated the Imperial Court, with only one interval of nominal retirement, from the early 1860's until after the opening of the twentieth century. She was the last of the great Manchu rulers, both loved and feared by her subjects. Only her firm hold on the reins of power sustained the dynasty as the dry rot of corruption and decadence, to which her own behavior contributed, prepared the way for the collapse that was to overwhelm it so soon after Tzu Hsi's death. For all her shrewdness and native ability, moreover, the Empress Dowager had a complete blind spot in so far as China's international relations were concerned. The strong anti-foreign feeling of the court even in 1858 was in part attributed to her influence, and she was never to become reconciled to the need for treating the nations of the western world on terms of equality. In the constant conflicts between her more forward-looking ministers and the anti-foreign reactionaries, it was the latter who could more generally count upon her support. She epitomized the innate conservatism of China, looking down with traditional scorn upon merchants and traders, opposing the introduction of modern means of transportation and seeking in every way to resist the persistent encroachments of western civilization.

Her approval of the Burlingame mission had not been based upon the idea that it should be an instrument for promoting further trade with China or encouraging missionary enterprise. On the contrary, she hoped it would ward off all such activity and forestall additional foreign demands. In direct contradiction to so much of what Burlingame was saying, supposedly in the name of the Imperial Government, the real Chinese attitude is revealed in a contemporary secret memorial to the throne from a high-ranking official. Concessions in regard to building railroads and telegraph lines, opening the rivers to steamboat transportation and further promoting trade in the interior, this document emphatically stated, would be disastrous for China. If the Imperial Government should again be compelled to give in through the superior force of western arms, the memorialist declared, the myriads of common people "in the extremity of their poverty would see how they could better themselves and rise to oppose the foreigners in a manner that all the authorities in China could not curb or repress."

A few years later both the arrogance and ignorance of Chinese officialdom were tellingly revealed in an important memorial from the Censor Wu K'o-tu, upon which the Empress Tzu Hsi approvingly cast "the Sacred Glance." It dealt with the disputed question of an imperial audience and actually advised concessions. But on what grounds? The foreign envoys were so far beneath contempt that it was unseemly for the

Throne to wrangle with them over matters of etiquette which they were incapable of understanding.

"They think only of profit, and with the meretricious hope of profit they beguile the Chinese people," this memorialist stated. "These men know not even the meaning of duty and ceremony, wisdom and good faith, yet we profess, forsooth, to expect them to act as if they were endowed with the five cardinal virtues! They know not the meaning of the Heaven-ordained relationship between Sovereign and Minister, between father and son, husband and wife, elder and younger brother, friend and friend—yet we propose to require them to conform to the five principles of duty. It seems to me that one might as well bring together dogs and horses, goats and pigs, in a public hall and compel these creatures to perform the evolutions of the dance!"

Burlingame at no point admitted the wide gulf still separating China and the western world as he so grandiloquently proclaimed the need for closer cooperation in our foreign policy. The situation, indeed, had a curiously paradoxical aspect. China was unwilling to recognize the equality of the foreign powers even though events had cruelly demonstrated their material superiority, and in trying to force upon China formal acceptance of such equality, the West was actually imposing upon her a degrading inferiority. The Chinese did not have the practical wisdom, and the West did not have the magnanimity, to make international equality a reality. Burlingame was vainly seeking to establish a relationship that circumstances in both the East and the West rendered impossible throughout the nineteenth century.

There was, however, one concrete result from his mission in the United States. In July 1868 a new treaty, or rather an amendment to the Treaty of Tientsin, was signed at Washington by the Chinese envoy and Secretary of State Seward. Its general articles, strengthening the provisions already incorporated in earlier treaties and once again disavowing any intention on the part of the United States to intervene in China's internal affairs, were not of great importance. There was, however, one innovation. The two nations mutually agreed to recognize "the inherent and inalienable right of man to change his home and allegiance, and also the mutual advantage of the free migration and emigration of their citizens and subjects, respectively, from one country to the other, for purposes of curiosity, of trade, or as permanent residents."

To the implications of this encouragement of immigration we shall return. It is sufficient to note at this point that the clause in question, incorporated in the treaty upon the suggestion of Secretary Seward rather than of Burlingame, clearly demonstrates that far from there being any official objection to the entry of Chinese laborers into this country in 1868, a principal objective of the treaty was to promote such immigration. Within a few years a quite different attitude was to prevail, and the United States adopted a policy aimed at the exclusion of all Chinese. These conditions were not foreseen when Burlingame and Seward so confidently signed their new treaty.

The Chinese mission left the United States soon after signature of this pact to proceed on its tour of the European capitals. In London it met a reception almost as cordial as that encountered in this country, and the British government officially assured Burlingame that it had no intention of applying any unfriendly pressure upon China. Paris and Berlin were somewhat cooler in their attitude and neither government would make any definite commitments as to their policy. The visit to St. Petersburg brought the mission to a tragic end. Burlingame was stricken with pneumonia and died in February 1870. While his Chinese colleagues went on to Brussels and Rome, no further efforts were made to enter into negotiations with the European governments.

In so far as relations between the United States and China were concerned, the Burlingame mission had served greatly to increase American interest in China. It both strengthened the traditional sympathy of the public for the Chinese people, and fortified the popular belief in the immense potentialities of the China market. Yet by raising far too high the hope for more practical cooperation on the part of the Imperial Government, and by painting a much too promising picture of China's progress along the road to internal stability and reform, it led to keen disappointments and a subsequent decline in the friendly relations it had hoped to promote.

Had Burlingame lived to return to China, the results might have been more favorable. Yet it is highly improbable that he could have done very much to convince the imperial authorities of the wisdom of the policy he had so sincerely proclaimed in their name. The Empress Dowager and her advisers interpreted the conciliatory attitude of the western powers as a sign of weakness. They were actually encouraged by the reception of the mission in the United States, and also in Great Britain, to believe that they need not be too conscientious in carrying out the terms of the treaties that had already been imposed upon them. Their resistance to foreign pressures was actually intensified. They renewed their efforts to block any further encroachments of a civilization they still considered so inferior to their own.

Burlingame's successor at Peking, J. Ross Brown, soon bore startling witness to this intransigent attitude. "An impression seems to have obtained in the United States that the government of China is peculiarly friendly to our country," he wrote soon after signature of the 1868 treaty, "and that great advantages to our commerce are about to accrue from this preference. . . . I need scarcely say these anticipations are without foundation. The government of China may have preferences; but it has no special regard for any foreign power. The dominant feeling is antipathy and distrust towards all who have come in to disturb the administration of its domestic affairs." And on a later occasion, he declared even more emphatically that since the United States had been the recipient of all favors gained by British or French arms, we were considered by the

Chinese to be "accomplices in the acts of hostility committed by those powers."

Anti-foreign disturbances, and especially attacks upon missionaries climaxed by the massacre of the members of a French mission in Tientsin in 1870, were a further discouraging sign of how completely Burlingame had misrepresented actual conditions in China. There was widespread unrest throughout the country, and it would continue to simmer not very far beneath the surface until the outbreak of the Boxer Rebellion, as a consequence of the Chinese people's deep-seated hostility toward all foreign innovations. The Imperial Government did nothing to meet the issue. On the contrary, its own attitude stimulated the fears of the peasants.

As a final example of how little China had in truth changed, the perennial audience question once again came up and was finally settled only by the most grudging concessions. In 1873 the young Emperor (in whose name Tzu Hsi had been ruling) came of age. The official reception of the foreign envoys could no longer be postponed, and in the spirit expressed in the memorial to the throne already quoted, preparations were finally made for this significant ceremony. The American minister at the capital, Frederick F. Low, was instructed to proceed with due regard "for the inveterate prejudices and grotesque conceit of the Chinese courtiers," but nonetheless to refuse absolutely to perform the kowtow. Only after four months of stubborn argument was an agreement reached between the court officials and the diplomatic corps in which three formal bows were accepted as sufficiently respectful of his Imperial Majesty.

When the great day dawned, the foreign envoys entered the reception hall together, and after a speech of congratulation by the Russian minister, as dean of the diplomatic corps, each in turn laid his letter of credence before the Emperor. Prince Kung then expressed the friendly sentiments of the throne and after their three formal bows, the envoys withdrew. Precedent had been shattered; foreigners had stood in the awful presence of the Son of Heaven. Yet the Chinese had the last word. The Emperor had neither risen from his throne nor spoken to the ministers. The audience had been held not in the Forbidden City, but in the Pavilion of Purple Light which custom set aside for the reception of the envoys of tributary states.

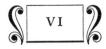

VI

"THE CHINESE MUST GO"

THE darkest chapter in Chinese-American relations centers about the immigration of Chinese laborers into the United States. There was justification for the vigorous demand of California and other Pacific Coast states that it should somehow be regulated and controlled. The problem of assimilation it presented could not be casually dismissed. But prejudice rather than fair play was allowed to dictate national policy, and the rights of the Chinese themselves were callously disregarded as the whole issue became entangled in the interplay of partisan politics. The United States found itself doing just what it had condemned China for doing. It adopted a program of rigid exclusion, and in so doing violated both the spirit and the letter of its treaty engagements.

The discovery of gold in California, in 1848, marked the real beginning of the entry of Chinese laborers. There was only a small handful in the country, perhaps fifty in all, when James Marshall wonderingly sifted through his hands the fine yellow particles he had found in the tailrace of Sutter's mill. Three years later, some 10,000 were reported to have arrived in California, and before the middle of the 1850's the Chinese population of the state was said to be more than 25,000. The news of the gold to be found in the Sierra Nevadas, and of the new opportunities for work and business on the Pacific Coast, had been carried by the China clippers to Shanghai and Hongkong with the same results as the news produced in New York, Philadelphia and Boston. The Chinese descended upon California in droves to take their place among the eager prospectors for gold, to set up retail shops and laundries, to work at every possible job in the rapidly growing mining towns.

Each succeeding year saw a further increase in this alien

element in the Pacific Coast's steadily rising population. Many Chinese returned home within a few years, after making more money than they could have saved in a lifetime in China, but others came to take their place. When opportunities for work in the mining towns fell off, a new demand for cheap labor sprang up with the building of the transcontinental railway. With annual arrivals averaging some 16,000, it was estimated in 1868, the year in which Seward and Burlingame signed their treaty encouraging immigration, that the total for all Chinese in the United States was 90,000. The great bulk of these immigrants remained in the Pacific Coast states, and California was far in the lead. Its Chinese population, rising from 35,000 to 75,000 between 1860 and 1880, represented approximately 9 per cent of the state total.

The Chinese were at first warmly welcomed. There was plenty of room for all newcomers and little feeling that they would in any way intrude upon the interests of other settlers. Racial prejudice had not yet been aroused. As the Chinese took over so many of the jobs that no one else was willing to do in communities where the major attention was always directed toward mining and prospecting, they played a highly useful role in society. Their willingness to work at almost anything was a great asset in the California of gold rush days, and the way in which they quietly went about their own business served to disarm criticism.

"Quite a large number of the Celestials have arrived among us of late, enticed thither by the golden romance that has filled the world," the *Daily Alta California* commented on May 12, 1852. "Scarcely a ship arrives that does not bring an increase to this worthy integer of our population. The China boys will yet vote at the same polls, study at the same schools and bow at the same altar as our own countrymen."

This cordial attitude did not last very long. The patient perseverance and unflagging industry of the Chinese began to awaken dislike and prejudice in the mining fields. Native Americans were unable to compete with what appeared to them to be almost inhuman concentration on work. The standard of living of the Chinese was also lower than that of other elements in the population, and wage scales seemed to be unduly held down by the continuing influx of cheap coolie labor. The feeling grew that California should be saved for native Americans and racial prejudice was inevitably added to the economic causes for anti-Chinese feeling. By the middle of the 1850's, the California legislature had already embarked upon its long course of discriminatory laws making the Chinese scapegoats for many of the developing evils in the labor situation for which they were in no way responsible. They were driven out of the gold fields by means of a special licensing tax for miners and subjected to a general state head tax for all oriental immigrants.

The new demand for labor resulting from the railroad construction of the 1860's led to a temporary decline in this antagonistic attitude. The employer class encouraged Chinese immigration. It was estimated that some nine-tenths of the workers in the construction gangs building the Central Pacific Railroad were coolies. Without this plentiful source of cheap labor, in fact, the line would never have been completed in time to receive the subsidies promised by the Federal government. The Chinese were playing the role in the construction of our west coast railroads that Irish immigrants had played in building eastern lines a few decades earlier.

This was the situation that inspired Secretary Seward's recognition of "the inherent and inalienable right of man to change his home and allegiance" in the treaty of 1868. In going so far as to provide, on a reciprocal basis, that the Chinese in this country should enjoy all the privileges of nationals of the most-favored nation, he had even further emphasized his feeling that everything should be done to encourage immigration in order to provide for the development of the new communities on the Pacific Coast. The Chinese were not granted the right of naturalization, and the Supreme Court was later to sustain the power of Congress to bar them from citizenship, but in every other way they were to be accepted on a basis of equality with all other aliens.

The conclusion of this treaty nevertheless marked a turning point in the national policy toward Chinese immigration. Even though no objections to its ratification were raised by west coast representatives in the Senate, it had hardly been approved before the movement that was eventually to lead to exclusion began to gather momentum. The completion of the transcontinental railway freed thousands of laborers, and as the Chinese appeared to be competing for other jobs with native Americans in a period of growing unemployment, all the old resentments against their frugality and lower standard of living flared up once again. An unreasoning and bitter hostility toward the Chinese spread from the ranks of labor to almost all elements in the population of the west coast. The immigration issue became a football of California politics, and soon made its way into national politics.

The economic basis for anti-Chinese agitation had another aspect. There had for long existed a nefarious coolie trade in the Far East whereby Chinese were transported as contract laborers, first from Hongkong, and then from the Portuguese port of Macao, for work on the plantations of Peru and Cuba. It had come to bear so close a resemblance to the old African slave trade that the conscience of the world was aroused. The overcrowding, filth and horrors of the transpacific voyages paralleled those of the Atlantic's notorious Middle Passage from Africa to America. When they reached their destination, the coolies were in effect sold to the planters in Peru and Cuba, at prices ranging from $400 to $1,000, for a contract term of service running into many years. While the Chinese government made some feeble efforts at control, it was estimated that more than 100,000 coolies were taken to Peru and some 150,000 to Cuba before this modern form of slavery was brought to an end.

Chinese immigration to the United States was not a part of the coolie traffic, and conditions governing the entry of workers in California were in no way comparable to those prevailing in Peru and Cuba. The Chinese coming to this country did so voluntarily, paid their own transportation charges across the Pacific, and great numbers of them returned very shortly to their native land after having made such money as they desired. Yet the fact that many immigrants had borrowed the funds for their passage, and were under contract to work off this debt under terms imposed by the lender, sometimes seemed to make the distinction between their status and that of the coolies forcefully transplanted to Cuba or Peru a rather narrow one. A Chinese organization known as the Six Companies largely controlled the business of financing immigration, and there appeared to be something mysterious, if not sinister, in its operations.

The people of California, in any event, refused to believe that the Chinese within their borders were actually the free agents they were supposed to be. They saw in the activities of the Six Companies an attempt to maintain a system of forced labor. They became convinced, under the pressure of their mounting prejudices, that the Chinese coming to the United States were the scum and riffraff of the treaty ports, kidnaped as many of the coolies transported to South America had been, and held like them in virtual slavery.

They were not actually the riffraff of the treaty ports. The majority of them were self-respecting peasants, and on the farms of the Pacific Coast, as well as in many other trades and occupations, they were contributing importantly to the growth and increasing wealth of this part of the country. Yet it was true that they represented the most ignorant and economically depressed class in China, and they were willing to work for lower wages than would provide an adequate living for white workers. Their presence created a situation that could not fail to foster resentment. The charges brought against the Six Companies had some justification in the peculiar conditions of employment that so generally prevailed. For the Chinese did not bring their families to the United States, and consequently they had no wives or children to support. They were not interested in the refinements of western civilization, and therefore spent nothing on luxuries. It was hardly surprising that native workers, trying to compete with them in the labor market, obstinately closed their eyes to any rights to which the Chinese might be entitled, and allowed prejudice wholly to govern their attitude toward the deepening problem.

The clannishness of the immigrants and their retention of their own way of life also awoke discomforting fears among the people of California. The Chinese made no effort whatsoever to adopt American customs. Speaking their own language, wearing their own native clothes, retaining the distinctive badge of the queue, eating their own food, insisting on being taken back to China for burial, and worshiping their own gods, they remained completely alien to the civilization which surrounded them. They lived by themselves, often in appalling conditions of overcrowding and poverty, in the Chinatowns which sprang up in almost every city. As cooks and houseboys, gardeners and laundrymen, the Chinese were liked and trusted, but *en masse* their aloof inscrutability caused them to be regarded with instinctive suspicion.

Their vices were greatly magnified. The Chinese were inveterate gamblers, many were addicted to opium smoking and prostitution was very common. But there was little warrant for condemning them all as vicious, treacherous characters because of the prevalence in the Chinatowns of gambling, opium smoking and prostitution. Comparable vices were not wholly unknown among native Americans. The Chinese had no monopoly on crime. Granted that differences in race, religion and culture appeared to make them unassimilable, and granted that their swelling numbers for a time gave some warrant to fears that they might ultimately become a majority in California, nothing could have been more unfortunate than the growth of the unreasoning prejudices which, in spite of the generally dignified attitude of the Chinese themselves, served at every turn to embitter racial relations.

The latent hostility toward the Chinese was sedulously fanned in the 1870's by labor agitators and political demagogues who saw an easy way of winning popular support for themselves by unashamed appeals to such prejudice. "Treason is better than to labor beside a Chinese slave," a virulent manifesto of the Workingmen's Party in California declared. "The people are about to take their own affairs into their own hands and they will not be stayed either by 'Citizen Vigilantes,' state militia, nor United States troops." In the sandlots of San Francisco, a wild and unprincipled Irish agitator, Dennis Kearney, preached a violent doctrine of riot and lynch law to drive the Chinese out of the country. Mobs of hoodlums, small-time thugs and unemployed rowdies were inspired to burn and wreck the property of the Chinese, to chase them about the streets for the sport of cutting off their queues, to pelt them with stones and brickbats, and sometimes actually to murder them.

"Dead, my reverend friends, dead," Bret Harte wrote in his classic obituary of Wan Lee. "Stoned to death in the streets of San Francisco, in the year of grace 1869, by a mob of half grown boys and Christian school children."

With the whole west coast ringing with the cry "The Chinese must go," both political parties in California took up the issue and vied with each other in promoting repressive legislation against the voteless Chinese. But the discriminatory laws passed by the state legislature could not solve the problem because control of immigration rested with Congress. In 1876, the state senate consequently sent an address and memorial to Washington appealing for a national policy of exclusion.

"During their entire settlement in California," this account of the Chinese stated, "they have never adapted themselves to our habits, modes of dress, or our educational system; have never learned the sanctity of an oath, never desired to become citizens, or to perform the duties of citizenship, never discovered the differences between right and wrong, never ceased the worship of their idol gods, or advanced a step beyond the traditions of their native hive. Impregnable to all the influences of

Anglo-Saxon life, they remain the same stolid Asiatics that have floated on the rivers and slaved in the fields of China for thirty centuries of time.''

Congress decided upon an investigation, and a joint committee of the House and Senate promptly visited the Pacific Coast. The resulting report was also a violent condemnation of the Chinese. Presented by Senator Sargent of California, it largely echoed the views of the original memorial with a mass of evidence emphasizing the degradation, immorality and vice that supposedly existed among the Chinese. Professing to fear that unless something were done, California's white population would in time be outnumbered by its yellow residents, the committee recommended that treaty arrangements with China be modified to permit Congress to bring relief to the Pacific states from "the terrible scourge" under which they were suffering.

A much more reasoned position had been taken by the original chairman of the committee, Senator Oliver P. Morton of Indiana. He stressed the contribution that the Chinese had made to the development of the west coast, asserted his belief that the hostility against them was due far more to the fact that they were different from Americans than to either their alleged vices or any actual injury to the white people of California, and warned against adopting a policy of exclusion which was the very thing for which China was so strongly criticized. Unfortunately, however, Senator Morton died before the committee made its final report, and the majority view reflected little of his moderation or sense of justice.

As Congress prepared to act upon the recommendation of its committee, a decided sectional split became apparent. The West wanted an immediate ban on immigration; the East favored less stringent action because of our treaty obligations. With some warrant, the representatives of the Pacific Coast states declared that if New England faced the same problem, its attitude would be quite different. "Let a colony of these Asiatic brethren," the San Francisco *Argonaut* said, ". . . camp down beside Boston Common, with their filthy habits, their criminal practices, and their nasty vices, and how long would it be before Beacon Hill would sniff the polluted atmosphere, and all the overgodly of New England would send up their prayers for relief." The most powerful factor blocking fair treatment for the Chinese, however, was that they had no vote, while those demanding their exclusion were in a position to make their political influence strongly felt.

The congressional measure that emerged from these debates was the so-called Fifteen-Passenger Bill, adopted in 1879, which prohibited any ship from bringing more than fifteen Chinese passengers to the United States. For all its devious approach to the problem, this proposed law was clearly a denial of the principles that had been written into the Burlingame treaty. President Hayes promptly vetoed it. The eastern newspapers hailed his forthright message as "saving the character of the country from humiliation among the family of nations." Those on the west coast bitterly attacked it. Realizing that the issue had to be met, Hayes consequently dispatched a special mission to China to undertake negotiation of a new treaty that would enable the United States, without violating existing commitments, to take such action as Congress felt to be necessary to protect the national interest.

The commission, headed by James B. Angell, President of the University of Michigan, held lengthy conversations with representatives of the Imperial Government in Peking. The latter were not very much concerned over immigration to the United States, nor with the status of the relatively few Chinese subjects who were residents there. Nevertheless the demand of the Angell Commission that China should admit the right of the United States to exclude Chinese, while freely admitting the nationals of other countries, was an affront to national pride and racial dignity that no government could accept. A compromise understanding was consequently written into the treaty that was finally concluded on November 18, 1880. It was agreed that the United States could regulate, limit or suspend the immigration of Chinese, but not absolutely prohibit it.

Moreover, such limitation or suspension was to be reasonable, apply only to Chinese who went to the United States as laborers and not to other classes, and should not affect the right of those already in the country to go and come of their own free will.

Concurrently with conclusion of this treaty, an agreement was also reached, at the request of the Chinese government, forbidding any further importation of opium into China by American citizens. While hardly to be considered as a *quid pro quo*, this move helped to reconcile the imperial authorities to their concessions on the immigration issue. But they shrewdly pointed out to the Angell Commission the implications of the attitude that the United States appeared to be taking. "If now, because of temporary competition between the Irish and stranger guests," the Chinese stated, "a decision is lightly taken to change the policy of the government, contradiction with the Constitution of the United States and with existing treaties cannot be avoided. . . ." The opportunity to remind the Americans of the lessons they had been trying to teach the Chinese in regard to international equality was too good to be neglected.

Congress at once prepared to act under the provisions of the new treaty. The whole issue had been injected into the presidential campaign of 1880, and with both parties adopting anti-Chinese planks in their platforms, as they had indeed in 1876, national sentiment appeared to favor drastic legislation. So virulent was the exclusion fever in California that Garfield had failed to carry the state after publication of a letter, subsequently shown to have been forged, that purported to reveal that he had declared himself in favor of "Chinese cheap labor." If concern over the problem was not as great in other parts of the country, west coast proponents of strict regulation were able to muster support for passage of a bill suspending all Chinese immigration for twenty years.

Could this measure be reconciled with treaty provisions for the "reasonable" suspension of immigration? With a measure of political courage even greater than that which had led President Hayes to veto the Fifteen-Passenger Bill, President Arthur, who had succeeded to the presidency after Garfield's assassination, declared in another ringing veto message that twenty years' suspension could not be construed as reasonable in the sense meant in the Angell Treaty. His action precipitated a sharp fight in Congress, but despite the bitter denunciation of west coast members, one of whom declared that the President would "empty the teeming, seething slave pens of China upon the soil of California," his veto was sustained.

Congress thereupon passed and President Arthur accepted another measure which provided for a ten-year suspension of the immigration of both skilled and unskilled Chinese laborers, and also stipulated that "hereafter no state court or court of the United States shall admit Chinese to citizenship." Even though it did not go so far as the original exclusion bill, this law nevertheless marked a complete reversal of our immigration policy in so far as it applied to the Chinese. It flatly denied the traditional principle that the United States was to be a haven and asylum for peoples of all nations, and it most certainly violated the spirit if not the actual letter of our treaties with China. As events were to prove, moreover, it established a precedent which was to lead to the permanent exclusion of Chinese laborers in later years despite the emphatic and indignant protests of the Imperial Government.

Some action to control or limit their entry, as previously suggested, was completely justified. The problem of assimilation in California could not have been handled if Congress had withheld all cooperation by refusing to enact any immigration laws. But a prejudiced minority exercised such powerful political pressures that Congress let itself be swayed by the most emotional arguments. It was an issue that directly affected only the west coast, due to the continued concentration of the Chinese population in these states. In effect, California was thus allowed to have its own way by the abdication of national responsibility and popular disregard of our obligations to China.

In the minds of the Chinese, our attitude paralleled that of the European governments which were encroaching upon their rights nearer home. "China had to look the fact in the face, that she had no friends," our minister in Peking, John Russell Young, reported the Grand Secretary, Li Hung-chang, telling him in August 1883. "Here was Russia menacing her on the north. Germany had invaded her territory at Swatow. Japan had taken the Loo-Choo islands. England held Hongkong, and was forcing upon her a traffic in opium that meant the misery and ruin of her people. France was sending an expedition to dismember her empire. The United States had passed an act excluding Chinese from her soil, Chinese, alone, of all the races in the world. . . . Why did not foreign nations, if they were friendly to China, deal with China as they did with themselves? Why have one kind of treaties with his empire and another kind with other empires?"

Even passage of the ten-year exclusion bill did not bring to an end the anti-Chinese agitation on the west coast. The following years saw not only the adoption of local laws further discriminating against the Chinese, but instances of still more violent mob action. The old sports of the San Francisco sand-lots—stoning the Chinese in the streets, cutting off their queues, wrecking their shops and laundries—spread to other parts of the west. If the victims of such attacks tried to go to court to win protection, they could not hope to get a fair hearing. The phrase "not a Chinaman's chance" had a grim and bitter reality.

The most spectacular of anti-Chinese outbreaks took place at Rock Springs, Wyoming. In the summer of 1885, a mob of white citizens in this mining town attacked the local Chinese community, burning and destroying homes, cutting down in cold blood the frightened and defenseless Orientals. When the riot finally subsided and the mob withdrew, twenty-eight Chinese were dead and fifteen seriously injured. A wave of indignation swept over the country upon news of this bloody massacre, yet there was no real abatement of the anti-Chinese feeling in western mining communities or on the Pacific Coast.

Shortly after the Rock Springs affair, a California legislative committee again went on record as to its attitude toward a situation which it felt could be met only by getting rid of the Chinese altogether. "For thirty years China has dumped upon our shores all its refuse," this committee stated; ". . . all the incapable, the idiotic, the unfortunate, the criminal, the diseased, the vicious, the outcasts, have remained with us. . . . the men the most degraded slaves upon earth . . . the women slave prostitutes . . . the children the product of the most promiscuous miscegenation on earth."

With such attitudes prevailing on the Pacific Coast, it was all too clear that the temporary suspension of immigration had solved no problems. At the same time, the Chinese government not surprisingly demanded redress for the mistreatment of its subjects who had been promised full protection. A further attempt was consequently made to find a new basis for coping with the issue through the negotiation in 1888 of another Chinese-American treaty.

China was now herself willing to prohibit the emigration of laborers to the United States in return for guarantees of the safety of the Chinese already there and indemnities for past outrages. The United States thereupon proposed a complete ban on immigration for twenty years, but it evaded the issue of both indemnities for the past and guarantees for the future on the ground that the Federal government could not interfere in the affairs of the several states. After some delay, however, it was agreed that an indemnity of $276,619 would be paid, although without recognition of the Federal government's responsibility, and such protection would be guaranteed as that afforded citizens of the most-favored nation. On this basis a twenty-year exclusion treaty was signed.

The Senate approved this pact, with amendments that actually tightened up its provisions by forbidding the reentry of

Chinese who had temporarily returned to their own country, but in the meantime the issue had once again been injected into the politics of a presidential campaign. Party leaders in both camps, anxious to win the votes of the west coast, eagerly sought an opportunity to demonstrate their determination to shut out the Chinese at whatever cost. Upon the pretext that Peking was unduly delaying ratification of the new treaty, a bill was introduced into Congress for immediate adoption of its exclusion provisions without waiting for Chinese approval.

The more conservative members of both the Republican and Democratic parties protested at once that to take such action before China had ratified the treaty was both unnecessary and dishonorable, a move that would not be contemplated were the nation concerned a stronger power. "It is a game of politics," Senator Butler of Tennessee declared. ". . . but for the fact that we are on the eve of a presidential election, this Senate would not now be engaged in this debate." Nevertheless the bill was passed and President Cleveland, failing to follow the precedent of the Hayes and Arthur vetoes, signed it on the ground that China had not cooperated with us.

While party newspapers with an eye on the west coast vote tried to make such capital as they could out of the situation, the independent press outspokenly condemned the course Congress had followed. It universally agreed that the Angell Treaty had been violated without even the courtesy of notifying the Chinese government. Delayed action on the proposed new treaty could in no way absolve the United States from its international obligations, it was asserted, and the whole business stood revealed as nothing more nor less than a political scramble for the votes of anti-Chinese hoodlums. Senator Sherman characterized the new legislation "as one of the most vicious laws that has passed in my time in Congress . . . a mere political race between the two houses."

The Chinese minister in Washington, who had been out of the country while the measure was pending, entered a vigorous protest upon his return to the capital. His government's slowness in ratifying the new treaty, he stated, had been due to its consideration of possible amendments. The pact had not been rejected. "I was not prepared to learn," he declared with dignity, "that there was a way recognized in the law and practice of this country whereby your country could release itself from treaty obligations without consultation or the consent of the other party; it can hardly be contended that my government was exceeding diplomatic practice or courtesy in following out the example of the Senate and proposing amendments."*

The situation in regard to treaty observance had indeed undergone an ironical reversal. The United States was now doing exactly what it had condemned China for doing so many times in the past. There was of course no question of the constitutional right of Congress to restrict immigration in any way it saw fit, but this did not free the United States of its responsibility to respect the rights guaranteed the Chinese in existing treaties. Our national attitude was determined by prejudice and political demagoguery just as surely as China's attitude had in the past been determined by prejudice and anti-foreignism.

The friction resulting from these developments led to a virtual breaking-off of all diplomatic exchanges between the United States and China throughout President Harrison's term of office. The hands of the State Department were completely tied through action over which it had no control. Moreover, in 1892 Congress made assurance as to the exclusion of the Chinese doubly sure by extending for another ten years the provisions of the 1882 legislation, and so broadening the definition of laborers that only merchants, teachers, students, government officials and travelers were permitted entry. Furthermore, the full burden of being always able to prove their right of

* It is probable that this note was written by John W. Foster or some other American advisor to the Chinese legation. Individual Americans played an important role throughout this period, and in the opening years of the twentieth century, in helping to direct the course of Chinese diplomacy and in drawing up constitutional reforms.

residence in the United States was placed upon the members of these exempt classes. Together with Chinese laborers who had entered the country prior to 1882, they had to meet any complaint with conclusive evidence that they were here legally.

As on all previous occasions, the congressional debates over this measure demonstrated the extent to which politics were allowed to dominate any thought of international fair dealing. The argument that it was unjust in its treatment of the Chinese already in this country, and could not fail to injure both our political and commercial relations with China, won no hearing. Advocates of rigid exclusion declared that some 30,000 Chinese had illegally entered the country in the guise of merchants, and consequently the provisions of earlier legislation had to be tightened up and more drastically enforced. They accused China of violating her own engagements and acting unreasonably in not ratifying the treaty of 1888. Even should it injure our commerce with China, the more rabid declared, this was of no real importance.

The Chinese minister bitterly denounced the law as "a violation of every principle of justice, equity, reason and fair-dealing between two friendly powers." Our disregard of Chinese rights certainly contrasted strangely with contemporary efforts being made to secure respect for American rights in China. Our merchants continued to demand all the benefits of special treaty concessions in their trade, and in their program of education and evangelization among the Chinese people, our missionaries expected full consideration of their privileged position. Yet Chinese protests against the severe enforcement of our arbitrary exclusion laws went unheeded.

Finally, in 1894, a new *modus vivendi* was reached with the negotiation of another Chinese-American treaty. The United States did not retreat from its position, but it did undertake to administer the immigration laws more leniently with respect to the rights of merchants, students, teachers, government officials and travelers. In return, China reluctantly acceded to the exclusion of all laborers for the ten years stipulated in the new legislation.

Upon expiration of this period, however, Congress quickly showed that it still did not feel itself in any way bound by treaties. Without considering the possible attitude of China any more than it had on previous occasions, it once again re-enacted the old exclusion laws—and this time on an indefinite basis. China's reaction was to terminate the treaty of 1894. That was all it could do, and its action awoke widespread popular support among the Chinese people. Boycotts on the import of American goods were declared in 1904 and 1905, and excitement in the treaty ports led to a wave of anti-American feeling. While the pressure of these boycotts, or perhaps an uneasy conscience, gradually led to fairer and more efficient application of existing laws, the rigid policy that the United States had adopted was not appreciably modified. We would admit no Chinese laborers and those already in the country were not entitled to citizenship. After years of persistent pressure, the west coast had completely triumphed in overriding all opposition to its anti-Chinese program.

The exclusion laws were to remain in effect for almost forty years longer. The whole issue was to be fought over again with another Asiatic power when the United States sought to keep out Japanese as well as Chinese, and the growing strength of Japan made the controversy in this instance a far more critical one. For many years the entry of Japanese immigrants was consequently governed by the Gentleman's Agreement negotiated by President Roosevelt in 1908. Finally, however, the policy enforced against the Chinese was extended to all non-Caucasians through the Immigration Act of 1924, barring the entry of persons ineligible to citizenship. To China this new law meant little. It merely confirmed the exclusion to which her people were already subject. Nevertheless, the discrimination which prevented Asiatics from entering this country under the quota provisions applicable to European immigrants did not rankle any the less because it was extended to the Japanese.

A proud people had never become reconciled to the injustice which had been done in the denial of those principles of equality which had been written into the Burlingame Treaty of 1868.

The United States was not to make redress for this wrong done the Chinese until the dramatic developments of the 1940's brought the two nations together as allies in their common war against Japan. Only then were the old laws repealed. Through legislation adopted at the close of 1943, the immigration of Chinese into the United States was placed upon the same general basis as that of Europeans. They were given an annual quota (in this instance, however, applying to all Chinese rather than to those coming directly from China), and they were made eligible for American citizenship. The quota was limited by the terms of our general immigration laws to only 105 entries annually—graphic evidence of how little such a concession actually affected our population—but it removed the stigma of discriminatory treatment.

"Nations, like individuals, make mistakes," President Roosevelt declared in appealing to Congress to pass this legislation. "We must be big enough to acknowledge our mistakes of the past and to correct them."

VII

MANIFEST DESTINY

ALTHOUGH the continuing controversy over immigration was almost the only reminder of the existence of China for most Americans during the 1880's and early 1890's, internal developments in that country had created a situation that very nearly led to the complete dismemberment of the Empire, and at least indirectly served to promote our own national expansion to the shores of Asia. The twentieth century was to open with the United States established as a Pacific power, ready to exercise a renewed influence in seeking to uphold the traditional objectives of its Chinese policy.

The cooperative program instituted by Anson Burlingame had largely broken down after his death. The attitude of the Imperial Government clearly revealed that far from being willing to welcome foreign commerce and foreign missions, as Burlingame had so optimistically promised, China was still stubbornly determined to resist all encroachments on her established way of life. Treaty obligations were avoided whenever the conservative mandarins dared to do so. Trade in the interior was hampered by obstructive local regulations. Further anti-foreign riots and attacks upon missionaries betrayed the persistence of old prejudices among the masses of Chinese peasantry.

The reaction of the foreign powers was to insist all the more severely upon what they regarded as their rights. In spite of the futile protests of the Imperial Government, the scope of extraterritoriality was constantly expanded, and force or the threat of force was employed to compel acquiescence in various new privileges infringing upon Chinese sovereignty more flagrantly than ever before. Complete control was established over the coastal trade; the 5 per cent limitation upon tariff rates was enforced in the face of rising domestic prices which gave foreign merchants every advantage in the Chinese market; concessions were obtained in the interests of foreign capital for the construction of railways and telegraph lines; increasing domination of Chinese finances resulted from the negotiation of loans secured by customs revenues collected by the Inspectorate of Maritime Customs; and the rights of the Imperial Government in the International Settlement at Shanghai were reduced to a mere technical recognition of sovereignty. The powers were promoting their own interests and Peking remained helpless.

The United States continued its policy of seeking neither territory nor outright concessions of any kind from China. Our goodwill was demonstrated on various occasions through attempts to aid her in meeting the problems created by the demands of other countries. We made various gestures of friendship. In 1872 and 1873, a cordial welcome had been accorded two groups of young Chinese students who came to this country and entered schools in Connecticut and Massachusetts; ex-President Grant visited China in 1879 and exerted his influence in trying to mediate the dispute with Japan over the Liuchiu Islands, and an indemnity which had been exacted in 1858 for damages to American property was generously remitted.

Whatever might be said in favor of a policy which sought to win respect for treaty rights by "moral suasion" rather than force or military pressure, however, we still insisted upon sharing all the new privileges won by the other powers. The United States had its part in the general movement that was steadily wearing down Chinese sovereignty, and forcing upon the empire what was virtually a semicolonial status in its relations with the West.

Assailed from all sides, China was unable to awaken from the lethargy of centuries and put up any effective resistance to these persistent foreign advances. One by one her former tributary states fell under the control of European powers. Great Britain established herself in Burma, France in what was to become French Indo-China, and Russia was a constant menace in the north. The final humiliation of China, however, and the most startling revelation of her utter impotency, resulted from a war with Japan over the status of Korea.

Under the terms of its treaties with China, the United States was prepared to offer its services as a mediator in this conflict. Yet its sympathies, in 1894, were divided between the two oriental nations. Our relations with Japan had been generally friendly since the opening-up of that country by Commodore Perry, and the friction that had developed with China over the immigration issue was not conducive, in this particular year, to any determined support for the Middle Kingdom. The United States refused to take part in a program of intervention whereby the powers would have guaranteed the independence of Korea, took occasion to warn Tokyo in the most friendly fashion of the risks of European interference in the dispute, and not until hostilities had run their course and resulted in a disastrous defeat for China, did it seek to employ its good offices in bringing the two nations together.

China was then compelled to relinquish all control and influence in Korea, and to cede to Japan both Formosa and the Pescadores. The war would also have meant a first step in the alienation of Manchuria had not Germany, Russia and France combined to persuade Japan to give up her demand for Port Arthur and the Liaotung Peninsula. Yet even more important than these immediate consequences was the further impetus given to European aggression through such a conclusive demonstration of China's military weakness. "The various powers," lamented Tzu Hsi, the old Empress Dowager, "cast upon us looks of tiger-like voracity, hustling each other in their endeavors to seize upon our innermost territories."

These assaults reached their climax in 1898. Germany made the murder of two missionaries a pretext for demanding the cession of the port of Kiauchow and establishing control over Shantung; Russia exacted leaseholds at Port Arthur and Talienwan, the very territory from which she had warned

Japan three years earlier, as part of her program to make Manchuria a Russian sphere of influence; Great Britain extended her control over the Yangtze Valley and secured a leasehold upon the port of Weihaiwei; and France tightened her grip upon the southern province of Yunnan and seized Kwangchow Bay. It was only when Italy tried to emulate the example of these stronger powers that China summoned the courage to call a halt in this rapid process of dismemberment. Otherwise she was unable to defend herself. Her futile, harassed government looked on hopelessly as the onetime magnificent Chinese Empire suffered such devastating blows.

The role of the United States as China was carved up into spheres of foreign influence remained that of a bystander. Washington watched these developments with apparent equanimity. Overtures from Great Britain for concerted action to safeguard the old principle of equality of trade were bluntly rejected by President McKinley in March 1898. There was no warrant, he stated in his reply to the British government, for any departure from the traditional American policy of avoiding "interference or connection with European complications." Nine months later, in his annual message to Congress, he declared that there did not appear to be any prospect of our trade being prejudiced through exclusive treatment in the newly leased foreign territories. Assurances against any such discrimination "obviated the need of our country becoming an actor in the scene."

Nevertheless, there was a feeling in some quarters that the United States could not remain aloof indefinitely, and concern over possible foreign monopolies in the Chinese market gradually awoke more interest in the affairs of eastern Asia. Our commerce had not lived up to mid-century expectations. The value of exports to China had risen to some $12,000,000 annually, but this represented only about 2 per cent of our total exports. The China trade was proportionately less important than it had been before the Civil War, and it was approximated in value by our growing commerce with Japan. Most of the old American firms doing business in China had failed or withdrawn; there had been a startling decline in our shipping; we were playing a very small part in railroad, mining or other industrial developments; and total American investments in China were less than $25,000,000, including mission property. The threat of exclusion from the Chinese market was all that was necessary, however, to revive the old concept of its tremendous potentialities for future development.

A series of articles in the *North American Review* in the early months of 1898 called graphic attention to "Our Future in the Pacific," "America's Interests in China" and "America's Opportunity in Asia." Could the United States stand aside while our commercial rivals preempted the field and set up their own monopolistic controls? "The markets of the Orient," wrote Charles Denby, Jr., a secretary of legation in Peking, "are the heritage of her merchants, and the time will inevitably come when the voice of the Republic will be heard in oriental courts with the same accent of authority as in the commonwealths of South America."

Commercial newspapers, eagerly canvassing outlets for what appeared to be a growing surplus of manufactured goods resulting from our phenomenal industrial expansion, looked to China as holding out greater possibilities for trade than any other part of the world. An article in the *Journal of Commerce* flatly stated that if we could circumvent our rivals in the Far East and gain more ready access to the Chinese market, the problem of disposing of our manufactures would be largely solved. At the annual meeting of the National Association of Manufacturers, deeply concerned with the development of foreign trade, speaker after speaker demanded strenuous efforts to develop our commerce in the Pacific and called for government support.

The New York Chamber of Commerce sent a memorial to President McKinley urging immediate action. "The administration at Washington," it stated, "seems to be supine about the present menace to these important interests of our citizens in China." Similar action was taken by other chambers of commerce and boards of trade, including those of Philadelphia, Boston, Baltimore, San Francisco and Seattle. It would be an exaggeration to suggest that the entire country had suddenly become aroused to the need for protecting our interests in China, yet the policies being pursued by Great Britain and Russia, Germany and France, caused widespread concern at least in commercial circles. Newspapers were generally agreed, as interpreted in a leading article in the *Literary Digest* as early as January 1898, that the scramble for exclusive privileges in China was "a conscious or an instinctive move of all Europe against all America, in competition for the markets of the world." The *Baltimore Sun* sounded a more belligerent note: "If American interests or American citizens are threatened by complications in the East, this country will know how to protect them and maintain its own dignity."

Against this background of apparent break-up in China and mounting concern in commercial circles over what it might mean to American prospects for trade, war with Spain suddenly and unexpectedly brought the United States to the very shores of Asia as a result of the Battle of Manila Bay. At a most critical time in the history of the Far East, we found ourselves, almost fortuitously, in a position to assert our national power in the Pacific as never before. If the American people were at first somewhat at a loss as to what we were doing in the Philippines, our historic interest in Pacific expansion and in Chinese markets soon convinced them that the opportunity offered for strengthening our position in Asia was one that could not be neglected.

"The booming guns of Dewey's battleships," an enthusiastic senator proclaimed in the exciting summer of 1898, "sounded a new note on the Pacific shores, a note that has echoed and re-echoed around the world, and that note is that we are on the Pacific, that we are there to stay, and that we are there to protect our rights, promote our interests, and get our share of the trade and commerce of the opulent Orient."

Only a handful of ambitious expansionists had foreseen the opportunities that war with Spain might open up for what Secretary of State John Hay was to call "our Pacific work." The occupation of the Philippines, however, did not fall wholly outside the pattern of earlier advances into this part of the world. We have seen that settlement of the west coast was in some degree motivated by the desire to win maritime control of the Pacific and thereby dominate Far Eastern trade. Seward had purchased Alaska as a drawbridge between America and Asia. Our ties with the Hawaiian Islands, which were finally to be annexed in the summer of 1898, had been first formed because of their importance as a way station on the route to the Orient. There was a deep stirring of imperialistic sentiment in the United States of the 1890's, born of industrial growth, the closing of the frontier and an instinctive urge toward further expansion. There was a growing feeling that Americans, in Captain Alfred Thayer Mahan's phrase, "must now begin to look outward." And they looked toward the Pacific as the inevitable field for expansion largely because of the vast potentialities of the Chinese market.

Business circles which had formerly opposed the war over Cuba because they were fearful of where the country's imperialistic sentiment might lead it, at once saw in possession of the Philippines a means to combat the threat to our interests in China resulting from the European powers' establishment of exclusive spheres of interest. With the American flag flying within five hundred miles of Hongkong, the *Journal of Commerce* confidently stated, our policy would in the future have "something more than merely moral support." The answer to the whole problem of keeping China's markets open, the *Banker and Tradesman* declared, "was given, as European nations very well know, when Dewey entered Manila Bay and won his glorious victory." It was constantly reiterated that the only way to counteract European influence in China was through the more active participation in Far Eastern politics that occupation of the Philippines at last made feasible.

James J. Hill declared that the people who controlled the trade of the Orient held the purse strings of the world; Frank A. Vanderlip, at this time Assistant Secretary of the Treasury, wrote in an article in the *Century* that the Philippines were the key to the Orient; and Senator Lodge carried through the argument in stating that Manila was the great prize "and the thing which will give us the eastern trade." Even more representative of what had become the view of the industrial interests largely dominating government was Mark Hanna's forthright answer to those who combatted as selfish and materialistic the idea of holding the Philippines for the sake of trade with China. "If it is commercialism to want the possession of a strategic point giving the American people an opportunity to maintain a foothold in the markets of that great Eastern country," he declared, "for God's sake let us have commercialism."

The idealistic impulses of American missionaries furnished another link between the Philippines and China. They saw the further extension of our influence in the Far East as aiding them in their immense task of bringing Christianity to the Chinese people. They discovered the working of Divine Providence in our new conquests. "Every American missionary from whom I have heard in recent months," Dr. J. H. Barrows wrote in the *Interior,* "has thanked God that the American flag has entered the Far East." Just as the Philippines were to be a base for our trade with China, so were they to be the gateway for missionary enterprise. There was as fervid support for the imperialism of righteousness as for the imperialism of commercial power.

Other factors entered into the final decision of President McKinley to retain the Philippines. There were questions of naval strategy and of the balance of Pacific power, the influence of imperialistic expansion for its own sake and a wholly sincere belief that the United States could not shirk the duties and responsibilities imposed upon it by the victory of Manila Bay. If the islands had been returned to Spain, the end result might well have been their purchase by Germany, or, in the event of Filipino rebellion, their seizure by that ambitious power. But McKinley, too, recognized the importance of matters of trade and commerce. "Incidental to our tenure in the Philippines," he wrote his peace envoys after eloquently dwelling upon our national obligations, "is the commercial opportunity to which American statesmanship cannot be indifferent."

There was strong opposition to our venture in imperialism and consequent entanglement in Far Eastern politics. A sharp division of opinion in the Senate corresponded to opposing views in the country as a whole. Only after what Senator Lodge, arch-expansionist, declared to be the stiffest political battle of his experience, was the treaty annexing the Philippines finally approved. The basic argument of the anti-imperialists was that colonial possessions could in no way be reconciled with democratic ideals and the republican form of government, but they also sought to combat the proposition that possession of the islands would promote trade in eastern Asia. Senator Caffery declared it to be absurd on the ground that few American products went to Asia because they were not wanted there, while western Europe took nine-tenths of our exports because of its need for them. He was not concerned over the scramble for concessions in China. "It is manifest," he stated, "that if we want markets for our surplus manufactures, our surplus cereals, all that we cannot consume, we must send them to the people who will consume them."

These were negative arguments, however. They lacked the driving force and imaginative appeal of those which connected possession of the Philippines with an effective challenge to European trade rivalry in China. The American public was swung to support of the Senate's action in upholding the treaty with Spain by the more glowing appeals to manifest destiny made by such forthright imperialists as Senator Beveridge.

"The Philippines are ours forever," this young Indianan declared in a speech, in January 1900, which grandiloquently expressed the expansionist fervor of the day. ". . . And just beyond the Philippines are China's illimitable markets. We will not retreat from either. . . . Our largest trade must henceforth be with Asia. The Pacific is our ocean. . . . And the Pacific is the ocean of the commerce of the future. Most future wars will be conflicts for commerce. The power that rules the Pacific, therefore, is the power that rules the world. And, with the Philippines, that power is and will forever be the American Republic."

It may well be debated whether the annexation of the islands was actually a move made in the interests of supporting our policy in China, or whether it resulted solely from that "cosmic tendency" toward imperialism which was so powerful an impulse throughout the world at the close of the nineteenth century. So eager an expansionist as Captain Mahan spoke of the nation as "staggered for an instant by a proposition so entirely unexpected and novel as Asiatic dominion." But however fortuitous the occasion for winning control of the Philippines, our new Pacific advance was clearly a projection of those forces which for over a century had led us closer and closer to the shores of Asia. Popular support for retaining the islands was certainly greatly influenced, perhaps more than by any other single consideration, by the idea that their possession would enable us to safeguard our interests in China at a time when they appeared to be so gravely jeopardized by that country's threatened partition among the European powers.

Such an interpretation of imperialism in the Pacific is not invalidated because our actual trade with China was so relatively slight in 1898, nor because so few people were actively concerned in its development. As already suggested, our national interest in China has for over a century been largely based upon the tremendous potentialities of her markets and an almost mystical faith in the promise of her national advance. In not wanting to be shut out from China, we have been consistently dazzled by great expectations.

THE OPEN DOOR AND THE
BOXER REBELLION

IN so far as public attention was directed toward the Far East in the immediate aftermath of the Spanish War, it was absorbed by the bitter struggle in which the United States unexpectedly found itself engaged in the Philippine Islands. The Filipinos had not shown themselves to be quite so happy over the extension of American rule as the imperialists had fondly hoped. They were prepared to fight for their independence, however hopeless their cause, and the military conquest of the islands was something on which most Americans had not counted. While the policy on which we had embarked was generally supported, it still awoke vehement criticism among the anti-imperialists. There was also a very definite cooling off in the popular ardor for further involvement in Asiatic politics.

In circles directly concerned with trade, however, considerable agitation continued for direct action to combat the possible partition of the Chinese Empire among our commercial rivals. The proposals put forward by Great Britain in favor of what was already being called "the open door" had received a good deal of support in leading newspaper editorials as early as September 1898. As interpreted by the press, the real danger in the Chinese situation came from Russia, whose persistent advance in Manchuria appeared to foreshadow imperialistic control over all north China. It was urged that the United States assume its share of responsibility not only in safeguarding equality of trade within the Chinese Empire, but in even more general support of Anglo-Saxon principles and traditions. The *New York Times* criticized the McKinley administration on the ground that our interest in China had "not been intelligently represented or adequately appreciated by the

State Department." The *New York Sun* stated emphatically that there should be more effective recognition of "the complete solidarity of interests" with England. The *Commercial Advertiser* also stressed the principle of Anglo-Saxon cooperation and the *Philadelphia Record* specifically urged President McKinley to act with Great Britain in opening up Chinese ports to world trade.

Further support for this point of view was derived from the propaganda of Lord Charles Beresford, who visited this country early in 1899 after a tour of the Far East as delegate of the Associated Chambers of Commerce of Great Britain. In public speeches, magazine articles and interviews with the press, this super-salesman for British interests in China employed all his persuasive powers to arouse greater popular interest in this country for the Open Door. Just what did he contemplate? "It means that England, America, Germany and Japan," Beresford wrote, "shall, by an agreement, maintain free and equal commercial relations for all time in the Orient." If such a policy were not adopted, he warned, Russia would soon become all-powerful in north China, there would be a general scramble over the rest of the helpless empire and the United States would lose out completely in the future development of the Chinese market.

The public as a whole, disillusioned over our adventure in the Philippines, was not greatly impressed. A few more memorials from business groups, especially those concerned with the cotton trade, were forwarded to Washington in support of such schemes. But other matters claimed national interest. It was actually as an almost complete surprise that toward the close of 1899 the public learned that Secretary of State John Hay was prepared to fulfill the promise of our expansion to the shores of Asia by intervening more directly than ever before in Far Eastern politics. The *Literary Digest*, in its issue of November 18, 1899, referred to a "widely credited report" of a definite move to ensure the Open Door that "has brought to public attention a development of world politics and international commerce that has been little thought of in this country."

It was not to take the form of concerted action with Great Britain. John Hay would undoubtedly have favored such a policy. He was always a strong Anglophile. There was also support for a cooperative approach to the problem from so influential a political leader as Senator Lodge. "I should be glad to have the United States say to England," he had written Hay while the latter was still serving as our ambassador in London, "that we would stand by her in her declaration that the ports of China must be opened to all nations equally or to none. . . ." But Hay was compelled to realize that in spite of newspaper editorials urging Anglo-American rapprochement, only independent action could hope to command popular approval. The American people were not likely to favor a policy that seemed to be taken under British pressure or could possibly be interpreted as pulling British chestnuts out of the fire. Moreover, it was more thoroughly in keeping with our historic policy toward China to insist on the basic principle of equality of trade on our own account.

The steps whereby Hay reached the decision to state his Open Door policy, all unknown to the public, make a curious story. For however strong the underlying forces that made this projection of our influence in Asia such a natural development, the notes themselves were inspired by two advisers to the Secretary of State whose views may well have reflected the influence of British agitation for the Open Door. These men were William W. Rockhill, an American who had diplomatic experience in the Far East and was serving as a special consultant for the State Department on Chinese affairs, and an English friend, A. E. Hippisley, who happened to be in Washington on his way home from service in the Chinese customs inspectorate.

It was Hippisley's original suggestion, conveyed to the Secretary of State with Rockhill's strong endorsement, that the United States should assume leadership in meeting the problem of China by itself seeking an international guarantee that there would be no interference with foreign trade in the various powers' spheres of influence. Hay at first hesitated. "I am fully awake to the great importance of what you say and am more than ready to act," he answered Rockhill on August 7, 1899. "But the senseless prejudices in certain sections of the 'Senate and people' compel us to move with great caution." This was an obvious reference to the anti-British feeling which Hay thought would cause any such move to be interpreted as playing into Great Britain's hands. But Hippisley was not to be discouraged by such nervous forebodings. He argued that political capital could be made out of the issue if it were handled carefully. "The public need know nothing of the steps taken by the Secretary of State till the negotiations have been consummated," he suggested, "and the announcement then that the United States had secured China's independence and so served the cause of peace and civilization would be a trump card for the Administration and crush all the life out of the anti-imperialist agitation of Bryan, Croker & Co."

Whatever the force of these arguments, Hay became convinced that the time for action had come. He asked Rockhill, still serving as the intermediary for Hippisley's views, to draw up draft instructions for our foreign envoys incorporating the proposed policy. Rockhill did so at once, embodying in this document almost word for word a memorandum Hippisley had submitted with his last letter. It was approved by both Secretary Hay and President McKinley, and on September 6 these instructions were dispatched to London, St. Petersburg and Berlin, and a month later to Paris, Rome and Tokyo.

Each of the several powers was asked to adhere to a threefold declaration of policy:

"First: [That it] will in no wise interfere with any treaty port or any vested interest within any so-called 'sphere of influence' or leased territory it may have in China.

"Second: That the Chinese treaty tariff of the time being shall apply to all merchandise landed or shipped to all such ports as are within said 'sphere of influence' (unless they be 'free ports'), no matter to what nationality it may belong, and that duties so leviable shall be collected by the Chinese Government.

"Third: That it will levy no higher harbor dues on vessels of another nationality frequenting any port in such 'sphere' than shall be levied on vessels of its own nationality, and no higher railroad charges over lines built, controlled, or operated within its 'sphere' on merchandise belonging to its citizens or subjects of other nationalities transported through such 'sphere' than shall be levied on similar merchandise belonging to its own nationals transported over equal distances."

These were the original Open Door notes. They were so highly limited in their scope that they clearly recognized existing spheres of influence, and they made no suggestion whatsoever of safeguarding China's political independence. They said nothing about equality in so far as it related to industrial or railroad concessions.

The influence of Great Britain in the evolution of our policy is clearly apparent. It is highly revealing to realize how the notes to the powers, so generally credited to John Hay himself, were inspired, if not actually written, by a British subject visiting in Baltimore. Nevertheless the United States had acted independently, and the principles that Hay sought to establish were in complete conformity with American doctrine throughout the nineteenth century. Hay's objective was to thwart discrimination against American trade from any quarter, and there were no distinctions in the requests he made to the powers. Where Great Britain had perhaps hoped to draw the United States into a common policy primarily directed against Russia, it was now made clear that we were playing no favorites and sought the same assurances of trade equality from everyone. It was this which gave the Open Door notes their real validity. Moreover, the step which Hay had taken would hardly have been feasible had not the recent extension of our influence in eastern Asia given him the authority to take such an independent stand.

After the dispatch of the notes Rockhill commented hopefully that "they will undoubtedly help to insure, for the time being, the integrity of the Chinese Empire." But despite his assertion of this more ambitious goal, it should be reiterated that the original notes themselves said nothing of Chinese independence. For all the interest it was to excite, and the importance of the developments that flowed from its first announcement, the Open Door policy, as formulated in 1899, was only a restatement of principles that had first been written into the Treaty of Wanghia over half a century earlier, and again and again reaffirmed by our mid-century envoys in China.

There was a marked reluctance on the part of the powers to accept even such limited commitments. They had no desire to subscribe to what was for them in effect a self-denying ordinance in respect to any future plans they might have for their spheres of influence and leased territories. But no one of them quite dared to betray what it might be contemplating by an outright refusal to accept the American proposals. The replies which Secretary Hay received were couched in evasive and somewhat ambiguous terms. Even the British answer, exempting Hongkong from any application of the new principle, was anything but enthusiastic, while that of Russia was so equivocal that only by the broadest stretch of the imagination could it be considered acceptance at all. Ironically enough, the reply of Japan perhaps went furthest in accepting the principles which Hay had advanced. Still an "innocent onlooker on international affairs," as one of her statesmen phrased it, Japan did not hesitate to endorse a policy which would prevent her European rivals from monopolizing Chinese trade or partitioning the empire while she was still too weak to claim a share in the plunder.

Hay refused to be discouraged by the ambiguities of the powers' answers. He decided to ignore the strings attached to their acceptance of his program, and to make the most of what he had in hand. Hoping to win such strong public support for his policy, at home and abroad, that no nation would in the future dare to do violence to the principle of the Open Door, he announced publicly, on March 20, 1900, that he had received satisfactory assurances from all the governments to which he had addressed his notes, and that in each case the assent to his proposals was "final and definitive."

Whatever the reservations in the minds of European statesmen, the American public generally accepted Hay's achievement at its face value. It was hailed as an outstanding triumph for American diplomacy, not only guaranteeing our trade in China "the fair field and no favor" which had always been our principal objective in the Far East, but also ensuring the Middle Kingdom against any further attacks upon its sovereignty. A move which at one and the same time promoted American commercial interests and demonstrated our friendship for the Chinese people created a warm glow of satisfaction over the new direction in which our foreign policy was moving. Party lines were broken in the chorus of approval that greeted Hay's announcement. Even anti-imperialist opponents of the McKinley administration could find little fault with a program that appeared to commit the United States to nothing, while vigorously asserting our new role as a world power.

"One of the most important diplomatic negotiations of our time," the *Journal of Commerce* stated, while the *Chicago Herald* declared even more expansively that "there has never been a more brilliant and important achievement in diplomacy." The *New York Evening Post* characterized the exchange of notes as "a noble work of peace." The *Philadelphia Press* expressed the opinion that history would record the agreement as a greater achievement and more important triumph than victory in the Spanish War—"it protects the present, it safeguards the future, and it establishes the United States in an impregnable position." The *New York Tribune*, the *Boston Transcript*, the *Chicago Evening Post* were equally enthusiastic, adding their editors' conviction that, with its new power and influence in Asia, the United States would be able to uphold its policy should any nation in the future dare to disregard it.

Almost alone among the nation's important papers, the *Springfield Republican* raised the question as to what had actually been accomplished. It had no criticism of the Open Door notes; they could do no possible harm. "But to suppose that such assurances, politely written and most blandly tendered, really amount to anything in themselves," this newspaper caustically stated, "seems rather funny. . . . Diplomacy has done nothing to change the situation, while the government has gone far toward placing itself in a position where, to be consistent, it must guarantee by military force the political integrity of China, or share in a possible partition. Underneath this showy concern for the interests of American trade and commerce in the Far East, there is a steady movement toward militarism."

At the very time that Secretary Hay was making his triumphant announcement of the powers' acceptance of the Open Door, a crisis was rapidly developing within China that was to subject his policy to its first critical test. In a fierce wave of resentment against the ceaseless pressure of the western powers, their seizure of territory and interference in internal affairs, a popular movement had flared up in north China to rid the country once and for all of the presence of the "foreign devils." Bands of Chinese, loosely organized in such secret societies as that of the Fists of Righteous Harmony, more popularly known as Boxers, took up arms to drive the barbarians into the sea. Foreign property and foreign lives were endangered as never before in all the history of the relations between China and the western world.

This new upsurge of anti-foreign feeling was largely due to the continual interference with native customs for which both western business interests and western missionaries were responsible. The building of railroads and telegraph lines, in such callous disregard of the people's sensibilities as often to disturb ancestral burial sites, had awakened the superstitious fears of the ignorant and intensely conservative peasants. The establishment of churches and mission schools had defied native religious belief in the way of Confucius and the rule of Buddhist and Taoist gods. Despairing of help from their own corrupt and decadent government, the Boxers turned against all foreigners in vengeful fury. Their armed bands roamed the countryside, at first burning the property and taking the lives of "secondary devils," the native Chinese converts to Christianity, but soon attacking the mission stations themselves with fire and sword.

"Peking, Tientsin, and Paotingfu," read a contemporary account of conditions in the spring of 1900, "are encircled by bands of maddened and fanatical people whose numbers are swollen by an excited crowd of vagabonds, and who, being maintained by leaders in high position, rob, pillage, burn and kill as they pass. For the moment their activity is directed against Chinese converts, Catholic and Protestant. . . . They do not conceal their object to get rid of all foreigners . . . by means of a destruction of religious missions and a general insurrection against European and American residents . . . and on their flags they now assert they act by imperial command."

The Empress Dowager Tzu Hsi, crafty, willful and imperious, had virtually deposed the Emperor, after a short-lived period in which he had tried to introduce a program of constructive reform, and there was little question that the Boxers had her secret sympathy. Their movement had originally been anti-dynastic, as well as anti-foreign and anti-Christian, growing as it did out of universal discontent and impoverishment among the Chinese masses. Tzu Hsi hoped by espousing it to divert wholly against the western barbarians any attacks that might otherwise be made upon the Manchus. She knew her own position on the Dragon Throne was none too secure. And she was still as anti-foreign herself as she had been in days past. Nothing would have pleased the Empress Dowager more than to have the Boxers rid the country of all foreigners. She half believed in the superstitious rigmarole which they claimed rendered them immune from foreign bullets. While she did not quite dare openly and frankly to adopt their cause, for she knew the heavy hand of the powers, she nevertheless gave their leaders aid and encouragement. She replied evasively to the protests that the Imperial Government was doing nothing to maintain order. When compelled to go through the motions of issuing decrees to the provincial officials for suppressing disorder, she couched her orders in such ambiguous terms that they felt more than justified in doing nothing whatsoever to check the growing rebellion.

The situation came to a head in Peking during June 1900. Powerful Boxer forces, armed with swords and spears, wearing flaming red sashes, burst into the Tatar City. Foreign buildings were plundered and put to the torch, over two thousand Chinese converts massacred, the chancellor of the Japanese legation and the German minister assassinated, and siege laid to the legation quarter where the foreigners had hastily taken refuge. The Empress Dowager made no effort to maintain order. While professing herself helpless to control matters, she was actually encouraging the Boxers. A contemporary Chinese diary tells vividly of the flaming hatred of the Old Buddha for the foreigners and her desire to see them all exterminated. On one occasion the Boxer bombardment of the legations suddenly came to a stop. Had Tzu Hsi finally intervened in the foreigners' behalf? No—the sound of the firing had disturbed the ladies of the court picnicking in the palace gardens.

When the first reports of the uprising reached the United States, Secretary Hay at once instructed our minister in Peking, E. H. Conger, to take whatever steps appeared necessary to safeguard American lives and American property. At the same time, he made it clear that the United States had no idea of allowing disorders in China to become a pretext, as they had so often in the past, for imposing new demands upon the Chinese government. American policy, Conger was told, had no other objective than "to protect with energy American interests." In pursuing such a goal, he was further instructed, he should act at all times independently. Except in cases of absolute necessity, he was not even to participate in any joint protests to the Imperial Government. Above all, Secretary Hay emphatically declared, "there must be no alliances." The old cooperative policy among the powers appeared to have been wholly abandoned in line with the new attitude represented by the Open Door notes.

The deepening crisis in Peking soon placed a somewhat different complexion on affairs. "Situation worse," the American minister cabled just before the Boxers finally closed in on the legation quarter. "It is possible we may be besieged in Pekin, with railroads and telegraphs cut. In that case, I ask, as my colleagues are doing, that necessary instructions be given Admiral [in command of American naval forces] to concert with other chiefs of squadron at Taku to take necessary measures warranted by the situation to eventually deliver Pekin." A few days later he cabled again, asking permission to join the envoys of the other powers in seeking an imperial audience, and to participate in whatever other joint steps might be taken for their mutual protection. "Answer quick," he urged.

Hay at once cabled the necessary permission, and waited, anxiously, for the next word from the Chinese capital. None came. The Boxers had broken all communications. Day followed day with no news at all from the besieged legations. Rumors from the treaty ports flooded the world. The Boxers had shattered the defenses of the legation quarter and demolished all foreign buildings. They had taken the foreigners themselves captive. They had massacred them all in cold blood. All hope was finally given up for the lives of the Europeans and Americans in Peking, and in London plans were made for a memorial service to be held in St. Paul's Cathedral.

At this point Secretary Hay received through devious channels a cipher message from the American minister. It brought a quick surge of relief to the entire country, to the entire world, and yet it also crystallized new fears. "For one month we have been besieged in British legation under continued shot and shell from Chinese troops," Conger reported on July 17. "Quick relief only can prevent general massacre."

Plans for relief had already been initiated. Foreign troops were gathered at Tientsin and preparations started for a possible allied military expedition to Peking. Uncertainty over what was actually happening in the capital, the ambiguous attitude of the Imperial Government and the general complexities of the situation had led, however, to prolonged delay in setting these plans in motion. A small contingent of some 2,000 troops had on one occasion advanced inland, but the threatening attitude of the Chinese had caused it to withdraw. Until mid-July, indeed, the United States still hoped that active hostilities could be avoided. When the forces of the other powers occupied the Taku forts, in startling parallel to events in the 1850's, the American naval commander would take no part in the operation. Unlike Commodore Tatnall, he ignored the appeal that "blood was thicker than water," and interpreted literally his orders not to make war on the Chinese.

Yet forthright action to raise the siege at Peking soon became essential if the foreigners were to be rescued. The Empress Dowager protested that intervention was not necessary for their safety, but she gave no assurances that the siege would be lifted. Nor could her promise to bring the foreigners to Tientsin under official escort, made only as preparations for the relief expedition neared completion, be believed when she was known to be secretly conniving with the Boxer leaders. After word reached Tientsin from the American minister that to leave the legations was to face "certain death," a final decision was reached to advance on Peking. The relief expedition at last got under way on August 4.

The United States, reiterating that its sole object was the rescue of the legations, was now fully committed, by force of circumstance, to joint action. It contributed some 2,500 men to the total allied forces of 19,000. The largest contingent was 8,000 Japanese troops, the Tokyo government cooperating fully with the western powers all along the line; the Russian force was 4,800; the British totalled 3,000, and the French some 800. There was no over-all command until German forces arrived considerably later. Then Count von Waldersee was given this post in token of the paramount interest of Germany in the affair as a consequence of the assassination of her minister.

The world waited with growing anxiety for reports on the progress of the expedition. It was engaged in a race against time. There was no telling when the legations might be compelled to surrender to the overwhelming forces massed against them. At any moment the Imperial Government might decide to back the Boxer attack in strength and make all further resistance in Peking entirely futile. Throughout the entire summer the fate of the foreigners really depended on the wavering whims of the Empress Dowager. Listening first to one and then to another set of advisers, she apparently could not make up her mind. One day she would send supplies to the beleaguered legations, and on the next, urge the Boxer chieftains to destroy them. At any time, she could either have raised the siege or crushed out the foreigners completely. She did neither.

As the allies advanced from Tientsin, they met only the slightest resistance. Whatever hopes Tzu Hsi may have had that the Boxers could put up any real fight against a foreign army were soon dissipated. As the relief expedition approached the capital, the fear of retribution consequently drove everything else out of her mind. She turned her back on the crisis. Disguising herself in peasant costume, the Old Buddha secretly escaped from the imperial palace and left Peking in headlong flight. Court officials and Boxer leaders alike were thrown into panic, and soon they too scattered to the four winds. When the relief expedition entered Peking on August 14, the leaderless rebels were already melting away. The siege was lifted; the legations had been saved.

For eight bitter weeks the foreigners—473 civilians and 451 foreign guards—and several thousand Chinese converts had been under intermittent attack. Some 76 of the defenders had been killed, and 179 wounded. All had suffered cruel privation, living on a scanty diet of rice and horse flesh. It was almost as if by miracle that they had survived.

The principal concern of both the American people and their government in regard to these dramatic happenings in China had been the fate of the besieged foreigners in Peking. Secretary Hay remained determined, however, to do everything possible to prevent the Boxer Rebellion from being made the occasion for either war against China or new demands upon her government that would revive the danger of partition. The Open Door was at stake. The full force of American diplomacy was to be thrown behind its maintenance by holding the powers to full responsibility for what Hay had interpreted as their acceptance of his proposals of the previous year.

With this end in view, a further declaration of just where the United States stood was made in a circular sent to the several powers on July 3. It went beyond a reaffirmation of the Open Door. Hay took the further logical step of declaring it to be American policy to sustain China's independence by limiting intervention in the existing emergency to the restoration of order and the protection of our treaty rights. The United States intended, the Secretary of State declared, to seek a solution of the situation which would "bring about permanent peace and safety to China, preserve Chinese territorial and administrative entity, protect all rights guaranteed by treaty and international law, and safeguard for the world the principle of equal and impartial trade with all parts of the Chinese Empire."

This assertion of our national interest in Chinese affairs went much further than the original Open Door notes. The emphasis upon preserving China's independence was a far more challenging statement of American policy. Secretary Hay's primary objective was still that of safeguarding our commercial interests in eastern Asia. To uphold the existing Chinese government, however weak it might be, was the best possible means of assuring equality of trade. Yet the fact remains that the promotion of our own interests through this association of Chinese independence and the Open Door also conformed to the best interests of China.

No one of the powers made any commitment to support this amplified policy. As the difficult negotiations proceeded in Peking for settlement of the questions rising out of the Boxer Rebellion, Hay found himself engaged in a single-handed struggle to uphold the American position. Germany was most concerned with further punitive expeditions against the Chinese; Russia was aggressively expanding her area of control over Manchuria. "There is . . . not a single power we can rely upon," Hay wrote bitterly on one occasion, "for our policy of abstention from plunder and the Open Door." The European nations were playing a diplomatic game all their own, and the veteran Chinese diplomat Li Hung-chang, to whom the fleeing Empress Dowager had confided full responsibility for dealing with the foreigners, cleverly took advantage of their rivalries to do what he could to protect China's interests.

The final Boxer settlement, concluded in September 1901, provided for the punishment of the ringleaders of the rebellion, secured guarantees that there would be no further recurrence of such attacks upon foreigners, and imposed a heavy indemnity upon the Chinese government for losses in lives and property. The powers were henceforth to have the right to maintain troops in Peking and Tientsin and to keep open the railway between these two cities. These were harsh terms and they represented still further infringements upon Chinese sovereignty. But there was no partition of the empire, as for a time had been expected, and the underlying principles of the Open Door were at least theoretically maintained.

Throughout the negotiations the United States had at all times sought to moderate the powers' demands, revealing a far less vengeful policy than the European nations and vainly trying to keep the indemnity down to reasonable levels to enable China to recover from the devastation caused by the rebellion.

We were later to give full proof of our good faith in this regard by remitting our share of the Boxer funds to the Imperial Government for the promotion of education. Nevertheless, it was the mutual suspicions of the powers and their entanglement in the power politics of Europe that really saved China in this emergency, rather than anything said or done by Secretary Hay. He had found it difficult to exercise even the limited measure of influence that he did because of the rather lukewarm attitude at home toward his policy. The public approved of the Open Door and preservation of Chinese independence. Yet when the question arose of keeping in Peking the troops which the Secretary of State believed essential to impress upon the powers that we meant business, it balked. Our forces had to be withdrawn for fear of possible political repercussions in an election year. A first proof was given of the reluctance of the American people, however willing to accept the Open Door in theory, to run any risk in its support.

Secretary Hay was so thoroughly disillusioned by this experience that by November 1900 he appears to have been ready to abandon the basic premises of his entire policy. Under pressure from the War and Navy Departments, he instructed our minister in Peking to seek to obtain for the United States a naval base and territorial concession at Samsah Bay, in the province of Fukien. A demand so at variance with our traditional attitude toward China was not pressed through, however, and one of the reasons for withdrawing it was objections from Japan. After suavely pointing out that any such concession would run counter to the declared policy of the United States not to make the Boxer Rebellion a pretext for seeking territorial grants from China, the Tokyo government declared that Fukien was within its sphere of influence and the proposed concession would violate Japanese treaty rights.

With the possible exception of this abortive move, our general attitude toward China during the entire course of the Boxer troubles had on the whole demonstrated a very real sympathy for the Chinese people. Still, our position in the Far

East had an air of unreality about it. When Japan, again entering the picture, inquired in February 1901 what we intended to do about the principles we had professed in the light of persistent Russian encroachments in Manchuria, Hay was compelled to answer that the United States was "not at present prepared to attempt singly, or in concert with other powers, to enforce these views in the East by any demonstration which could present a character of hostility to any other power."

Nor would we, indeed, for another forty years. We had taken our stand, primarily in the interests of our trade and commerce, as an avowed supporter of China's independence. It was a policy reflecting both the practical and idealistic impulses of the American people, but one that we would not effectively carry out until this same Japan, seeking a free hand to carry out her conquest of eastern Asia, struck directly at the United States.

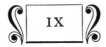

ADVANCE AND RETREAT

It was Russia which most seriously challenged the Open Door policy in the years immediately following the Boxer settlement. The troops that had poured into Manchuria when disturbances first flared up in 1900 were not withdrawn when order was reestablished. In complete control of the Manchurian railways, as well as her leased territory on the Liaotung Peninsula, Russia gave every sign of maneuvering for position to impose new demands upon China. It was apparent that she had no idea of observing the principle of equality of trade in any of the vast area north of the Great Wall where her influence was predominant.

Hay several times protested strongly against the presence of these Russian troops in Manchuria and the discrimination which was being practiced against American trade. On each occasion, he was assured that all military forces would be withdrawn and that Russia was not seeking exclusive commercial privileges. But there was no real change in policy at St. Petersburg. Hay fulminated hopelessly over trying to deal "with a government with whom mendacity is a science." At one meeting he told Count Cassini, the Russian ambassador in Washington, that if the count's country continued on its course, there would be nothing for the powers to do except take over control of other Chinese provinces. "This is already done," Cassini stormed in reply to this veiled threat. "China is dismembered and we are entitled to our share."

Under such circumstances, there was little that our Secretary of State could accomplish. As he had intimated to Japan, the United States was not prepared to enforce its policy in the Far East by a demonstration of hostility toward any other power. He discouragedly wrote Theodore Roosevelt, now

President following the assassination of McKinley in 1901, that the United States might as well recognize Russia's "exceptional position" in Manchuria and be done with it. Roosevelt was unwilling to accept so meekly what he regarded as an attempt to organize China against American interests. "I have not the slightest objection," he told Hay, "to the Russians knowing that I feel thoroughly aroused and irritated at their conduct in Manchuria; that I don't intend to give way and that I am year by year growing more confident that this country would back me in going to an extreme in the matter."

Just what he meant is hardly clear. There was little public concern over what might happen in far-away Manchuria—even less than some thirty years later—and Hay was far more realistic in his appraisal of the situation than the President. There could be no "going to an extreme in the matter," as he indicated in explaining the futility of State Department protests to St. Petersburg. "I take it for granted," Hay stated, "that Russia knows as we do that we will not fight over Manchuria, for the simple reason that we cannot. . . ."

He made one move in 1903, however, to obtain assurances from the Peking government that our position in Manchuria would at least become no worse than when the territory was under unquestioned Chinese control. A new commercial treaty was negotiated which pledged the ultimate relinquishment of our extraterritorial rights, reaffirmed observance of the Open Door principle in Chinese-American relations and opened up to trade the Manchurian cities of Mukden and Antung. From the point of view of our commercial interests, this was nevertheless a barren achievement in view of Russia's tightening grip on all territory north of the Great Wall. No one realized better than Hay himself that it could not possibly halt the Czar's advance.

There was one power, however, which could not afford to condone further Russian advance, for it directly blocked her own aggressive ambitions. This was of course Japan. With Russia firmly entrenched in both Korea and Manchuria, every possibility that Japan might herself expand overseas and win a foothold on the Asiatic continent would be forever gone. The Japanese Empire would be at the mercy of an overwhelmingly powerful neighbor. War was a more acceptable alternative than submission for a nation so determined to win a larger place in the sun. Having concluded an alliance with Great Britain which assured her of support should any other country come to Russia's assistance, Japan was ready to accept the challenge of Czarist imperialism. When peaceful negotiation failed to settle the issue, she struck swiftly and surely. In circumstances that were to be strangely paralleled forty-odd years later when the United States rather than Russia stood as the chief obstacle to her continental expansion, Japan opened hostilities on February 8, 1904, with a surprise attack upon the Russian fleet at Port Arthur.

There was little realization in the United States at this time of Japan's ambition to win political supremacy in eastern Asia. The Tokyo government had apparently accepted the Open Door policy. No attempt was made during the Boxer Rebellion to secure special privileges from China, and Japanese troops had acted with more restraint in Peking than those of several of the other powers. The attack on Russia was consequently widely interpreted as a move to safeguard China's independence. Where the United States had stood aside, Japan was valiantly accepting the Czar's challenge to the Open Door policy. There was no question of the United States taking any position other than one of neutrality, but a survey of newspaper opinion upon the outbreak of war revealed overwhelming popular sympathy for Japan. Conservative and liberal papers were in full agreement in their hope of quick defeat for Russia.

"Japan is not only fighting the battle of progress and civilization," the *Journal of Commerce* declared. ". . . She is standing as the champion of commercial rights in whose maintenance no nation is so vitally interested as the United States." "In this war Russia stands for reaction and Japan for progress," an editorial in the *Arena* stated. "The organization and control of the millions of China by Russia is far more dangerous to the rest of the world than would be their control by the Japanese."

President Roosevelt fully shared this popular view of the issues at stake in the Far East. Two days after the attack at Port Arthur, he wrote his son how thoroughly pleased he was with Tokyo's first victory—"Japan is playing our game." According to a later statement, he even went so far as to notify both Germany and France that, should either of them intervene in the struggle, he was prepared "to side with Japan, and proceed to whatever length was necessary in her behalf." There is no evidence that he actually took such an unprecedented step, yet our friendly attitude toward Japan, and the role of American bankers in financing Japan's war efforts, made us almost a silent partner in the Anglo-Japanese alliance.

At the same time, the State Department did everything possible to bolster the Open Door policy by seeking guarantees from both Russia and Japan that they would observe China's neutrality and "in all practicable ways her administrative entity." This was a futile gesture. Manchuria was the inevitable battleground of the war and each of the belligerents, as a Russian note bluntly stated, had to consider its own interest.

Japan's spectacular victories on both land and sea dampened the early enthusiasm for her cause. It was with shocked surprise that the American public suddenly realized that Japan had become a powerful nation with political ambitions that might well run counter to everything for which the United States stood in the Far East. In decisively defeating Russia it was obvious that she would fall heir to the Russian position in Manchuria. Although the Tokyo government had given assurances that it intended to restore this area to China, the horrid doubt arose whether a completely victorious Japan would prove as solicitous over the Open Door as when Russia was swinging it shut. For all our original confidence in Japan's good intentions, it began to be feared that her imperialist ambitions might prove quite as disturbing as those of the Czar.

Roosevelt's policy became one of seeking to maintain a balance of power in eastern Asia that would provide a more favorable basis for protecting our interests in China than too decisive a victory for either Russia or Japan. With such purposes in view, perhaps quite as much as any more general interest in peace, he was ready to mediate in the Russo-Japanese conflict, and through his good offices peace negotiations were begun at Portsmouth, New Hampshire, in August 1905. While Japan was eventually induced to modify somewhat her original demands upon Russia, notably in regard to an indemnity, the settlement finally concluded represented a substantial Japanese triumph. Russia was compelled to withdraw entirely from Korea, surrender the southern half of the island of Sakhalin, and hand over to Japan both her leased territory in the Liaotung Peninsula and all her railway holdings in south Manchuria. Japan had almost overnight become a world power, with a firm foothold upon the Asiatic mainland and a position that would enable her to exercise an important influence in the future political developments of the Pacific.

Having failed to secure recognition of China's rights during the war, the United States could not block this substitution of Japanese for Russian controls in south Manchuria. No protest was made when the Tokyo government compelled China to sign new treaties acknowledging Japan's title to the former Russian concessions, nor were any objections raised when it became quite clear that Japan intended to annex Korea. Indeed, a bargain was struck in July 1905 through a secret memorandum signed by Secretary of War Taft and Foreign Minister Katsura. The United States recognized the transfer of Korea to Japanese suzerainty in return for Japan's disavowal of any aggressive designs upon the Philippines.

Three years later the ambiguities of our position were even more clearly demonstrated in the Root-Takahira agreement of 1908. This pact provided at one and the same time for acceptance by the United States and Japan of the existing status quo in the general area of the Pacific, and for the maintenance of trade equality within a sovereign and independent China. Yet the status quo as it applied to Manchuria drastically infringed upon Chinese political authority north of the Great Wall. The United States was seeking to come to terms with Japan, rather than insisting upon the principles Secretary Hay had asserted in 1900. Roosevelt was in retreat before Japanese aggression just as Hay had been forced to back down in the face of Russian advances. The United States did not wholly abandon the Open Door. Its maintenance continued to be the theoretical basis of our Far Eastern policy. But as Japan proceeded to annex Korea and further consolidate her position in Manchuria, we tacitly acquiesced in moves that were, in fact, definite violations of Chinese sovereignty.

How far Theodore Roosevelt had modified his earlier ideas upon upholding the Open Door doctrine is graphically revealed in a letter written two years after conclusion of the Root-Takahira agreement to his successor in the White House. American policy, he told President Taft, should be the careful avoidance of any move that could possibly make the Japanese feel that the United States was hostile to them or a menace to their interests. Any alliance with China for the protection of our mutual rights, he argued, would not be an additional strength to this country but an obligation that we could not afford to assume.

"I do not believe," Roosevelt stated emphatically in 1910, "in our taking any position anywhere unless we can make good; and as regards Manchuria, if the Japanese choose to follow a course of conduct to which we are adverse, we cannot stop it unless we are prepared to go to war, and a successful war about Manchuria would require a fleet as good as that of England, plus an army as good as that of Germany. The Open Door policy in China was an excellent thing, and I hope it will be a good thing in the future, so far as it can be maintained by general diplomatic agreement; but, as has been proved by the whole history of Manchuria, alike under Russia and Japan, the Open Door policy, as a matter of fact, completely disappears as soon as a powerful nation determines to disregard it, and is willing to run the risk of war rather than forego its intention."

The realistic, and also prophetic, nature of this statement hardly needs comment. Usually depicted as belligerently prepared to promote American interests at whatever risk, Theodore Roosevelt reveals himself as strongly opposed to overseas commitments that he did not feel the American people would uphold by force. He wielded "the big stick" to show Japan that the United States could not be pushed around in the controversy during these same years over Japanese immigration into the United States, but he did not favor an aggressive policy in support of Chinese sovereignty when Japan had so much more at stake than did the United States.

Taft did not follow Roosevelt's advice. In the final result no more successful in upholding the Open Door than either Hay or Roosevelt, he followed a course which established among all Japanese the idea that the United States was the one obstacle in the path of their overseas expansion. Coming into office at a time when matters of foreign trade and foreign investments were even more in the forefront of public interest than they had been at the close of the nineteenth century, his administration sought to promote our commercial expansion by every means in its power. Both in Manchuria and in China proper, "dollar diplomacy" lent active support to American business and financial interests.

These activities were also a means to a further end. The nations which financed the new railway and industrial projects in China were bound to exercise a predominant influence in that country. The Taft administration sought American participation in all such undertakings, so that the United States, in the phraseology of a State Department memorandum in 1909, would have "more authority in political controversies in that country which will go far toward guaranteeing the preservation of the administrative entity of China." We had first reached out for more political influence in the Far East in order to safeguard our trade. We now tried to expand our industrial stake in China as a means of strengthening political influence.

Efforts by American capitalists to promote the construction of railways in Manchuria opened this chapter in our Chinese policy. At the close of the Russo-Japanese war, the great railroad builder E. H. Harriman, carried away by dreams of a round-the-world transportation system wholly under American control, tried to obtain an interest in the South Manchuria Railway from the Japanese government. Failing in this scheme, he then sought to secure concessions from the Chinese government to build a new line more or less paralleling the South Manchuria. His agent in these negotiations was Willard Straight, for a time American consul at Mukden, and no one better epitomized the new American spirit of commercial enterprise. Keen, far-sighted, imaginative, Straight felt himself to be both an advance agent of capitalism on the new frontiers of Asia, and a generous knight-errant fighting the battles of China against Japan. He was convinced that the concessions he sought would prove to be of equal benefit for the Chinese people and the United States.

For all his zeal, the attempt to secure the entry of American capital into Manchuria failed. It was naturally opposed by Japan, and when despite this Straight appeared to be on the verge of success, the support he hoped to get from the State Department was withdrawn as a result of conclusion of the Root-Takahira agreement. Straight angrily characterized this move as "a terrible diplomatic blunder to be laid at the door of T. R.," and at least temporarily it effectively blocked his plans. Further political complications, lack of financial support and finally the death of Harriman thereupon caused their complete collapse.

Philander C. Knox, Secretary of State in the Taft administration, was nevertheless intrigued by the possibilities for American investment in Manchuria. In order to combat Japanese opposition, he evolved a scheme, soon after coming into office, for the commercial neutralization of this territory. He officially suggested, in November 1909, that measures should be adopted to bring "the Manchurian highways and the railroads under an economic and scientific and impartial administration by some plan vesting in China the ownership of the railroads through funds furnished for that purpose by the interested powers willing to participate."

This was an ambitious application of the Open Door principle going much further than anything Hay had ever contemplated. It was enthusiastically hailed in this country as "startling for its audacity" and "striking at the very heart of the Far Eastern Question." Whatever the plan's theoretical value, however, neither Japan nor Russia had the slightest idea of giving up her special concessions in Manchuria in order to allow American participation in a general program of development. Both nations summarily rejected Knox's proposal. The principal result of his attempted intervention in Manchuria's tangled railway politics was to bring Russia and Japan, so recently at war, into one another's arms in joint opposition to the United States. Nor was England, allied to both Russia and Japan, prepared to support us. There was nothing Knox could do but withdraw his suggestion.

In the meantime, somewhat comparable problems of participation in railway loans in China proper had aroused American interest. Here again Willard Straight, having become the Chinese representative of a group of New York bankers, was the spearhead of capitalist finance. When it appeared that the United States might be frozen out of an international project for the construction of railways in Szechuan province, involving the so-called Hukuang loan, he succeeded in prevailing upon President Taft to intervene directly on behalf of American rights.

"I have an intense personal interest," the President cabled to the Prince Regent of China in July 1909, "in making the use of American capital in the development of China an instrument for the promotion of the welfare of China, and an increase in her material prosperity without entanglements or creating embarrassments affecting the growth of her independent political power and the preservation of her territorial integrity."

Taft's carefully phrased—and quite unprecedented—demand was based upon the ground that only American participation could assure China that her interests would be protected and the Open Door duly preserved. The representatives of the other powers were not so confident of the purity of American motives. They found the United States, our minister in China reported, pursuing "an active and aggressive policy, which is competitive if not hostile to all other foreign interests in China." When the Chinese government acceded to the President's proposal, they nevertheless had no alternative other than to admit American capital to the Hukuang loan. A four-power financial consortium was organized, with the inclusion of American, British, French and German financial interests. It then went on from the Hukuang loan to arrange an even more ambitious undertaking for the reform of Chinese currency and vast industrial developments in Manchuria. When an agreement on this loan was finally reached with the Chinese government in April 1911, the hopes of Willard Straight and Secretary Knox soared. "Dollar diplomacy is justified at last," the former wrote home exultingly.

But these hopes were not to be realized. They were shattered in the first instance by a revolutionary upheaval in China, hardly foreseen by the international bankers, which overthrew the Manchu dynasty and led in 1912 to the creation of the Chinese Republic. To the events responsible for this cataclysm we shall return. Their immediate effect on the consortium was to compel a complete readjustment of its plans and to involve it in the most complicated political negotiations. Proposals were made for an entirely new loan to the republican government, and on their insistent demand, both Japan and Russia were admitted to a reorganized banking group. In the meantime, however, a change in administration in the United States had brought up for reconsideration the whole question of our taking part in these transactions. The result was President Wilson's withdrawal of all official support for the proposed new loan, and the consequent resignation of the American bankers from the six-power consortium.

The basis for Wilson's action was that the conditions of the proposed loan, involving the right of the powers to supervise the collection of the taxes which were to serve as collateral, appeared "to touch very nearly the administrative independence of China itself." Whereas Taft had called upon the principles of the Open Door to force our participation in China's industrial development, Wilson found in them a compelling reason for the United States to abstain from any move along such lines restricting China's own freedom of action. "Our interests," he stated emphatically, "are those of the Open Door,—a door of friendship and mutual advantage. This is the only door we care to enter."

The bankers welcomed rather than opposed Wilson's withdrawal of official support. They were actually looking for a way out. Their position in 1913, in trying to discover the attitude of the new administration, was that they would seek a share in Chinese loans only if the State Department definitely asked them to do so. Their earlier ventures had not paid dividends. The Taft administration had driven them into the consortium in order to preserve American political influence in China. They were themselves interested in immediate financial profits, which were not forthcoming, rather than in any vague future benefits to be derived from keeping an American finger in the Chinese pie.

Sometime later, when the advantages gained by the other powers through their loans to China became more apparent, President Wilson was to reverse his original stand. He promoted American membership in a revived consortium in order that the United States might be in a more favorable position in respect to both its political and economic interests in the Orient. But in 1913 the consortium's loan policies led him to adopt a strictly hands-off policy. If the United States could not induce its commercial rivals to observe the principles built around the Open Door doctrine, it at least would not join them in still further undermining Chinese independence through financial pressure.

The dollar diplomacy of the Taft era neither promoted American interests in the Far East nor succeeded in safeguarding those of China. Wilson was repudiating a policy that had already failed. The cycle of successive advances and retreats in attempting to maintain the Open Door had left the United States in just about the same position that it had held in 1900. There had been no dismemberment of China, but foreign infringements on her sovereignty had by no means been halted. And in its championship of Chinese independence, the United States found itself gravely challenged by the rising imperialism of Japan.

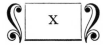

WARTIME DIPLOMACY

"THE awakening of the people of China to a consciousness of their possibilities under free government," President Wilson declared in hailing the Chinese Revolution, "is the most significant, if not the most momentous, event of our generation. With this movement and aspiration the American people are in profound sympathy."

Beyond the repudiation of dollar diplomacy, however, there was no change in our Far Eastern policy. Although the revolution drew tighter our bonds with the Chinese people, the United States was no more willing than it had been in the past to run the risks of possible war in upholding their independence. When Japan shortly seized upon the opportunity presented by both the weakness of the new republic and the western world's absorption in the First World War to renew her aggressive advance on the Asiatic mainland, we were not prepared to intervene beyond the stage of diplomatic protests in support of our own treaty rights. Our State Department was convinced, as Acting Secretary of State Lansing replied to Chinese appeals for aid, that "it would be quixotic in the extreme to allow the question of China's territorial integrity to entangle the United States in international difficulties."

The movement to overthrow the Manchu dynasty was the culmination of the long-standing discontent of the Chinese masses that had already found expression in the terrible Taiping Rebellion and the incensed fury of the Boxer uprising. Unable either to offer any effective resistance to foreign exactions or to adjust itself as had Japan to the impact of western civilization, the Chinese Empire had for more than a century been steadily losing both power and prestige. More conservative even than the Chinese people, the Manchu rulers had shown themselves incapable of understanding the modern world. Some reforms had been adopted and a hesitant beginning made toward establishing parliamentary rule. But these moves came too late, and were carried forward too half-heartedly, to create any real confidence in either the good faith of the Manchu dynasty or in its ability to meet effectively the challenge of westernization.

The revolutionary party was convinced that only the overthrow of the empire and establishment of a republic offered China any chance of taking its place in the march of modern progress. Its leader, Sun Yat-sen, had for many years dreamed expansively of his country's great future as a democracy. Students, intellectuals and merchants were won to his cause by their despair over the slow progress of reform under existing conditions. Driven into exile because of his revolutionary agitation, Sun had also obtained the support of the Chinese overseas who contributed substantial funds for the revolutionary cause.

American missionaries and educators had always favored the reform movement in China, and their influence also played a considerable part in feeding the fires of revolutionary discontent among their converts and the students of the treaty ports. They preached the gospel of democracy as well as of Christianity. Since Senator Benton had first spoken of science, liberal principles in government and the true religion casting "their lights across the intervening sea," and Anson Burlingame had so eloquently declared that the Chinese invited us "to plant the shining cross on every hill and in every valley," the idea of America's mission to lead China along the path of progress had never been lost to sight. Sun Yat-sen drew much of his inspiration and almost mystical zeal from American sources. His theories upon China's future grew at least in part out of the tremendous impression made upon him by American ideals and American institutions. It was with all this in mind that President Wilson could speak of our "profound sympathy" for the aspirations of the Chinese people in finally overthrowing the decadent dynasty that had for so long blocked all advance.

In spite of such a background for revolution, the uprising in October 1911 that precipitated the collapse of the empire found the revolutionary leaders unprepared. Sun Yat-sen was out of the country. A revolt whose immediate cause was opposition to foreign control over railroad construction in Szechuan nevertheless spread rapidly and the imperial authorities found themselves helpless to stem it. Manchu rule was dramatically revealed as little more than a hollow façade, and the boy Emperor commanded almost no popular support. Hurriedly returning to China, Sun Yat-sen undertook organization of a provisional government, with himself as President, and demanded the Emperor's immediate abdication.

In Peking, in the meantime, the Prince Regent had appointed as his chief minister the redoubtable Yuan Shih-kai, who had already proved himself to be a powerful figure during the Boxer Rebellion when he had sternly maintained order in Shantung. Instead of attempting to rally support for the throne, however, Yuan saw the handwriting on the wall and entered into negotiations with the revolutionaries. He was prepared to force abdication of the Emperor if he was chosen to head the new republican government. Accepting in good faith a pledge that the principles of the revolution would be maintained, hoping to establish national unity and avoid civil war, Sun Yat-sen agreed to this program. The Emperor was thereupon compelled to relinquish all his rights, and in February 1912 the new republic was officially proclaimed with Yuan Shih-kai as its President. Governmental power was nominally exercised by a national assembly, but it actually reverted to the strong and capable hands of the Emperor's former first minister.

As events were soon to prove, Yuan Shih-kai had little interest in the idea of a Chinese republic. He believed the revolution to be one of China's periodic dynastic upheavals and ambitiously pictured himself as ascending the Dragon Throne to found a new dynasty. His plot to become emperor was to be thwarted. The Chinese people were opposed to the reestablishment of imperial rule. But they were equally unprepared to understand a new form of government departing so radically from the pattern of the past. The revolution had broken out before Sun Yat-sen had been able to prepare the country for it. Despite the wellsprings of democracy in village life, the Chinese masses had no experience in the forms and institutions of a republic. While unwilling to accept Yuan Shih-kai as a new emperor, they consequently submitted passively to the dictatorial personal rule he set up in complete defiance of Sun Yat-sen's bitter protest that he was betraying the purposes of the revolution which had swept him into power.

Yuan Shih-kai died in 1916 soon after the final collapse of his plan to make himself emperor, and the power he had so firmly held devolved upon the parliament. But while it elected a new president, such semblance of unity as China had appeared to have completely collapsed. A virtually independent government was set up in the south by Sun Yat-sen, there was civil war in Szechuan, and the north was ridden by militarists whose real interest was building up their own political power. For ten dreary years China was to be torn by civil strife as the provincial warlords fought intermittently among themselves, and at Peking a government whose control hardly extended beyond the city's walls staggered through successive political crises that were a travesty of democratic rule. It was not until a revived Nationalist party under Chiang Kai-shek took up once again the immense task of unifying the country that China had any real central government whatsoever.

The first reports of the Chinese Revolution in October 1911 had been greeted in the United States with a scepticism that subsequent developments were in considerable part to justify. While the revolutionary leaders from the outset sought to win American support by declaring that their objective was to make their government "like that of the United States," it was widely believed that China was not ready to become a republic. The *New York World* dismissed the whole idea as "an absurdity"; the *New Orleans Picayune* said it was "simply preposterous," and the *Philadelphia Ledger* declared that the Chinese people were totally unfit for self-government. The general reaction in this country was that the revolution would interrupt such progress as China was actually making, obstruct trade and endanger foreign interests. Such papers as the *New York Tribune*, the *New York Sun* and the *Atlanta Journal* were agreed that the principal result would be to heighten the old danger of China's dismemberment at the hands of the European powers.

Our official policy was at first one of complete neutrality between the Peking government and the provisional republic. Early in 1912, Secretary of State Knox declared that the United States would make no move whatsoever unless a threat to foreign interests demanded concerted intervention. After the abdication of the Emperor and the elevation of Yuan Shi-kai to the presidency, however, our attitude began to change. The State Department was prepared to support the reorganization loan promoted by the six-power consortium, as already noted, and it welcomed what appeared to be the firm control established by Yuan Shih-kai. Official recognition was withheld until May 1913, but even so the United States was the first power to welcome the Chinese Republic into the family of nations.

By this time, indeed, the original scepticism over the possible consequences of the revolution was giving way to the enthusiasm displayed by President Wilson when he termed it the most momentous event of his generation. Comment upon the roseate future now facing China became as extravagant as it had at first been reserved. The avoidance of protracted civil war in 1912 and establishment of a strong government momentarily swept away all doubts as to the ability of the Chinese to govern themselves. Newspapers throughout the country could hardly have been more sanguine in their confidence of peace and stability in the Orient. Outdoing its contemporaries, the *Journal of Commerce* declared the Chinese Revolution to be not the greatest event of the twentieth century, as was generally agreed, but the most remarkable historical development since the fall of Rome.

A little more than a year after American recognition of the Republic of China, the sweeping ramifications of the First World War spread to eastern Asia with Japan's entry into the conflict in conformity with the terms of the Anglo-Japanese alliance. China was at once alarmed and sought from the United States concrete proof of our declared friendship. Convinced that Tokyo's real object was to find an excuse to encroach further upon Chinese sovereignty, Yuan Shih-kai urged President Wilson to induce the belligerent nations to observe China's neutrality and refrain from hostilities in either Chinese territory or marginal waters.

Before anything was done along these lines, Yuan Shih-kai's fears were proved to be well founded. Having seized all German island possessions in the north Pacific, Japan demanded of Berlin the immediate surrender of the leasehold at Kiouchow and all other concessions in Shantung. When the German government rejected this ultimatum, Japanese troops attacked the German leasehold, completely ignoring China's protest against this flagrant violation of her neutrality, and in November 1914 captured and occupied Kiouchow. There was no question where American sympathies lay. Here was new proof of the Japanese threat to our Chinese policy. But there was nothing the United States could do without running the risk, against which Lansing so forcibly warned, of becoming inextricably involved in dangerous international complications.

Within a few months Japan further showed her hand. In January 1915 her Minister in Peking secretly presented to Yuan Shih-kai a series of proposals, the notorious Twenty-One Demands, that not only sought to compel China to acquiesce in the seizure of Germany's possessions in Shantung, but also to grant an extension of Japanese privileges in south Manchuria. In addition, a supplementary fifth group of demands, whose bare-faced effrontery led even the Japanese government to designate them as "wishes" or "desires," stipulated further political and economic concessions that would have transformed China into a virtual Japanese protectorate. Her government was to employ Japanese advisers, agree to the purchase of munitions from Japan, and in important cities provide for joint Chinese and Japanese police administration.

When the reports of this new assault upon Chinese sovereignty reached the United States—for Yuan Shih-kai allowed the news to get abroad despite the Japanese injunction of secrecy—there was an immediate outburst against the "perfidious villainy" of the Tokyo government. The Twenty-One Demands were viewed as a treacherous consequence of Japan's penetration in south Manchuria, her rejection of the Knox scheme for neutralization of the Manchuria railways and her seizure of Shantung. Japanese policy was violently attacked as a contemptuous denial of the whole concept of the Open Door to which Tokyo no less than Washington stood pledged.

Nevertheless, popular opinion as expressed in the nation's press showed considerable confusion as to what could be done. While there was some agreement with the *New York Sun's* emphatic statement that "this country cannot by any possibility let Japan's forward movement go by default," other newspapers were quite as convinced that we should do nothing that might create the danger of open conflict. From Paul Reinsch, our minister in Peking, came repeated pleas for a forthright defense of the mutual interests of the United States and China, but other officials felt that the world situation demanded greater caution.

"I have had the feeling," President Wilson finally cabled Reinsch, "that any direct advice to China, or intervention in her behalf in the present negotiations, would really do her more harm than good, inasmuch as it would very likely provoke the jealousy and excite the hostility of Japan. . . ." Even more circumspect, if possible, was the note dispatched by Secretary of State Bryan after he had received in March the full text of the

Twenty-One Demands. Remarking that the United States had
treaty rights which would warrant the strongest objections to
the Japanese proposals in regard to both Manchuria and Shantung, he nevertheless pointed out that we had to recognize
"that territorial contiguity creates special relations between
Japan and these districts." He took a somewhat stronger line in
respect to the fifth group of demands, so patently infringing
upon China's political independence, but at best his note was a
weak and faltering response to China's fervent appeals for help.
It was clearly in the spirit of retreat from the Open Door policy
already marked in the Root-Takahira agreement.

The crisis in eastern Asia was naturally overshadowed by the
war in Europe. It nevertheless gained world-wide attention,
and, under the pressure of foreign opinion and spirited Chinese
resistance, Japan finally agreed to withdraw the fifth group of
her demands "for future discussion." But she continued to
insist upon immediate acceptance of her position in south
Manchuria and Shantung. With no direct aid forthcoming from
the United States or any other nation, the Chinese government
prepared to make this concession.

The United States now made one definite move. In notes forwarded to the Japanese and Chinese governments in May 1915,
Secretary Bryan made it clear that we at least wished to keep
the record straight. "The United States," he declared, ". . . cannot recognize any agreement or undertaking which has been
entered into between the governments of Japan and China,
impairing the treaty rights of the United States and its citizens
in China, the political or territorial integrity of the Republic
of China, or the international policy relative to China commonly known as the Open Door policy."

Seventeen years after the dispatch of this note, when under
somewhat comparable circumstances Japan renewed her offensive against China and seized control of all Manchuria, the
United States sent a protest to Tokyo that was couched in
virtually identical terms. William Jennings Bryan rather than
Henry Stimson first enunciated the non-recognition doctrine

that bears the latter's name. In neither 1915 nor 1932, however, did our policy have the slightest effect upon Japan. Two weeks after Secretary Bryan's statement of our position, China signed under duress two treaties specifically acknowledging Japan's special rights and privileges in both Manchuria and Shantung.

During the next two years, American and Japanese diplomacy continued to clash over the status of China. The Tokyo government employed every possible stratagem to win international acceptance of its new position; the United States sought to uphold as strongly as it could Chinese sovereignty. It was an uneven contest. For once again what happened in China was a vital matter for Japan, and awakened only minor concern among Americans. Moreover the steady drift of the United States toward intervention in the European war drove Far Eastern affairs even further into the background. Japan was able to exert increasing influence over the faction-ridden government which was nominally in power at Peking.

Upon our final declaration of war against Germany in April 1917, the confusion of Asiatic politics was still further heightened by a tug-of-war over the possible belligerency of China. It became the popular belief that the Peking government, resisting counterpressure from Japan which did not like the idea of Chinese participation in the peace conference, responded bravely to President Wilson's appeal that China join the crusade to make the world safe for democracy. Actually, the United States was opposed to this move even though it was for a time highly favored—and strongly urged upon the Chinese—by the American minister. "The entry of China into the war with Germany, or the continuance of the status quo of her relations with that government, are matters of secondary consideration," Lansing, who had succeeded Bryan in the State Department, advised Peking on June 6. "The principal necessity for China is to resume and continue her political entity and to proceed along the road of national development on which she has made such marked progress."

We feared, in other words, that any diversion of Chinese

energies from the immense task of internal reconstruction would create still further political turmoil and consequent openings for interference by Japan. When the reactionary clique in control in Peking disregarded our advice, declaring war on Germany primarily in the hope of obtaining American financial aid, these fears were realized.

Japan succeeded in obtaining assurances from the Allies, through a series of secret treaties, that her territorial acquisitions in the Pacific and on the Asiatic mainland would be recognized. She thereupon sought to secure a comparable guarantee from the United States. The fact that the two nations were fighting side by side against Germany appeared to present a unique opportunity for removing this last obstacle to the consolidation of her wartime gains. To this end, Viscount Ishii was sent to the United States on a special mission in the summer of 1917, and took up the whole question of Japanese-American relations with Secretary Lansing.

The views of the two statesmen were at opposite poles. Lansing suggested a reaffirmation of the Open Door policy, together with an undertaking that neither nation would take advantage of the war to exact new privileges from China. Viscount Ishii urged acceptance by the United States of what he termed Japan's "paramount position" in China. Neither could give way entirely—any more than could the American and Japanese diplomats in the negotiations at Washington twenty-four years later. The result in 1917, however, was a compromise into which anything at all could be read. The Lansing-Ishii agreement both reaffirmed the two nations' adherence to the principles of the Open Door policy, and also embodied recognition of what was ambiguously described as Japan's "special interests in China, particularly in the part to which her possessions are contiguous." And still further to confuse the issue, a secret protocol was added stating that neither the United States nor Japan "would take advantage of the present conditions to seek special rights or privileges in China." This final pledge was not announced, through some curious aberration of the diplomatic mind, as being "superfluous."

What did the agreement really mean? Viscount Ishii maintained that it implied full recognition by the United States of Japan's newly obtained concessions in Manchuria and Shantung. Secretary Lansing insisted that it had no such significance and that its real purpose was to reassert the two nations' adherence to the Open Door policy. Each statesman read into the document exactly what he wanted. It emphasized the distance between the American and Japanese positions.

China was bitterly disappointed. She could not fail to see in this official acknowledgment by the United States of Japan's "special interests" in China an encouragement for further aggression which far outweighed the vague pledges respecting the Open Door. But our traditional interest in the maintenance of Chinese sovereignty and equality of trade was still very much alive. Expediency dictated the Lansing-Ishii agreement. It had been concluded under wartime pressure to assure Japan's continued cooperation in the struggle against Germany. Asiatic observers were to be greatly mistaken in so far as they interpreted the accord as marking American withdrawal from the Far East.

This was emphatically demonstrated at the Paris peace conference. When Japan launched an intensive drive to have her right to former German possessions in Shantung acknowledged in treaty form, President Wilson stubbornly demanded that the disputed province be returned to China. The United States reassumed its role of friend and guardian of Chinese independence, employing every diplomatic weapon in its armory to uphold this basic principle.

China could hardly have been in a weaker position to defend her own interests. Her envoys, somewhat anomalously, represented both the Peking government and the rival regime that had been set up at Canton. The confused and shifting political scene at home left them in continual doubt as to whether any commitments they might make would be approved. Actually, the two chief delegates, Wellington Koo and C. T. Wang, both of them "returned students," were speaking for China and the people of China rather than for any Chinese government. They symbolized the young new republic that was struggling to win its freedom from the Japanese-controlled reactionaries who were entrenched in Peking. Their valiant fight to secure the return of territories seized by Japan and to win full recognition of Chinese sovereignty was a personal battle. In view of the virtual anarchy in the country whose cause they so eloquently pleaded, the wonder was that they received any hearing at all.

The combined American-Chinese forces, however, did not have a chance of prevailing against the determined stand of Japan. She had entered the European war to take over all German possessions in the Pacific, and she had no mind to be deprived of her wartime spoils. Through the treaties imposed upon China in 1915, reinforced by additional concessions exacted in 1918, she had built up her legal position. Her secret pacts with the Allies meant that they had already decided the case in her favor, and both Lloyd George and Clemenceau brought strong pressure to bear upon Wilson to follow their lead. Unless the United States also recognized her rights, especially those in Shantung, Japan let it be known that she would withdraw from the peace conference and refuse membership in the League of Nations. China's legal or moral position did not concern her.

President Wilson finally succeeded in persuading the Japanese delegation to recognize China's political sovereignty in Shantung and agree eventually to restore to her the former German leased territory. But the Japanese made it clear that they proposed to retain a concession in the port of Kiouchow, renamed Tsingtao, and all commercial privileges, including railways and mines, which Germany had held in other parts of Shantung. Nor would they commit themselves, as Wilson himself later admitted, to any definite date for surrendering even the empty shell of the province in which they had so strongly entrenched themselves.

Wilson reluctantly accepted this settlement—and it was written into the Treaty of Versailles. He had become convinced that he had no alternative if the adherence of Japan to the general terms of peace, including the League of Nations, was to be secured. Although Secretary Lansing and other members of the American delegation felt that further pressure upon Japan might prove effective, he could not agree. "They are not bluffers," he told Ray Stannard Baker, "and they will go home unless we give them what they want." He had no illusions about what was happening. But where Lansing indignantly characterized the settlement as "a sacrifice to propitiate the threatening Moloch of Japan," the President maintained that it "was the best that could be had out of a dirty past."

Wilson realized that Japan would feel triumphant and China would be bitterly disappointed; he knew American public opinion would strongly disapprove his concessions. Yet he felt that he had to make whatever sacrifice circumstances demanded in order to obtain his major goal of a league for peace. And for that Japanese cooperation was essential. "The only hope," the President later told Baker in another conversation during these critical days in Paris, "was to keep the world together, get the League of Nations with Japan in it, and then try to secure justice for the Chinese not only as regarding Japan but England, France, Russia, all of whom had concessions in China. . . ."

The reaction in Asia was what Wilson had expected. The American minister in Peking reported a general attitude among the Chinese of "indignation, and discouragement and despair." The Japanese openly boasted that all further opposition to their ambitions was now shown to be wholly futile. Nevertheless, the former acknowledged Wilson's support. They fully realized that the United States was the only nation which had sought to uphold China's cause, and that from us alone could they hope for any future aid in inducing Japan to restore Shantung.

Public opinion in this country, aroused as never before by Japanese policy, almost universally condemned the position Wilson had taken at Paris. It is true that the virulent press campaign on the Shantung issue was in part inspired by isolationist opposition to American membership in the League of Nations. The President had given his foes a powerful weapon of attack by a surrender so clearly violating his own principles of self-determination. Yet a growing alarm over Japanese aggression combined with our traditional friendship for China to give a further significance to the whole affair. There was ample evidence that the American people had no mind to allow Japan free rein in the Far East.

The Hearst press, always bitterly anti-Japanese, raged against the perfidy of "wily, tricky, fight-thirsty Japan"; the conservative *Boston Transcript* found itself almost echoing such editorials with its own tirades against "insolent and Hunlike spoliation," and the socialist *New York Call* swelled the chorus of dissent in describing the Shantung agreement as "one of the most shameless deeds in the record of imperialistic diplomacy." Whatever his motives, Senator Lodge was responsible for an attack on Japan in the halls of Congress which at the time appeared wildly extravagant, but may today be seen to have had a somber prophetic note.

"Japan is steeped in German ideas," Lodge told the Senate, "and regards war as an industry because from war she has secured all the extensions of her Empire. . . . She means to exploit China and build herself up until she becomes a power formidable to all the world. It is not merely that she will close the markets of China and obtain commercial and economic advantages. . . . Japan will be enabled to construct in that way a power which will threaten the safety of the world. . . . But the country that she would menace most would be our own, and unless we carefully maintain a very superior navy in the Pacific, the day will come when the United States will take the place of France in another great war to preserve civilization."

President Wilson's answer to the attacks on his surrender at Paris was to emphasize the importance of the League of Nations as an agency that could redress whatever wrong had been done in China, and also enable her to secure a hearing for adjustment of the whole problem of extraterritoriality. He believed the Shantung settlement itself to have been unavoidable, and that nothing could be done for China except through the League. But with the League the future was bright with promise. "Henceforth, for the first time," Wilson declared, "we shall have the opportunity to play effective friends to the great people of China, and I for one feel my pulses quicken and heart rejoice at such a prospect."

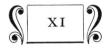

XI

THE WASHINGTON CONFERENCE

PRESIDENT WILSON was not to have the opportunity to give effective expression to his friendship for the Chinese people. Two years after the Paris conference, however, another international parley was summoned by his successor, President Harding, to meet at Washington for the discussion of naval limitation and general political settlements in the Pacific. Even though its action on the first of these issues was in some ways more important, a new international agreement reaffirming the Open Door policy in its broadest sense made the Washington Conference of 1921-1922 an outstanding milestone in American-Chinese relations.

Various threads of interest were drawn together to bring about this meeting. The need to bring naval rivalry in the Pacific to a halt as part of a general program of national economy was a first consideration, but this was possible only if some political accord was reached blocking any further Japanese expansion on the Asiatic mainland. "We have seen the eyes of the world turned to the Pacific," President Harding was to state at the conference's opening session. "With Europe prostrate and penitent, none feared the likelihood of any early conflict there. But the Pacific had its menaces, and they deeply concerned us." If the proposed meeting was to have any chance of success, strong pressure had somehow to be exerted upon Japan. If there was to be any arms limitation, she had to be compelled to relax the paralyzing grip she had fastened upon China during the war.

The forward march of Japanese imperialism had placed the Tokyo government in a position almost comparable to that which it was to hold some twenty years later. Japan was in full control of Russia's Far Eastern maritime provinces as an aftermath of allied intervention in Siberia in 1918. She held Germany's former island possessions in the north Pacific as mandates. She had special privileges in both Manchuria and Shantung that added up to complete economic domination. While there were no forces of occupation in other parts of China, as would be the case in 1941, Japanese influence was paramount in Peking, and the chaotic internal situation placed China almost wholly at Japan's mercy.

Aroused by this startling evidence of what Japan had been doing while war was raging in Europe, American newspapers and magazines in the spring of 1921 were repeatedly telling the public that the principal foreign issue before the country was whether or not the Japanese were to become masters of the Pacific. Books and articles appeared under such titles as "The Menace of Japan," "The New Japanese Peril," "Must We Fight Japan?" and "The Next War." Anti-Japanese feeling was especially strong on the west coast, where the immigration of Japanese laborers had created a situation comparable to that caused by the influx of Chinese coolies half a century earlier. Senator Phelan, among many others, foresaw a day when Japan would threaten the entire world unless the United States at once took forceful measures to restrain her.

At the same time, opinion in Japan saw in the pro-Chinese policy of the United States the principal obstacle to the development of Japanese interests in Asia. The United States was charged with drawing a wholly false picture of the Japanese menace solely because of its own ambition to extend the Monroe Doctrine to the Far East. The alarmist articles in the American press had their counterpart in Japan. Newspapers featured grave warnings of possible invasion by an imperialistic United States, and public debates were held upon the question of "Shall Japan Fight America?"

Whatever the basis for these alarms on either side of the Pacific, the growing tension disturbed official circles in Washington. There were cabinet discussions in March 1921 upon the advisability of transferring our entire fleet to the Pacific, and orders were reputedly sent to army and navy officials in our island possessions to be ready for any eventuality. Actually, of course, Japan was in no position to launch the war which was to be started by the attack on Pearl Harbor in 1941. The United States still had effective naval supremacy in the Pacific, and even more important, it was not confronted with any European threat to its peace and security. Its hands were free to defend its Pacific frontier. Nevertheless, many observers doubted if there could be any peaceful solution of the underlying conflict between American and Japanese policy in eastern Asia. How could Japanese imperialism and the Open Door policy be reconciled? "The conflagration appears as certain," an international expert in one of the leading French newspapers wrote, "as lightning which leaps from two clouds charged with opposing currents."

As these circumstances gave a heightened tension to American-Japanese naval rivalry, and as this rivalry in turn emphasized the inherent dangers of a possible clash between the two nations, public support for an international arms conference gathered increasing strength. Senator Borah had introduced a resolution asking the President to invite Great Britain and Japan to such a meeting as early as December 1920. The resolution was unanimously approved by the Senate in May 1921 and a week later acted upon favorably by the House of Representatives by a vote of 332 to 4. In part urged on by such congressional pressure, and in part because of a desire to take some step to relieve the crushing economic burden of armaments and lessen the possibility of war, the Harding administration decided to act. The original Borah proposal was broadened to suggest a general disarmament conference which would include France and Italy, as well as the United States, Great Britain and Japan.

In the meantime, developments in another part of the world served to emphasize even more strongly the need for Pacific settlements. At an imperial conference of the British dominions, held that summer in London, one of the most important issues under discussion was the Anglo-Japanese alliance. The United States had already intimated that it could hardly view with favor the renewal of a treaty under whose protection Japan might feel free to challenge American interests in Asia. This position was warmly supported in London by Canada. In order not to endanger American goodwill and yet avoid offending her Japanese ally, Great Britain was consequently interested in exploring the possibilities of concluding a more comprehensive agreement in the Pacific to replace the Anglo-Japanese alliance. It was decided to ask the United States to summon a conference which might take up both the political and naval problems affecting the Far East.

By one of the most curious of diplomatic coincidences, a cable dispatched from Washington on July 8 proposing an international disarmament conference, crossed a message from London conveying the British suggestion that the United States call a conference on Far Eastern affairs. Secretary Hughes at once undertook to combine the two plans. After clearing with the British government, he enlarged the scope of the original American proposal. "The question of limitation of armament has relation to Pacific and Far Eastern problems," he cabled in new messages to the powers, "and therefore it would seem appropriate that proposed conference should also embrace discussion by interested powers of all Far Eastern questions and that China should be invited to participate in that discussion."

In so far as it dealt with political questions, the Washington Conference was thus in part the inspiration of the British government. The Harding administration had at first been very vague as to its purposes in calling a disarmament parley and it had not included China among the original participants. But if the United States may be said to have acted upon a British suggestion in including the Far East in the conference agenda, "the menaces of the Pacific" were very much in the mind of Secretary Hughes. He realized that the issue presented by Japanese imperialism could not be avoided in seeking to limit naval power.

Invitations were officially dispatched to Great Britain, France, Italy, Belgium, the Netherlands, Portugal, Japan and China. Soviet Russia was ignored. They were at once accepted without reservation by all but Japan. The Tokyo government was interested in possible naval limitation, but it had no desire to discuss political issues. From the Japanese point of view, there was nothing to discuss. In a vain effort to limit the scope of the negotiations, Japan proposed that "problems such as are of sole concern to certain particular powers or such matters that may be regarded accomplished facts should be scrupulously avoided." It was a technique that Japan was also to employ throughout the 1930's in her reiterated insistence that Japanese-Chinese relations affected only Japan and China. On this occasion, Secretary Hughes ignored Tokyo's reservations. It was announced that invitations to the conference had been accepted and that it would open in Washington on November 11, 1921.

Three major treaties grew out of the negotiations at Washington. A Five-Power Naval Treaty, proposed under dramatic circumstances by Secretary Hughes on the very first day of the conference, provided for over-all limits for the capital ships of the signatory nations. In so far as the United States, Great Britain and Japan were concerned, it was agreed that the approximate totals should be 500,000 tons each for the first two countries and 300,000 tons for Japan—the famous 5-5-3 ratio. These powers also undertook, even more significantly in the light of subsequent developments, not to fortify any further their island bases in the Pacific. In compensation for the stricter limitation imposed upon her fleet, Japan was assured of a greater measure of security in her own home waters.

Supplementing this accord, the United States, Great Britain, France and Japan entered upon a Four-Power Treaty that in effect replaced the Anglo-Japanese alliance. The powers mutually agreed to respect one another's insular possessions in the Pacific, and to consult should any development arise threatening the status quo. There was no machinery to enforce the provisions of this treaty, but it brought Japan into a common agreement which it was hoped would remove any further threat to the Philippines or other American possessions in the Pacific.

The final settlement was the Nine-Power Treaty, to which the Netherlands, Belgium, Portugal and China were signatory as well as the major powers. It definitely bound the powers to respect China's territorial and administrative integrity, to provide her with the fullest opportunity to develop an effective and stable government, to use their influence in maintaining equal opportunity for trade and industry and to refrain from taking advantage of existing conditions in China to seek special right or privileges. In short, the underlying principles of the Open Door policy were not only reaffirmed, and very much broadened, but definitely written into an international understanding accepted by all countries with direct interests in eastern Asia.

"The willingness of the American government to surrender its then commanding lead in battleship construction and to leave its positions at Guam and in the Philippines without further fortifications," Henry L. Stimson was later to write as Secretary of State, "was predicated upon, among other things, the self-denying covenants contained in the Nine-Power Treaty, which assured the nations of the world not only of equal opportunity for their eastern trade but also against the military aggrandizement of any other power at the expense of China."

Throughout the negotiations leading to conclusion of the Nine-Power Treaty, the community of interests between the United States and China was clearly apparent. The Chinese delegates depended upon the good offices of the United States in putting forward their own claim to full recognition of Chinese sovereignty. In many ways it was the Paris peace conference all over again. But this time the United States was determined that there should be no such concession to Japan as President Wilson had felt compelled to make to win her support for the League of Nations. Our attitude was founded upon self-interest—the protection of our trade and commerce in eastern Asia—but once again it also conformed to the best interests of China.

In accepting the Nine-Power Treaty, Japan gave up, in so far as the agreement had any validity at all, her whole program of continental expansion. It was a diplomatic retreat for Tokyo all along the line. Moreover, the general provisions of this accord were reinforced by specific concessions apparently confirming that her delegates meant what they said. Japan cancelled the fifth group of the Twenty-One Demands with full acknowledgment of the right of foreign capital to participate in Manchuria's economic development and undertook to restore Chinese control over Shantung. Direct negotiations were held with China on this latter problem, Secretary Hughes and Premier Balfour acting as mediators, and the eventual agreement fully met China's demand for the recovery of the disputed province. As a capstone to this general relinquishment of former claims, Japan also agreed, shortly after the Washington Conference, to terminate the Lansing-Ishii agreement with its ambiguous recognition of special Japanese interests in China.

Did these concessions on so many points, this abandonment of the position so stoutly maintained at Paris, represent a sincere acceptance of the underlying principles of the Open Door policy? Japan signed the Washington treaties in the winter of 1921-1922 under pressure from a united international front forged by the United States. Our potential naval strength enabled us to exercise a greater influence in Asiatic politics than ever before in our history. Japan's leaders may well have felt that under existing circumstances, there was no other course to follow than acceptance of American views. Later events may, indeed, be interpreted as showing that these concessions were made only as a means to gain time for building up Japanese military and naval strength to a point where the United States could be challenged with greater impunity. Nevertheless, it cannot be stated unequivocally that this was the hidden motive of the Tokyo government, or that our acceptance of Japanese good faith in the Nine-Power Treaty was wholly unwarranted. There were at least some Japanese leaders, in 1922, who may have sincerely hoped that a peaceful, non-imperialistic policy would adequately assure the fulfillment of Japan's national aims and aspirations.

At the time, the nationalist press in Tokyo showed little disposition to approve the results of the Washington Conference as an equitable solution of Pacific problems. "Hateful and haughty America" was assailed for forcing upon Japan "a peace without liberty, a slavish peace." One newspaper declared that "the preposterous sacrifices and concessions made by Japan have furnished the United States and Britain with unexpectedly great successes and satisfactions, diplomatically and strategically." Another stated that Japan had "sustained such a loss as she would have suffered had she been defeated in her desperate war with Russia." Mass meetings were held in Tokyo at which the conference delegates were excoriated for signing treaties so inimical to their country's welfare.

Liberal opinion, however, was apparently ready to accept the conference accords and supported a program of international cooperation in the Pacific. It seemed anxious to substitute for the aggressive assertion of Japanese power, a more moderate program of economic expansion. "Japan is ready," Admiral Kato, Premier in the years following the parley, stated, "for the new order of thought—the spirit of international friendship and cooperation for the greater good of humanity—which the conference has brought about."

American opinion on the results of the Washington Conference reflected the view that the United States had won a splendid diplomatic triumph in the cause of Far Eastern peace, and it largely ignored the possible strategic consequences of our naval concessions. There were observers who believed that Japan's acceptance of our point of view had no real validity, and that we had actually purchased temporary peace in eastern Asia at the expense of the Open Door policy. Naval experts were gravely concerned over the implications of the 5-5-3 ratio and the non-fortification agreement in respect to our insular possessions. But these were minority protests. The American delegation declared officially that the relation of confidence and goodwill established through the Four-Power Treaty and the Nine-Power Treaty fully justified the reduction in armaments. "The Open Door policy in China," it stated, "has at last been made a fact."

Newspaper comment was even more optimistic. The *Cleveland Plain Dealer* said that it was now inconceivable that "Japan and the United States would ever approach the brink of war," while the *New York World* confidently proclaimed that "the threatening questions of the Pacific and the Far East have been removed from the category of war breeders."

A year after the conference, a future national leader who was to play the major role in determining American policy toward Japan between 1933 and 1941 emphatically affirmed his faith in the new policy of the Tokyo government. Writing in the magazine *Asia,* Franklin Delano Roosevelt declared that Japan had fully demonstrated her desire "to prove to the world that suspicions of the past are no longer justified." He proposed that this country recognize in some form Japan's real need for access to the raw materials and markets of Manchuria, and on such a basis seek her assistance in strengthening the new international order. "Why, in all reason," Roosevelt asked, "should not Japan, shoulder to shoulder with us, provide her aid as well? If instead of looking for causes of offense, we in all good faith confidently expect from Japan cooperation in world upbuilding, we shall go far toward insuring peace."

In addition to the naval and political settlements based on the international guarantee of China's independence, the conference also took up the question of foreign rights and privileges in China. The Chinese delegation was highly gratified by the course of negotiations over both the Nine-Power Treaty and the restoration of Shantung. Its members were anxious, however, to persuade the powers to surrender their control over the Chinese tariff, and to relinquish their rights of extraterritoriality. Independence for their country would be illusory, they declared, so long as these special privileges were maintained.

There was strong American sympathy for Chinese claims on this score, but a far more cautious attitude was shown than in other phases of the Far Eastern problem. Our support of the Open Door did not by any means imply a willingness to give up extraterritoriality. Foreign concessions in treaty ports, the International Settlement at Shanghai, rights of navigation on the Yangtze, the stationing of foreign troops at Peking and Tientsin—these and other concessions exacted from China through earlier treaties affected our commercial activities in China much too directly to be easily surrendered. The demands of the Chinese delegation could not be ignored. Their position was too sound in principle. But theory gave way before what were regarded as the practical aspects of the situation. The United States was no more willing than the other powers to forego existing special privileges in China, however much they impaired that country's sovereign powers.

The tariff issue was consequently settled by provision for an increase in existing customs duties and agreement upon a future conference to consider further possible adjustments. China was *not* granted tariff autonomy. As for other special rights, the powers would go no further than to authorize a commission "to inquire into the present practice of extraterritorial jurisdiction. . . ." Minor concesisons were made in abolishing foreign postal services in China and modifying foreign controls over radio communications, but consular jurisdiction was not relinquished. China won what were believed to be important guarantees against future aggression at the Washington Conference, but she still remained closely bound in the intricate mesh of special treaty rights that the powers had been weaving about her for almost a century.

In public debates upon ratification of the various accords, there were many expressions of our popular friendship for China suggesting that the United States should have gone much further in upholding her sovereignty. Senator Borah strongly supported the Nine-Power Treaty, but he warned that it should not be considered as acquiescence "in the wrongs which have already been committed against China." Senator Underwood declared that as far as he was concerned, he would be glad "to give China complete tariff autonomy tomorrow in the control of her tariff rates. I want to see China as independent and as sovereign a nation as possible." And Senator King vigorously criticized our hesitant attitude on these issues as "an affront to China, a grave wrong committed against a foreign state and against the honor and dignity of a great people." Perhaps the American public agreed with such statements. The fact remained that we gave up no existing rights.

Interpretations of the significance of the Washington Conference—whether it actually marked an advance or a retreat in our Far Eastern policy—have varied greatly since its several treaties were concluded. Did our naval concessions represent too heavy a price to pay for a diplomatic victory? Japan's brutal and successful assault upon China in the 1930's, leading as it eventually did to Pacific war, is often advanced as irrefutable proof that we did give away far more than we obtained. A starry-eyed idealism is said to have blinded the United States to Japan's determined imperialism. This criticism of the Washington Conference, however, disregards the historical fact that the American people had never shown themselves willing to uphold our Far Eastern policy by force—and would not in the future until the United States was itself attacked at Pearl Harbor. The only means whereby any administration could hope to support the Open Door, as John Hay, Theodore Roosevelt and Woodrow Wilson had each in turn come to realize, was by diplomatic pressure.

In a subsequent comment upon the situation prevailing in 1921, Elihu Root told his biographer that it had not entered the head of any President, or Secretary of State, or the chairman of any congressional committee on foreign relations, that the United States "would ever send forces to China to maintain the Open Door." Root had himself been Secretary of War during the Boxer Rebellion, later Secretary of State and a delegate at the Washington Conference. He knew what he was talking about. Our success in securing international adherence to our views upon Asiatic policy, even though it did not prove to be permanent, was under such circumstances an achievement for which we could afford to pay a substantial price.

And what was the price? The United States did not give away anything that it really had. We sacrificed what looked like an unapproachable lead in battleship construction, but there was every indication, in 1921, that Congress did not intend to carry through the great building program upon which the country was then embarked. Both Senator Lodge and Senator Underwood, members of the American delegation at the conference, assured Secretary Hughes that the necessary appropriations for outbuilding Japan would not be forthcoming. In holding Japan to a 300,000-ton limitation in capital ships, we were thus sustaining our relative naval power in the Pacific in the face of a determined congressional drive for economy. Our failure to build up our navy even to treaty limits during the next fifteen years would appear to confirm the force of this argument.

Such considerations also underlay the agreement, even more strongly criticized than naval limitation itself in the light of subsequent developments, not to fortify American naval bases in the western Pacific. In undertaking not to strengthen the Aleutians, Guam, Samoa and the Philippines, the United States was again putting into treaty form a policy upon which an economical Congress had already decided—and winning in return similar pledges from Great Britain and Japan in respect to their naval bases. The reluctance of the country to follow any other program in the Pacific than that adopted at the Washington Conference is once more revealed, moreover, in the failure to fortify adequately our bases in the western Pacific even after the treaty restrictions had expired.

The United States was not surrendering to Japanese imperialism at the Washington Conference. It was summoning the rest of the world to back up its traditional policy, symbolized by the Open Door, in clear recognition that only through united action could Japan be restrained. We never had been prepared to act alone. If there was any retreat here, it was only retreat from the exuberant imperialism of the opening of the century, when the United States had aspired to complete domination of the entire Pacific. We were prepared, in 1921, to sustain a system of collective security in this part of the world, in striking contrast to our withdrawal from Europe, that had as its basis an international guarantee of Chinese political and territorial integrity. The ultimate failure of that program did not lie in the concessions we made, but in the failure to provide the means for collective enforcement of the Nine-Power Treaty.

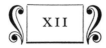

XII

THE RISE OF CHINESE NATIONALISM

DURING the years immediately following the Washington Conference, conditions within China were in a state of almost complete political anarchy. The Peking government, officially recognized by the powers, exercised little effective control beyond the walls of the capital city. Its authority was challenged not only by Sun Yat-sen's government at Canton, but by the rival warlords of the several provinces. Incessant political intrigue, intermittent civil warfare and a general interruption of trade and commerce once again underscored the old "problem of China." Repeated efforts were made by the Chinese leaders to bring about greater unity and a new union government, supposedly representative of both the north and south, was formed at one time. But the revolutionary upheavals of nationalism had still to be undergone before any real semblance of order was brought out of the existing chaos.

In order to divert attention from its inability to cope with domestic problems, and also in partly justified complaint that internal order could not be effectively established while China retained a semicolonial status, the Peking government repeatedly demanded that something be done about tariff autonomy and extraterritoriality. The powers had agreed at Washington to take up these issues, as we have seen, and it was insisted that they make good their pledges. Popular opinion in China vigorously backed this policy, whatever disagreements existed on other counts, and an embittered anti-foreign feeling began to sweep the country. The demand for ending the unequal treaties was the one thing on which all Chinese were united. The resentment against imperialism was particularly strong in the treaty ports, and it led almost inevitably to student riots and attacks upon foreign property.

The Chinese were encouraged in their campaign to rid themselves of foreign controls by the rifts that had already occurred in the extraterritoriality system. Germany and Austria had been compelled in the peace treaties following the First World War to surrender all their former privileges. With the exception of its interests in the Chinese Eastern Railway, the Soviet Union had voluntarily given up its special rights. What China was demanding of the other western powers and of Japan was that they follow this lead in complete revision of all existing treaties that were a legacy of nineteenth century imperialism.

The American attitude toward China became highly confused under these difficult circumstances. Our idealistic sympathy for her goal of complete independence warred against the practical considerations involved in surrendering our special privileges. Could we give up extraterritoriality when the Chinese government showed so few signs of being able to maintain internal order? And as always in the past, our policy could not be divorced from that of the other powers. We were at once unwilling to associate ourselves completely with them, and yet afraid that independent concessions would endanger our economic interests. "America has to steer a course," the *Detroit Free Press* commented in analyzing the situation, "which, while avoiding the old fogyism of other powers with entrenched interests in China, must also guard against too rash a submissiveness to China's ultra-nationalists." Somewhat similar advice came from the *Cleveland Plain Dealer*. It expressed its sympathy for the Chinese and demanded a policy of vigorous leadership in meeting their legitimate demands, but it warned that if such a program should appear inimical to the general interests of the powers, "the United States may well pause for consideration."

A special conference on American relations with China was held in Baltimore in 1925, attended by some two hundred educators, labor leaders, missionaries, businessmen and other persons with special interest in the Orient. Its discussions showed a highly friendly attitude toward China in the crisis through which she was passing, and reflected a belief that unless she was given the right to control her own affairs the anti-foreign movement might gather dangerous headway. A declaration of policy was adopted urging that the United States take an independent stand, should this prove necessary, in giving up extraterritoriality and tariff controls. Public opinion was generally approving, but in circles more immediately concerned with business enterprise in eastern Asia there was sharp criticism of such benevolent views. "It is well enough for a lot of professors and missionaries to get together and make speeches at each other," the *Philadelphia Record* declared, "[but] what right has this conference to vote instructions to the government in matters that the State Department is now considering?"

This agency was in the meantime moving very carefully. In accordance with the agreements reached at Washington, the United States cooperated in establishing a tariff commission that increased the rates the Chinese government was allowed to levy on foreign imports. It also proposed a survey of Chinese law codes as a preliminary move looking toward the end of foreign consular jurisdiction. Beyond this, in common with the other powers, it would not go. The prevailing disorder in China, and the inability of the government to prevent attacks upon foreigners, were candidly emphasized by Secretary Hughes as hardly creating an atmosphere very favorable for giving up extraterritorial rights. However, the United States refused to associate itself with any retaliatory action against anti-foreign outbreaks, and when conditions appeared to have improved after another cabinet reshuffle at Peking, it took the lead in urging the powers to continue negotiations on all issues in dispute.

A new tariff conference was consequently opened in Peking in October 1925, and three months later an official extraterritoriality commission started the proposed investigation of Chinese legal practices. At least limited progress was made in both undertakings. The tariff commission authorized the immediate levying of a customs surtax; acknowledged in principle China's full right to tariff autonomy; and provisionally agreed, subject to the removal of all internal barriers to trade, to accept a national tariff law which would go into effect on January 1, 1929. The extraterritoriality commission, in a report made public in September 1926, outlined a program of reform for China's judicial system as a possible basis for the future surrender of consular jurisdiction. "When these recommendations shall have been reasonably complied with," it was stated, "the several powers would be warranted in relinquishing their respective rights of extraterritoriality."

Further advance along such lines was now interrupted, however, by the rise of the Nationalist movement and the even more violent outburst of anti-foreignism which it fostered. Such slow progress toward the recovery of complete independence did not satisfy China's new leaders, and they were also ready to make the most of popular resentment against the foreigners as a means of winning adherents to their own revolutionary program. The Nationalists demanded the immediate and unqualified abolition of all unequal treaties.

It was not a question of what the powers might wish to grant China, Eugene Chen, the Foreign Minister, stated emphatically, but of what China might justly grant the powers. He warned that protection of foreign lives and property could no longer depend upon foreign bayonets. In asserting their rights, the Nationalists were prepared to make full use of the powerful weapon of economic boycott. "The liberation of China from the yoke of foreign imperialism," Chen significantly concluded his forthright statement, "need not necessarily involve any armed conflict between Chinese Nationalism and the foreign powers. For this reason the Nationalist government would prefer to have all questions outstanding between Nationalist China and the foreign powers settled by negotiation."

Chen was speaking with a voice of authority that no foreign

minister in Peking had been able to command. What had happened to helpless, prostrate, ineffective China? How dared Chen covertly threaten instead of plead in stating his country's position?

The forces making for a powerful Nationalism had been slowly gaining strength throughout the early 1920's. The movement stemmed from the government maintained at Canton by Sun Yat-sen, and the leader of the first revolution was its guiding spirit. Foreigners tended to dismiss Sun Yat-sen as a visionary and impractical dreamer. Continuing to hope for the emergence of some strong man in the north,. to pull the country together under a conservative government which would restore order and safeguard foreign property, they believed him to be the most formidable obstacle to real Chinese unity. But his ideas were steadily winning converts among all politically-minded Chinese. Despairing utterly of the weak and corrupt regime in Peking, they looked more and more to his Nationalist party—the Kuomintang—to save the country.

Sun Yat-sen had set forth as his program for China his famous doctrine of the Three Principles—Nationalism, Democracy and the People's Livelihood. Knowing that they could not be put into effect overnight, he also outlined the steps whereby the ground could be prepared for their effective application. The first was establishment of national unity by military conquest of both the decadent Peking government and the provincial warlords; the second, creation of an authoritarian government for a period of political tutelage; and the third, provision of democratic self-government for the Chinese masses. Dr. Sun was ready to accept help from any quarter in carrying through this program. When the western powers, including the United States, showed no interest in it, he turned to Soviet Russia. The response from Moscow was enthusiastic. After formation of a united front between the Kuomintang and Chinese Communists, Sun Yat-sen was able to call upon Russian military and political counsel in planning a great northern drive from Canton to extend Nationalist control over all China.

In the midst of plans for this campaign, in March 1925, Sun Yat-sen died. The impetus he had given the Nationalist movement carried it forward, however, and the leadership of the northern expedition fell into the strong and capable hands of General Chiang Kai-shek. He was to prove to be more than a military commander. An apparently firm believer in the Three Principles, an astute politician willing during these early days to make the most of Communist support without surrendering to Communist control, a soldier trained in the tactics of modern warfare, Chiang Kai-shek steadily grew in stature. He came in time to represent Chinese Nationalism more than any other political figure, and to symbolize his country's new spirit of unity.

The northern expedition, finally launched in the summer of 1926, met with almost uninterrupted success. As the Nationalists and their Communist allies advanced victoriously to the Yangtze Valley, they won not only new territory but increasing numbers of adherents. All China was electrified by the emergence of a party that not only promised unity and democracy, but dared to defy the foreigners and hold out the promise of an end to imperialism. By the close of the year, the Nationalists had successfully overrun more than half of China.

The powers watched these developments with conflicting emotions. The anti-imperialist tone of Nationalist propaganda, the new aggressiveness of Chinese leadership and the insistent demand for immediate revision of the unequal treaties caused a profound searching of the soul in foreign capitals—not excepting Washington. In all their dealings with China, the powers had been accustomed to making demands, not receiving them. The Nationalist threat to boycott all foreign trade showed that they now faced the alternatives of either coming to terms with the new China or having to maintain the old privileges by force of arms. Anti-foreign disturbances were increasing. Enraged mobs overran the British concessions in Hankow and Kiukang. There were fears of a general uprising directed against foreigners throughout the Yangtze Valley.

The American position was made clear in a statement of policy made by Secretary Kellogg on January 27, 1927. The United States had always desired the unity, the independence and the prosperity of China, he declared. We were ready not only to put the customs surtax into effect, but fully to restore to China complete tariff autonomy. Upon assurance of adequate protection for American lives and property, we were also prepared to accept the recommendations of the extraterritorial commission and eventually surrender consular jurisdiction. But the question at issue, he implied, was the responsibility of any Chinese government in representing or speaking for China as a whole. Unless order were maintained, the United States could not neglect its duty to protect the lives and property of its citizens.

The pressure of business interests, the age-old desire to see that the United States did not lose any privileges enjoyed by other powers and the latent fear of Communist influence in the Nationalist regime induced a cautious and conservative policy in Washington. The "old China hands" in the treaty ports, whose often arrogant attitude toward the Chinese had done so much to stir up anti-foreign feeling, were continually demanding additional protection. Their warnings against the radical influences at work in China strengthened the tendency of the State Department to move slowly and carefully.

Public opinion at home was more friendly toward the Nationalists. The American people could not help being greatly impressed with their revolutionary zeal, and they naturally sympathized with aims and aspirations that for the first time appeared to hold out the promise of democratic government in China. They had no desire to uphold the corrupt, reactionary regime which had for so long held sway at Peking, nor to stand in the way of final triumph of the Nationalist cause. It was popularly felt that the time had come to break away entirely from any concert of powers, and to aid the Nationalists by surrendering at once the special rights which blocked their full assertion of authority over all China.

Spirited debates in the House of Representatives revealed little support for the old treaty status. Representative Connally urged that the United States at once make clear that it would accord "great, old China the rights of sovereignty and the rights of nationality, and that in her aspirations along these lines America will stand by her side in time of peace as China stood by our side in the time of the [First] World War." Representative Linthicum stoutly declared that "the friendship of the Chinese people is more valuable to us than any extraterritoriality or jurisdictional rights we now have." In support of a resolution to initiate negotiations for giving up all such privileges, Representative Porter of the Committee on Foreign Affairs vigorously urged prompt action. "Every day's delay in the adjustment of differences between the United States and China," he said, "would increase the feeling among the Chinese that force alone could be depended upon to secure justice and make more difficult the settlement of these differences on the basis of mutual friendliness and fair dealing."

The conservatism of the State Department and new disturbances in China, however, continued to make the course of any such adjustment anything but smooth. With the Nationalists continuing their violent anti-imperialist campaign, aided and abetted by their Communist advisers, further outbreaks of violence directed against foreigners almost inevitably invoked retaliation. Relations between China and the western world drifted perilously close to open conflict.

The most spectacular clash took place in Nanking in March 1927. With the Nationalists' capture of the city, systematic attacks were made upon the foreign community, including the consulates, with widespread looting, destruction of property and some loss of life. Many of the foreigners, including Americans, took frightened refuge on what was called Socony Hill—the property of the Standard Oil Company. The danger of still further violence was averted only after both British and American gunboats opened fire on the mobs seeking to break into the company's compound and laid down a barrage for the foreigners' protection.

On the heels of this news came other reports of anti-foreign outbreaks. All China was said to be echoing Foreign Minister Chen's statement that "the time has come to speak to foreign imperialism in the language it understands." A graphic description of conditions appeared in the *Boston Globe*:

"Daily, down the huge Chinese rivers, come white men and women—missionaries, officials, business men and their families—escaping from anti-foreign mobs in the interior. Hundreds of these have been cut off for months; hundreds more have not been heard from yet.

"In the cities there have been riots, killings. At China's leading ports (all under the domination of foreign interests) European colonies throw up barbed wire, drill their residents and call home for troops. . . . Kuomintang political agents tour the whole country, organize locals and arouse the whole people against the 'foreign devils,' who deprive China of her ports, limit and collect her tariffs, run gunboats up and down her rivers at will and live in the country under their own laws, not the laws of China. . . . President Coolidge orders marines and battleships to protect the 12,000 American citizens in China. Great Britain embarks a division of soldiers for Shanghai. . . . Obviously the present trouble is not 'just another war in China.' "

The United States—in joint action with Great Britain, France, Italy and Japan—had at once protested in the most vigorous language against "the outrages against American nationals" at Nanking. Immediate punishment was demanded of those responsible, together with an apology from the commanding officer of the Nationalist army and adequate reparation for the damage done. Foreign Minister Chen denied the responsibility of the Nationalists for the attack, but he promised reparation wherever it could be shown that either property damage or loss of life was due to their troops. This reply was not considered satisfactory by the powers, and it was proposed that they should take concerted action to enforce their demands for immediate and complete restitution.

The United States, however, refused to be a party to any joint display of force. It broke away from the united front the powers had so far maintained, and decided to continue direct negotiations with the Nationalist government for a peaceful settlement of the issue. And on this occasion, contrary to developments that had so many times in the past led to Anglo-French pressure upon China while the United States stood aside, our lead was followed by the other powers. They too entered upon individual negotiations with the Chinese authorities.

The nation as a whole strongly supported our stand against joint action. Sympathy for the Nationalists asserted itself. Although some newspapers flatly stated that the United States should not allow questions of sovereignty to interfere with the protection of American lives and property, the more general feeling was that we should not resort to force under any circumstances or allow ourselves to become involved in pulling the other powers' chestnuts out of the fire. The concessions in China were not of vital importance to the United States, according to those who upheld our policy, and there was no obligation upon the government, in view of the civil war in China, to protect all Americans. They should leave China if they were in danger, and if necessary the government should furnish them the necessary transportation. From such newspapers as the *New York World*, the *Boston Globe*, the *Ohio State Journal*, the *Topeka Capital* and the *New York Herald Tribune*, among many others, came forthright praise for the moderation that had saved China from further disorder and bloodshed.

Soon after the Nanking incident, drastic changes in the internal political situation gave additional confirmation to the wisdom of our non-intervention policy, and also made our path much easier in dealing with China. Growing tension between the moderates and the radical left-wing elements of the Kuomintang led to an open split in their combined ranks, and for a time rival capitals were maintained at Nanking and Hankow. Chiang Kai-shek thereupon threw all his influence behind the movement to align the Nationalists with conservative interests, and turned violently upon the Communists and their adherents. The radical Hankow regime was overthrown, the Nanking government took over entire direction of the Nationalist campaign and relations with Moscow were completely broken off. In these new circumstances, the whole tone of Nationalist propaganda became greatly subdued and anti-foreignism gave way to a greater willingness to reach an understanding with the powers.

At the same time, the Nationalists renewed their northern advance and in the late spring of 1928 completely routed the militarists seeking to uphold the old Peking government. Conditions within China still fell far short of complete unification. There was continuing and bitter strife with the Communists driven out of the Nationalist ranks, and in many other parts of the country the provincial warlords refused to accept the authority of Nanking. Nevertheless the Nationalist government dominated by Chiang Kai-shek had been able to assert a larger measure of control over China than any regime since that of Yuan Shih-kai. The progress China had made in two short years appeared to be little short of miraculous.

Greatly influenced both by the Nationalists' successes and also by the more moderate and conservative character of their policies after the expulsion of the Communists, the United States had early in the year decided to recognize their government and try to work out with it a solution of all existing problems. A first step was settlement of the Nanking incident. The renewed negotiations were successful and a full agreement was reached in March.

The Nationalist government expressed its profound regret for what had happened, accepted full responsibility and promised reparation after an investigation by a special Chinese-American commission. On its part, the United States declared that while its naval authorities had no alternative to the action they had been forced to take, it deplored the fact that circumstances beyond their control should have forced them to open a bombardment for the protection of American citizens.

Having taken the initiative in resolving what might have proved a highly critical issue, the United States proceeded in this new atmosphere of cordiality to take up the tariff issue. Confirming the concessions already promised in the negotiations at Peking, China was in July granted full tariff autonomy in the first foreign treaty to be concluded by the Nationalist government. As the other powers gradually fell in line, China consequently found herself, by 1930, wholly freed of all foreign control over her tariff for the first time in almost a century. If the activities of Japan were soon to restrict this freedom, an important principle had finally been established.

Negotiations over extraterritoriality did not prove quite so successful. The strengthening of authority and complete consolidation of the position of Chiang Kai-shek led the Nationalist government to renew its insistence upon the immediate abrogation of all unequal treaties. In notes to the several powers it was categorically stated that, with unification of the country fully achieved, the time had come "to negotiate—in accordance with diplomatic procedure—new treaties on the basis of complete equality and mutual respect for each other's sovereignty." The new foreign minister at Nanking, C. T. Wang, ably argued that the old treaties were an unhappy legacy of the past. With such rapid progress being made in reforming the country's legal and judicial system, he maintained, there was no further warrant for delay in carrying out the reforms to which the powers had pledged themselves at the Washington Conference.

The reply of the powers was "not so fast." There was general sympathy for China's position on the issue of consular jurisdiction, but they were unwilling at this time to go any further than some slight modification of the prevailing system. For all its concessions on other points, the United States accepted this thesis quite as emphatically as other foreign governments. Secretary Kellogg reiterated that there would have to be more adequate guarantee for the safety of American lives and property before any surrender of our extraterritorial rights could be made. He countered the Nationalists' repeated demands for action by making further reform of the Chinese legal code an essential requisite for even continued negotiations on the issue.

Impatient over such delay, the Nationalist government undertook to do away with extraterritoriality on its own responsibility. It declared that all special rights and privileges heretofore enjoyed by foreigners would automatically end as of January 1, 1930. The Nationalist bark, however, was worse than its bite. When the powers still showed no signs of accepting such a policy, the desire to avoid an open break led Foreign Minister Wang to declare that the Nationalist mandate should be considered as an expression of principle rather than a threat of action. It should be regarded, he said in a conciliatory statement, simply as a step toward removing what remained the only real cause for friction between China and the powers. Negotiations were then renewed in a more friendly atmosphere.

Developments entirely unexpected in Washington were once again to interrupt their course, but as the first decade after the Washington Conference drew to a close, the general promise of Far Eastern peace and stability implicit in the conference accords appeared to be fulfilled. As the focal point in Asiatic politics, China was in a stronger position than at any time in the whole modern era. She was asserting her independence with increasing success. It was true that Japan had attempted to block the Nationalists' northward march, and regarded with misgivings the extension of their influence into Manchuria. Nevertheless, she had duly recognized the new regime. If she was reluctant to surrender her extraterritorial rights in China, so too were the United States and the European powers. But it was believed that time would surely lead to an equitable settlement of this problem as it had already to that of tariff autonomy. In inaugurating, at the beginning of the 1930's, the period of political tutelage prescribed by Sun Yat-sen for the establishment of self-government, China could view the future with renewed confidence. There was still civil strife in many parts of the country. The Communists refused to accept Nanking's authority. But the power and prestige of the new government were steadily rising.

In reacting to these important developments, American policy had undergone a definite shift. The United States was at first highly reluctant to give the Nationalists any support or encouragement. Alarmed by the anti-foreign movement and its threat to property rights, we had for a considerable period clung to the old hope of a strong leader emerging from the Peking regime who would prove more friendly to our interests. We had used force when American lives and property seemed to be endangered. The conservative influences which appeared to direct our policy toward China followed a line that could hardly be reconciled with popular expressions of sympathy for the revolutionary cause. "Your statesmen talk in a more friendly way," Chiang Kai-shek told an American correspondent on one occasion, "but in the end they sign the same treaties as the British and Japanese, and we like an attitude of straightforward opposition better."

The Chinese opinion of us was greatly modified, however, when the United States refused to take part in any further demonstrations of force after the Nanking incident, assumed the lead in recognizing the Nationalist regime and agreed to grant China complete tariff autonomy. Even though we still hesitated to surrender extraterritorial rights and were unwilling to make any further concessions unless the other powers also did so, we once again proved ourselves to be a friend of China when there was very real temptation to intervene more forcibly in her affairs. The strength of Chinese Nationalism, and its increasing moderation after Chiang Kai-shek's split with the Communists, both contributed importantly to this revised policy. It was dictated more by circumstance than by sentiment. Nevertheless there was a declared willingness, fully supported by the American public, to review our relations with China along more liberal lines in recognition of the new spirit that was permeating the Chinese people.

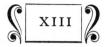

OUR STAKE IN CHINA

POPULAR interest in China had continued to grow all through the 1920's. The Nationalist revolution had a highly dramatic appeal for the American people. As the armies of Chiang Kai-shek surged northward, bringing more and more of the country under the control of the new government, popular attention was turned toward eastern Asia as at no time since the Boxer Rebellion. There were those who felt that the direction which the revolution was to take might become the most critical issue of the twentieth century, holding in balance future relations between the Orient and the western world.

More was written about China, and more widespread discussion and debate took place on America's attitude toward the resurgent republic, than ever before. Books poured from the presses upon every phase of Chinese civilization—descriptions of the country, accounts of its political struggles, analyses of its nationalism. The question of China's future was posed from every possible point of view. Some of these books were sound studies giving the background of Far Eastern history. Tyler Dennett's *Americans in Eastern Asia*, E. T. Williams' *China: Yesterday and Today*, H. B. Morse and H. F. MacNair's *Far Eastern International Relations*, A. N. Holcombe's *Chinese Revolution* and Paul S. Reinsch's *An American Diplomat in China* were a few such titles. There were also scores of books on the current situation. Nathaniel Peffer wrote on *China: the Collapse of a Civilization*; Putnam Weale on *Why China Sees Red*; Rodney Gilbert on *What's Wrong with China*; Scott Nearing on *Whither China?*; L. M. King on *China in Turmoil*; Hallet Abend on *Tortured China* and Anna Louise Strong on *China's Millions*.

While the authors of these books, as obvious from their

titles, were primarily concerned with the revolutionary throes through which China was passing, other writers discovered the cultural heritage of the Middle Kingdom and opened up for American readers new vistas of oriental art, literature, poetry and drama. In highly romantic terms, the Princess Der Ling described court life under the Manchu dynasty in *Old Buddha, Lotus Petals* and *Kowtow*. Florence Ayscough wrote the *Chinese Mirror*, compiled the *Autobiography of Tu Fu* and in collaboration with Amy Lowell brought out new translations of Chinese poetry in *Fir-Flower Tablets*. Among other studies of Chinese philosophy, Richard Wilhelm published his *Short History of Chinese Civilization* and *The Soul of China*. Still other facets of Chinese life were revealed in J. C. Ferguson's *Chinese Painting*, A. E. Zucker's *The Chinese Theatre* and E. H. Wilson's *China, Mother of Gardens*, the latter book obtaining a wide circulation among the members of the country's innumerable garden clubs.

Perhaps the peak of literary interest in things Chinese was reached in 1931 with publication of *The Good Earth* by Pearl Buck. A popular best seller, destined to win for its author the Nobel Prize, it presented an entirely new picture of China to thousands of persons whose previous knowledge had been based upon absurd misconceptions of the "heathen Chinee" as peculiar people who perversely insisted upon doing everything backward—from their manner of writing to the way they buttoned their gowns. The status of many of the Chinese in this country, it had also to be recognized, had done little to broaden such ideas. Chinese laundries, the exotic flavor of local Chinatowns, violent outbreaks of tong warfare and chop suey restaurants had become symbols of China and the Chinese for which *The Good Earth* was a valuable corrective. It gave an authentic and sympathetic description of how Chinese peasants actually lived, and also portrayed through its characters how they experienced the emotional conflicts known to mankind everywhere.

An even broader range of topics was treated in magazine

articles than in books. It was indicative of the general be-
wilderment over just what was happening in war-torn China
that so many of the titles of these articles were in the form of
questions. "What Is Happening in China?" "What's All This
About China?" "Whose War in China?" "Can the Powers Keep
Their Rights?" "Yellow Peril or White?" "Shall America Intervene?" "Shall the United States Drift into War With China?"
portrayed a confused quest for more adequate understanding
of the Orient. Yet there was no general agreement upon the
answers to these questions. Even the so-called experts were often
at a loss as to how the Nationalist revolution would affect
China's relations with the outside world.

Exchanges of visits by Americans and Chinese were more
general during the 1920's than in any previous period. Chinese
students attended American colleges and technical schools in
considerable numbers, and there were various official and unofficial missions from China to the United States. An unusual
cultural contact was the American tour of the great Chinese
actor Mei Lan-feng—"the Foremost of the Pear Orchard"—who
aroused both interest and widespread acclaim when he performed before wondering American audiences with his reper-
tory company. Visits to the Orient on the part of Americans
were a natural consequence of the great boom in tourist travel
during the decade. While such travelers may actually have
learned little of China in the course of fleeting visits to Peking
and Shanghai, even such superficial contacts served to heighten
interest in what was still a distant and somehow mysterious
country.

The United States also generously aided China in meeting
her chronic problems of flood and drought. At the opening
of the 1920's, and again toward their close, famine took its toll
of millions of Chinese lives, and nation-wide campaigns were
held in the United States to raise relief funds. The China International Famine Relief Commission was the principal
agency in carrying forward this program, and the American

Red Cross also made large contributions toward meeting China's tremendous need for outside help.

As the Nationalist movement came to its climax, one of the most compelling causes of popular concern over China was the position of American missionaries in the face of the anti-foreign movement. The activity of church organizations in spreading Christian doctrine among the Chinese people had steadily expanded with the passing years. The general interest in what was happening in Asia was perhaps most pronounced, except in some commercial circles, among the multitude of people who either directly or indirectly were associated with missionary enterprise.

Secretary Stimson was to bear witness to the missionary-inspired interest in China in discussing the later development of American policy in the 1930's. There was hardly a town in the United States, as he pointed out, where some church organization was not contributing to the support of a missionary in China. The letters home of such unofficial envoys, often mimeographed for general distribution, and their talks and lectures when on furlough, fostered a sympathetic understanding of China that played no little part, as already suggested, in developing popular attitudes upon foreign policy.

The number of American missionaries in China had risen by the opening of the century to some 1,000, representing thirty different societies, and in the early 1920's it was estimated to have increased still further to total about 2,500. While evangelical and organized religious work was still their main line of endeavor, they had continued to organize both schools and colleges, and especially promoted the study and practice of modern medicine. Throughout the entire history of American missionary activity in China, emphasis was always placed upon the general diffusion of western culture, sometimes with unfortunately little toleration for the Chinese people's own religious or philosophic ideas. It had been said that the Protestant missionary movement in China was "more of a subverting force than a converting proselytism." In so far as this was true, it was due to the greater receptivity of the Chinese to social reform than to religious conversion. Yet the missionaries never lost sight of their major goal, and one of the chief causes for the Nationalists' growing resentment against mission schools was their insistence upon religious instruction.

The activities of the Protestant missionaries were supplemented by those of American Catholics. The organization of the American Board of Catholic Missions in 1920 was both a sign of growing interest in such enterprises and a further spur to their expansion. Many missionaries were trained at Maryknoll, near Ossining, New York, for work in the China field, and others, including both priests and nuns, were sent to the Far East by religious orders scattered throughout the country.

After the close of the First World War, the American missionary societies had hoped to win many more Chinese to Christianity, and for awhile their "China for Christ" movement appeared to have given new impetus to their work. An increasing number of converts was reported, and a great deal was made of those who could be fairly said to be among the country's national leaders. Sun Yat-sen had been baptized, both his wife and other members of the Soong family were Christians and Chiang Kai-shek also professed the foreign faith. The most spectacular of converts in the early 1920's was the provincial warlord Feng Yu-hsiang. He was not only himself converted but was responsible for the wholesale adoption of Christianity by his army. His troops were reported to hold daily religious meetings, General Feng often preaching to them; to say grace regularly before meals, and to march into battle singing a Chinese translation of "Onward Christian Soldiers."

The number of Protestant converts did not make any real impression upon the Chinese population, however, and probably never totaled more than about 800,000 out of China's more than 400,000,000. The non-religious influence of the educational and medical work promoted by the missionaries and other philanthropic agencies was far more important and affected every phase of Chinese life. American mission schools not only provided the education of thousands of young Chinese, but helped to set the standard and influence the general pattern of the modern schools set up by the Chinese government. Foreign colleges and universities played the same role in higher education, and American teachers helped to inspire the intellectual renaissance that paralleled the growth of political nationalism. The visit of John Dewey, who lectured in Peking during 1919, was a case in point, but more important was the role of many returned students who brought American educational ideas back to China. Y. C. James Yen, the founder of the Mass Education Movement for combating illiteracy among the peasants, was but one of many such men.

Apart from missionary enterprise, which could be traced back over a century, an important sign of American interest in this phase of Chinese life had been the remission, first in 1908 and then even more generously in 1924, of the Boxer indemnity payments. This money was made available to the Chinese government for educational purposes, and it provided the funds both for Tsing Hua College at Peking and for sending to the United States every year some sixty Chinese students for further study in American colleges.

Among the thirteen American-supported colleges in China in the 1920's were St. John's University in Shanghai; the University of Nanking; Ginling College, for girls, also in Nanking; Canton Christian College; Boone University, at Wuchang; and Yenching University, in Peking. A number of Chinese colleges also received special aid and support from sister institutions in the United States. There was a Yale-in-China at Changsha, and in the northern capital a Princeton-in-Peking.

The broad role of the United States in furthering medical progress in China received great impetus at the beginning of the decade with the formation of the China Medical Board, a subsidiary of the Rockefeller Foundation. It established the Peking Union Medical College and erected a notable group of buildings, opened in 1921, which at one and the same time conformed to the best traditions of Chinese architecture, and rivaled in modern and up-to-date equipment the best of western medical schools and hospitals. There were also American-supported schools of law, journalism, agriculture and forestry associated with a number of the larger universities.

For all the progress being made along these lines, American educational institutions, as well as American missions, found themselves everywhere on the defensive with the rise of the anti-foreign and anti-Christian agitation of the mid-1920's. The missionaries were at first confronted by a movement, with which many of them were in sympathy, for Chinese assumption of complete control in both churches and schools. But following the firing upon a mob of students by the police of the International Settlement in Shanghai, in May 1925, the continued presence of foreign missionaries in China was bitterly denounced by the Nationalists. Although many Kuomintang leaders had been educated in American schools, the missionaries were accused of being the "running dogs of the imperialists." Patriotic demonstrations, often sponsored by students intolerant of all foreign control or influence, soon led to the outbreaks of violence in the treaty ports that have already been noted. Missions in the interior were also attacked, property looted and destroyed and a number of Americans killed in a crescendo of anti-foreignism reminiscent of Boxer days.

The result of such disturbances was the beginning of a general foreign exodus from China. No longer willing, as they had been in the past, to seek special protection from their government, and generally sympathetic with the Chinese demand for abolition of the unequal treaties, American missionaries were ready to pull up stakes rather than cause further friction in international relations. Out of a total of some 8,000 Protestant missionaries from all countries, more than 5,000 were reported to have left China by 1927. The Catholics did not suffer as severely as the Protestants, partly because they were not so deeply involved in higher education, but in general the missionaries' role in inspiring the Nationalist movement had been an important one, and they were among the first victims of the anti-foreignism which it strongly encouraged.

Most of them were to return as the agitation against them gradually subsided and diplomatic ties were formally concluded with the Nationalists, but the missionary movement as a whole had suffered a tremendous blow. In going back to their work, moreover, both missionaries and educators were compelled to adapt themselves to new conditions. Leadership and direction in both churches and mission schools were largely taken over by native Christians. The Chinese owed a great deal to what Americans had done for them and they fully acknowledged this debt. But China was coming of age. Intellectual tutelage to the foreigner was no more acceptable than political tutelage.

For all the popular interest in China aroused by the drama of Nationalist revolution and the dilemma of the missionaries, trade remained the most substantial bond between China and the United States. Since the opening of the century there had been a progressive increase both in its volume and in its relative importance. On the eve of the First World War, it had risen to some $51,000,000 annually, and by 1930 its value was almost four times this figure, or about $190,000,000. A growing market was being developed for American cotton, tobacco and kerosene, and there were also substantial exports of flour, iron and steel products and machinery. In return, the United States imported raw silk, tung oil, peanuts, eggs and egg products, furs, carpet wool, straw hats, tungsten and antimony.

Another factor in economic relations was American investments in China. This had been a matter of concern ever since the Chinese first began their foreign borrowing for the construction of railways and other modern improvements. It has already been noted that on the eve of the First World War, the United States had withdrawn from the international consortium which planned to loan the new Chinese Republic very considerable sums. But while President Wilson had opposed our participation in such an undertaking on the ground that the loan conditions infringed on Chinese sovereignty, he was soon taking the lead in organizing a new consortium. Political rather than economic considerations largely accounted for this shift in policy. It was felt that only international loans could prevent Japan from winning a dominating financial position in China that would pave the way for closer political controls. The new consortium was to enforce a financial Open Door paralleling our insistence upon equality of trade.

Its members were the United States, Great Britain, France and Japan, and an agreement finally reached, in 1920, provided for international participation in future Chinese loans applying not only to China proper but also to Manchuria. While Japan was assured that no support would be given to any enterprise inimical to either her national economy or her national defense, she was supposedly to allow other financial interests to cooperate in the further economic development of even that part of China which fell within her sphere of special influence. For all the apparent promise of the new consortium, the Chinese nevertheless remained fearful of its influence. Even though it was designed in part to keep Japan in check, they saw in it a threat of international control over Chinese finances no less dangerous to national sovereignty. The consortium consequently failed to provide any real opportunities for investing American funds in China, and blocked rather than promoted additional loans.

There was, nevertheless, some increase in other types of American investments and their total was estimated, in 1930, to be almost $250,000,000, or approximately ten times the figure reported in 1900. Business holdings made up the great bulk of this figure, and were valued at $155,000,000. Commercial firms accounted for about a third of the total, with public utilities (concentrated in Shanghai), banking and financial institutions, manufacturers and transportation companies following in order. American holdings of Chinese government securities and missionary property in China amounted to approximately $42,000,000 each. Some 566 American firms were doing business in China and the total American population, including missionaries, educators and all other residents, as well as businessmen, was about 7,000.

In the case of both trade and investments, it is clear that in spite of steady growth since the opening of the twentieth century, our economic stake in China still did not bulk very large over against world totals of American foreign trade and investment. The trade was less than 3 per cent of our total commerce, and investments were only about 1.3 per cent of total foreign holdings. Various efforts were made to provide more favorable conditions for doing business. The China Trade Act, first passed in 1922, allowed American companies operating in China to take out federal charters of incorporation in order to give them the greatest possible latitude in taking advantage of extraterritorial rights. But both trade and investment lagged. Our economic stake in China was not as important as that in Japan, with which our commerce was more than twice as great, let alone our interest in many European and Latin American countries.

All such statistics, however, had little bearing upon the attitude of either the business world or the general public toward the significance of our commercial relations with China. It was once again, as so many times in the past, the potentialities of the Chinese market, its apparently limitless possibilities of future expansion, that made the protection of our economic rights appear to be an important national interest. In the nineteenth century, it had been believed that China was destined to absorb our surplus wheat and cotton crops; in the twentieth, her potential capacity to consume the excess products of our industrial plant made an even greater appeal to the imagination. Americans were prone to think of the Chinese, as characterized in the title of a popular book by Carl Crow, as Four Hundred Million Customers. The realities of Chinese economic conditions, with a vast population bound to the soil and living in such poverty as often to leave countless numbers on the verge of starvation, were ignored in the beautiful vision of these millions of customers happily buying whatever the United States might want to sell them.

This hopeful attitude toward the future of Chinese trade was clearly brought out in the congressional debates on the China Trade Act. Representative Dyer emphasized in glowing terms the opportunities offered for economic development in the construction of new railways; Senator Cummins stated his belief that nowhere else in the world were there greater possibilities for commercial expansion, and Representative Husten echoed such sentiments with the further comment that our prospects in China were all the greater because "the Chinese people are probably more friendly to us than they are to any other nation in the world."

Such glowing hopes were perhaps expressed most exuberantly in *America's Future in Asia*, a book published some years later, on the eve of the Pacific war, by Robert Aura Smith.

"There will be not miles of road, or hundreds of miles of road, or thousands of miles of road," Smith wrote; "—there will be literally millions of miles of road from one end of China to the other. Someone will supply the cement and asphalt for these highways; someone will supply the scrapers and the steam rollers and the concrete mixers. And when China is ribboned from top to bottom there will be inevitable filling stations—and someone will supply the pumps, and the gasoline that goes into them. On these roads will be millions of motor cars and there will be at least four tires to the car. Someone will supply the materials and the skill that build those automobiles and those multiplied millions of miles of rubber on which they roll."

The dream of selling things to China in such huge quantities as to ensure our own prosperity had persisted, in spite of all disappointments, ever since the first China traders rounded Cape Horn and the early clipper ships built up the tea trade. Whatever its relation to the actualities of Pacific commerce, it has remained a fundamental factor governing our relations with China since the late eighteenth century. American policy has again and again, in the course of the past one hundred and fifty years, shown a generous sympathy for China, and this has been in part animated by a sincere concern for her best interests. But underlying our policy, possibly more than in the case of our relations with any other nation, has been the concept that the potential buying power of Four Hundred Million Customers makes it, above everything else, good business to be friendly with the Chinese people.

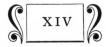

CRISIS IN MANCHURIA

Toward the close of 1931, largely unknown to the American public, events in Asia were hurrying toward a new crisis that was to have world-wide and devastating consequences. As the power of the Chinese Nationalists was gradually extended to Manchuria, Japan sensed a serious threat to her interests in the entire area lying north of the Great Wall. Her recognition of the new government at Nanking did not mean that she had any idea of allowing it to gain full control in territory that was regarded as a Japanese sphere of influence. Moreover the militaristic elements in the country, driven into the background since the Washington Conference, saw an even greater menace in the growing strength of Chinese Nationalism. Their ambitious program for Japanese expansion, postponed but not abandoned by the treaties which had been signed for preserving China's sovereignty, would be gravely endangered should the Nanking regime be allowed to become too powerful. Political and economic conditions in Japan, and in Manchuria itself, also contributed to the explosion in 1931, but its underlying cause was Japan's desire to gain an unassailable foothold on the Asiatic mainland before a resurgent China became strong enough to offer her effective resistance.

The campaign that was to lead to the occupation of Manchuria was launched on September 18. Seizing as a pretext a bomb explosion on the South Manchuria Railway, the Japanese attacked and occupied Mukden. Once again Japanese imperialism was on the march.

The full implications of this assault were not at once realized. Only subsequent developments were to reveal how neatly it fitted into the general pattern of imperialistic aggression. The Mukden incident was in the line of advance already plotted by war with China in 1894, the attack on Russia ten years later, the seizure of Shantung in 1914 and the notorious Twenty-One Demands. It foreshadowed the establishment of the puppet Japanese state of Manchukuo and the undeclared but full-scale war that broke out against China in 1937. Moreover, the Japanese militarists' successful defiance of all treaty obligations was to have even wider repercussions. Notice was served upon Rome and Berlin that the peace-loving nations were not prepared to take effective action against an aggressor. The Second World War began in September 1931. The attack upon Mukden was the first link in a tragic chain of events that ten years later led to Japan's bombing of Pearl Harbor in an effort to block American interference with her dreams of conquest.

All this was in the future. Far more deeply concerned with domestic affairs, the American public refused to become greatly alarmed, in September 1931, over anything that might happen in Manchuria. Japan had chosen well the time to strike. On the day after cables from the Far East told of the first clash between Japanese and Chinese, the New York stock market perversely celebrated the second anniversary of its 1929 peak by plunging to the lowest levels since 1924. On September 21, the ominous news was reported that England had abandoned the gold standard. The continuing impact of world-wide depression diverted popular attention from the political scene in Asia. With the American Legion, assembled at its annual convention, calling upon President Hoover to declare a national emergency, the Manchurian story was soon relegated to inside pages in the nation's press.

The State Department could not be so casual. China had at once appealed both to Geneva and directly to Washington for aid. As "sponsor of the sacred engagements" of the Kellogg-Briand anti-war pact, to which both Japan and China had adhered in 1928, the United States was asked "to take such steps as will insure the preservation of peace in the Far East." Two years earlier when hostilities had for a time been threatened between China and Russia over the status of the Chinese

Eastern Railway, Secretary Stimson had tried to invoke this treaty only to be sharply rebuffed. Nevertheless he was again ready to do whatever he could to fulfill what he regarded as American commitments both in respect to international engagements not to resort to war as an instrument of national policy, and also in supporting our traditional policy of upholding Chinese sovereignty. In stating the willingness of the United States to associate itself with the League of Nations in reminding both China and Japan of their obligations to maintain peace, however, he advised a policy of extreme caution. In the belief that the civilian elements in the Japanese government would soon reassert their authority over the military chiefs whom he held responsible for the Mukden attack, Stimson was at first unwilling to take any action that might intensify nationalistic feeling in Japan.

It soon became clear, however, that the militarists were in complete control of the Japanese government and not to be diverted from their program by mild reminders of possible treaty obligations. Whatever was said by Japanese diplomats, whether in Tokyo or Geneva, the army went blithely ahead on its predetermined course. China's rights of sovereignty were completely disregarded as almost all south Manchuria was quickly brought under Japanese domination. Any hope that liberal influences might restrain the military had to be wholly abandoned.

With China once again appealing for support and urging the United States to cooperate with the League in investigating the situation, Stimson was to take a stronger stand. He informed Geneva that this country was ready, acting independently, to reinforce whatever the League might do to uphold world peace. Moreover, he now urged forthright intervention. "It is most desirable," the Secretary of State said in a note sent to Geneva on October 5, "that the League in no way relax its vigilance and in no way fail to assert all the pressure and authority within its competence toward regulating the action of China and Japan in the premises."

Sharply breaking with all past precedents, he even went so far as to instigate, and then accept, an invitation for an official representative of the United States to participate in all discussions in the League Council relating to the Far Eastern situation. When the Council failed to take any decisive steps at its first meetings and adjourned to Paris, Ambassador Dawes was instructed to continue to represent American interests. Stimson suggested that he should move carefully in supporting any action proposed by the members of the League, but he made it clear that the United States was "anxious not to discourage them or put any obstacles in their path."

While generally upholding his Secretary of State, President Hoover was apparently more conservative in his ideas as to the extent of possible cooperation with the League. He insisted that it be restricted to moral support. "We will not go along on war," he is reported to have told his cabinet, "or any of the sanctions either economic or military, for these are the roads to war." In his opinion, neither our obligations to China nor our own interests nor our national dignity required us to run the risk of possible involvement in the Asiatic quarrel. In his message to Congress in December, he soberly reassured the country that in spite of our gesture toward collaboration with the League, the United States retained complete freedom of judgment and action.

The League made no determined move to restrain Japan. Its members may have felt that they could not count upon American support in view of President Hoover's attitude, but their inaction was basically due to the blindness of England and France toward the challenge to the whole system of collective security raised by Japanese aggression. In December, it was finally agreed to send the Lytton Commission, on which the United States was unofficially represented by Major General Frank R. McCoy, to investigate the entire situation. But Geneva would have nothing to do with either economic sanctions or any other form of direct pressure upon Tokyo. The opportunity to take advantage of American cooperation, even though there was no guaranty of how far it might be carried, was lost. Japan was tacitly allowed to go her own way despite the fact that in employing force against a friendly neighbor she was violating her obligations under the League covenant and the Nine-Power Treaty signed at Washington.

What was the reaction of the American public toward our tentative gestures of collaboration with Geneva? Did Secretary Stimson, ready to back up whatever the League might decide to do, or President Hoover, refusing to be drawn beyond moral support of its policy, more nearly reflect the popular attitude?

Not until October 24, after designation of an American representative to take part in League discussions of the crisis, did the nation appear to become very much concerned over our policy. There was sympathy for China. Our friendship for her people caused the public generally to favor her cause. As Secretary Stimson was himself to write later, however, Manchuria was too far away and too unknown, even had there been less concern over domestic problems, for the issues at stake to strike home. And the interest finally aroused by our mild flirtation with Geneva reflected the confusion which was to characterize the popular attitude toward Far Eastern policy for another ten years.

The press as a whole upheld the idea of cooperation with the League and found little to criticize in the stand that had been taken. There were complaints from isolationist newspapers. The *New York American*, heading its editorial "Stimson's Folly," declared our policy to be "nitwit diplomacy" and vociferously called upon even the cautious Mr. Hoover to "rid his internationalist mind of the Wilsonian delusion that he is President of the world." The *New York Daily News* was more succinct: "Let's shinny on our side of the street." However a long list of papers, including the *Springfield Republican*, the *Baltimore News*, the *New York Times*, the *New York Journal of Commerce* and the *Washington News*, were wholly approving. "More power to Mr. Stimson," declared the *Milwaukee Journal*, and the *New York Herald Tribune* congratulated him "on being able to approach Geneva without regarding its ground as either holy or bewitched."

Such praise for Stimson did not necessarily imply approval for economic sanctions. As reflected in editorials, popular opinion was apparently more in agreement with Hoover's concept of going no further than the exercise of moral pressure in support of either Chinese sovereignty or of collective security. Even when such pressure had proved to be wholly unavailing, and China again tried to prove how closely allied American and Chinese interests were in resisting Japanese aggression, the attitude of the press did not change. Early in December, the *Literary Digest* took a telegraphic poll of the nation's editors. A few expressed the opinion that if the League should institute a boycott of Japan, it should be respected by the United States. The overwhelming majority were opposed to our making any such commitment, and were emphatic in their warnings against allowing the United States to become involved in such a dangerous situation.

As so many times in the past, we were not prepared to make good our treaty commitments for upholding Chinese sovereignty and maintaining peace in eastern Asia if to do so involved the risks of possible war. Our national interests were not deemed to be sufficiently affected to justify any sort of coercive action. There was little popular realization, in 1931, that Japanese imperialism threatened not only our China policy, but the peace of the Pacific and of the world.

Secretary Stimson was more alive to these issues than the public. His first concern, as he had already demonstrated during the Russo-Chinese quarrel of 1929, was to uphold the principle of collective security. After the League had failed to act in the Manchurian crisis, however, he began to consider the more direct effects of Japanese aggression on American interests in eastern Asia. The forceful occupation of Manchuria was a blow to our political prestige as the champion of China's integrity, and Stimson was thoroughly in sympathy with our historic policy along these lines.

"For several centuries," he was later to write in *The Far Eastern Crisis*, "eastern Asia has owed its character mainly to the peaceful traditions of this great agricultural nation. If the character of China should be revolutionized and through exploitation become militaristic and aggressive, not only Asia but the rest of the world must tremble. The United States has made a good start in the development of China's friendship. It would have been the most short-sighted folly to turn our backs upon her at the time of her most dire need."

He was determined to demonstrate our friendship and at least keep the record clear whatever Japan might do, and to this end he dispatched similar notes to China and Japan, on January 7, 1932, clarifying American policy. They expressly stated that the United States would refuse to accept any treaties or engagements between the two governments that impaired American treaty rights, including those relating to the sovereignty of China and the Open Door policy, and would not recognize any situation, treaty or agreement brought about in violation of the Kellogg-Briand pact. In this move he was clearly taking a leaf out of Secretary Bryan's book. With the exception of the clause referring to the anti-war treaty, his notes were identical in their wording, as previously noted, with those sent to China and Japan at the time of the Twenty-One Demands. And as in 1915, the United States reserved its right to any future action dealing with the situation that it might choose to take.

Stimson had hoped that England would join the United States in this statement of policy. The British Foreign Office, however, not only refused to take similar action, but declared its confidence in Japan's protestations that there would be no infringement of Chinese sovereignty. An editorial in the *London Times* casually commented that China's political integrity was after all an ideal rather than an actuality.

China gladly accepted the implications of what was to become known as the Stimson Doctrine and, in replying to the Secretary of State's note, merely upheld the peaceful course she had followed throughout the Manchurian crisis. Japan naturally interpreted the statement of our policy as further evidence of American hostility and made no secret of her resentment. The unsettled conditions in China modified any possible application of either the Kellogg-Briand pact or the Nine-Power Treaty, the Foreign Office declared, and Japan had been acting entirely in self-defense in safeguarding her interests in Manchuria. There was no question either of violating treaty rights or of territorial aims and ambitions. If the United States was not specifically told to keep out of affairs that were none of its concern, the thinly veiled sarcasm of the concluding lines of the Japanese reply were revealing. "It is agreeable to be assured," Tokyo stated, "that the American government are devoting in a friendly spirit such sedulous care to the correct appreciation of the situation."

There was general approval in this country for Stimson's stand, but a highly varied reaction as to how effective it might prove to be. In some quarters it was interpreted as locking the barn door after the horse had been stolen; in others, the non-recognition doctrine was enthusiastically hailed as a most important contribution to the cause of world peace. A few commentators felt that in view of the more cautious policies being pursued by England and France, the United States should not go even this far in "sticking pins into Japan."

Shortly afterwards, on January 28, 1932, a new turn of events suddenly appeared to jeopardize China's independence even more seriously than anything that had yet happened in Manchuria. Although unable to defend their northeastern provinces, the Chinese had vigorously countered Japan's blows at their sovereignty by adopting an anti-Japanese boycott that was cutting heavily into normal trade. To meet this challenge of economic warfare, forces of the Japanese navy attacked the Chinese section of Shanghai and inflicted heavy losses of life and property upon its civilian population. For a time a single Chinese army put up a valiant resistance to this unexpected offensive and the Japanese had to land military reinforcements, but the Nationalist government still felt itself too weak to declare war and was also greatly influenced by appeasement elements within its own ranks. It appealed once again to Geneva and Washington for the help that had not been forthcoming the previous fall.

These startling developments awoke an immediate response in the United States that contrasted strongly with the slow and even apathetic reaction to the attack on Manchuria. The entire Asiatic squadron was concentrated in Shanghai to safeguard American interests, and public opinion turned wholly against Japan for her overt and brutal use of force. Editorial comment was studded with such phrases as "insane imperialism," "running amok," "beyond the pale of civilization" and "outlawed by her campaign of brutality." While popular sympathy for China had been gradually increasing during the winter months, our aroused resentment was also greatly influenced by geography. Many American nationals lived in Shanghai and the attack endangered business interests in the International Settlement of much greater importance than any in Manchuria. The significance of an independent China took on a new meaning. It appeared to be doubly necessary, as Secretary Stimson phrased it, to "convince China that we were not oblivious to our responsibilities in the situation."

There was a popular demand on the part of some peace leaders for the immediate application of economic sanctions as the only possible means for calling Japan to account. They were strongly urged by an imposing group of educators and editors, headed by former Secretary of War Baker and President Lowell of Harvard, and a petition with five thousand signatures was forwarded to President Hoover calling for American participation in an international boycott of all Japanese trade. "Economic pressure," it was stated, "would almost certainly stop the present bloodshed." An American Boycott Association, with the somewhat qualified backing of the Federal Council of Churches, also tried to promote an unofficial ban on all imports from Japan.

The movement received no official support. President Hoover again expressed his opposition and in a letter to Secretary Stimson declared that he was still "inflexibly opposed to the imposition of any kind of sanctions except purely public opinion." Moreover, after the first flush of enthusiasm, even popular interest quickly subsided. On second thought, newspapers generally toned down their first editorials, and with few exceptions warned against any precipitate action. It was "a time to keep cool," the *Boston Herald* urged, while the *St. Louis Globe Democrat* demanded that the administration "keep us out of war." Any direct involvement in the Chinese-Japanese quarrel, the *Washington Evening Star* stated unequivocally, "would be a monstrous injustice to the American people, a sacrifice of American lives and American treasure, for which there would be no justification."

Upon the first outbreak of hostilities in Manchuria, some four months earlier, one of the strongest advocates of sanctions had been the *Nation*. Its attitude had now undergone a complete reversal. "An attempt at this hour to enforce an economic blockade, or to withdraw diplomatic recognition from Japan," it stated editorially on February 10, "could hardly have any effect but to inflame still further the Japanese militarists." It was too late to prevent Japanese aggression by peaceful means, according to this thesis, and yet not too late to be drawn into war by reckless interference. The *Nation* wholly agreed with President Hoover that "economic boycott is not a peace instrument, but one of the deadliest of war weapons."

In the meantime, Secretary Stimson was exercising such influence as he could, in cooperation with Great Britain, to settle the Shanghai affair through mediation. These efforts were successful and the Japanese eventually withdrew their troops. The passing of the crisis was not primarily a result of foreign intervention, however. Japan was not yet prepared for military operations in the Yangtze Valley. The attack upon the Chinese in Shanghai had been perhaps inadvertent, due to the navy's desire to share the honors the army had been winning, and Tokyo's policy demanded the consolidation of the gains already made in Manchuria before making any direct moves against China proper. Settlement of the Shanghai affair was not retreat for the Japanese warlords but a matter of strategic timing. The offensive was to be undertaken in full force in another five years.

Before the Japanese finally withdrew from Shanghai, Secretary Stimson again took occasion to put American policy clearly on record. Japan had claimed that conditions in China made the Nine-Power Treaty inoperative, and he wished to emphasize that the United States intended to stand by its terms. He tried a second time to get England to collaborate in such a move, and once more the British Foreign Office refused to go along with him. To avoid giving Japan a chance to rebuff our overtures, he consequently made this further statement of policy in the form of a letter to Senator Borah which was given to the press on March 24, 1932.

The United States continued to regard the Nine-Power Treaty, Secretary Stimson declared, as a carefully developed and matured international policy intended to meet the very conditions that presently existed in the Far East. It was intimately related to the other treaties concluded at Washington in which the United States had undertaken to limit battleship construction and not to fortify its naval bases in the Pacific. Abrogation of the Nine-Power Treaty was consequently said to be impossible without also reviewing the provisions of these other treaties on which it was directly dependent. Having given this hint of possible revision of the naval accords should Japan persist upon her course, Stimson then went on to state that the situation that had developed in eastern Asia could not possibly be reconciled with either the Nine-Power Treaty or the Kellogg-Briand Treaty. He reaffirmed the determination of the United States not to recognize the government that Japan was trying to establish in Manchuria, and he called for similar action by other governments as a means of assuring eventual restoration to China of the territory of which she had been deprived.

This frank exposition of our policy, with its veiled threat of a renewal of naval rivalry in the Pacific, had no influence on Japan. The extremists were in full control, not stopping at assassination to strengthen their hold on power, and regardless of all diplomatic protests they aggressively went ahead in setting up the puppet state of Manchukuo. "Let the League of Nations say whatever it pleases," General Araki, Minister of War, shouted at a public meeting in Tokyo, "let America offer whatever interference, let China decry Japan's action at the top of her voice, but Japan must adhere to her course unswervingly."

Secretary Stimson had at least succeeded, however, in keeping the record straight, and shortly after publication of the letter to Senator Borah, the League of Nations followed his lead. Early in March, it adopted a resolution incorporating the non-recognition policy which the United States had already officially adopted. Japan might proclaim that so far as she was concerned the question of Manchukuo was settled, but the world refused to condone her resort to force.

The final chapter in the story of the Manchurian incident was the presentation of the report of the Lytton Commission to the League. At one and the same time it condemned Japan for her aggressive policy and proposed a solution of the whole problem that went part way in meeting her original complaints. But the time for any such settlement had long since passed. Japan was in full control of Manchuria. When the Assembly finally adopted its committee's report, in February 1933, the only result was Japan's resignation from the League.

During these latter stages of the controversy, the United States stood on the sidelines. Secretary Stimson had done what he could to uphold Chinese sovereignty in putting forward his non-recognition policy. No further action was feasible. Whatever chance there might originally have been to restrain Japan through economic sanctions or any form of forceful pressure had long since been lost by the failure of such proposals to command support either at Geneva or in the United States. The united front of the powers, which at the Washington Conference had brought Japan into line, was broken. The failure to incorporate in the Nine-Power Treaty any effective means for its own enforcement was bearing bitter fruit. It had to be recognized that the victory won at Washington for our policy of maintaining China's independence and the Open Door had proved to be a barren one.

Throughout these days of crisis in the Far East, and for almost the entire decade following the occupation of Manchuria, China was the helpless victim of Japanese aggression. Even though the Nationalist government had made remarkable headway in uniting China, it had not succeeded to the point where truly effective resistance could be made to the far stronger force of Japan's military power. Sensing the futility of war under such conditions, China had relied wholly upon her appeals to the United States and to the League for maintaining her national sovereignty. She had been bitterly disappointed that they had proved unavailing. It was particularly resented that the United States had not taken a stronger stand in blocking the Japanese advance. If Japan had violated her pledges under the Nine-Power Treaty to refrain from taking advantage of China's difficulties, the United States was held only less guilty of betraying the conference accords by limiting its action to futile protests and note-writing. It was recognized in China that American sympathy was with the Chinese people, but there was widespread disillusionment that such sympathy was not expressed in more concrete form.

Public opinion in this country was not unaware of this feeling in China, and realized there was some justification for it. Yet it was also critical at times of China's insistence that we should come to her aid when she was doing so little to defend herself. Our policy had the unhappy consequence of arousing Japanese hostility because of our opposition to her imperialistic designs, and impairing Chinese friendship because our assistance had not been more forthright and effective.

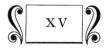

XV

THE CHINA INCIDENT

THE paradoxical aspects of a policy that irritated Japan and failed to satisfy China were to be even further emphasized when the Roosevelt administration came into office in 1933. It was of course far more concerned over domestic problems than anything that might happen in eastern Asia. The immediate emergency confronting the country, and the drastic measures initiated by the New Deal in its efforts to stimulate economic recovery and provide for the unemployed, largely absorbed the national energy. Nevertheless little time was lost in making it clear that no change was contemplated in Far Eastern policy. Friendship for China and support for her territorial integrity remained basic considerations, and there would be no recognition of Japan's territorial gains in Manchuria. Still, no move was made to implement our policies by direct action. Secretary of State Hull, indeed, was even more prepared than his predecessor to explore every possibility of reconciling conflicting American-Japanese aims in order to reach a more friendly accord with Tokyo.

This cautious approach to the problems of Asia was first demonstrated in Hull's testimony on a proposed bill for banning the export of arms to aggressor nations. Appearing before the Senate Foreign Relations in May 1933, just before China and Japan had concluded the so-called Tangku truce setting up a demilitarized zone in north China, the Secretary of State declared that the administration had no idea of applying an arms embargo against Japan, and would not even participate in any international measures of this kind without substantial guarantees against possible retaliation. He sought to uphold his position on the ground that China would not be aided through such a policy, but it was impossible not to read into his statement a reassurance to Japan that under existing circumstances the United States was not prepared to intervene further in the Far Eastern situation.

A year later, our lessening concern over what might happen to China and increased interest in good relations with Japan were further demonstrated. In reply to overtures from the Japanese Foreign Minister, Secretary Hull agreed "that there are in fact no questions between our two countries, which if they be viewed in the proper perspective in both countries, can with any warrant be regarded as not readily susceptible to adjustment by pacific processes." Even when a spokesman for Tokyo followed up this exchange by bluntly stating that Japan was opposed to any attempt on the part of China "to avail herself of the influence of any other country in order to resist Japan," Hull refused to take umbrage at what was in effect a warning that the United States had better stay out of Asia. He reasserted our stand that no nation could "rightfully endeavor to make conclusive its will" in situations involving the treaty rights of other nations, but the mildness of this protest once again showed China that she need expect no important help from the United States in combating Japanese encroachments.

Since at about this same time the final steps were being taken to grant the Philippine Islands their independence, the Tydings-McDuffie Act for establishment of the Philippine Commonwealth having been approved on March 24, 1934, the belief was widespread that the United States was withdrawing from the Far East altogether. Just as our acquisition of the Philippines had been interpreted as a move to safeguard our interests in China when that nation was threatened by partition at the close of the nineteenth century, so the granting of Philippine freedom gave the impression that we were no longer seriously concerned over our stake in eastern Asia's political and economic future.

The Roosevelt administration, however, soon gave concrete evidence that a more friendly attitude toward Japan, and independence for the Philippines, did not mean that it would allow itself to be maneuvered into a position where Tokyo could ignore American interests in the Far East with complete impunity. The United States undertook to build up its navy to the limits agreed upon at the Washington Conference, and in negotiations for renewal of the supplementary London Treaty, which had been concluded in 1930, it resolutely opposed Japan's demand for naval equality. When these developments led to the failure of efforts to continue naval limitation in the Pacific, with Japan's abrogation of the Five-Power Treaty and the breakdown of the London Naval Conference of 1935-1936, our naval construction was pushed ahead vigorously, culminating with appropriations of $1,000,000,000 in 1938.

In the field of diplomacy, the long-delayed recognition of Soviet Russia was also a move that was in part dictated by the desire to strengthen our position in Asia. Other factors entered into this situation, perhaps more importantly, but there can be no doubt that Japan's growing power emphasized the desire on the part of both the United States and Russia for closer collaboration. "Some move in the direction of normal relationships with Russia at this time," Senator Johnson stated early in 1933, "would do far more to remove perils from the Far East, and therefore from the world in general, than any other single act."

Popular interest in all such problems had greatly subsided with the end of Japan's military operations in north China and the withdrawal of her troops from Shanghai. The danger of possible war appeared to have been averted, and the more subtle forms of pressure that Japan exerted against China hardly made newspaper headlines. Ambassador Grew warned the State Department of Japan's ambitions and on one occasion intimated that unless the United States was prepared to accept a *Pax Japonica* in eastern Asia, we should be prepared for all eventualities, including possible war. But the public knew little of what was actually happening and did not feel that important national interests were in any way involved.

In some ways our ties with China had been weakened as a result of developments in Manchuria and the failure of the Chinese to defend themselves against Japanese aggression. An economic mission investigating the possibilities of Far Eastern trade ran true to form in stressing above everything else the immense potentialities of the Chinese market, but its report did not arouse much interest. Such attention as the American people could spare from their own deep concern with the continuing efforts of the New Deal to bring about economic recovery was directed toward Europe rather than Asia. The rising tide of Fascist aggression as Mussolini attacked Ethiopia, Hitler defiantly marched his troops into the Rhineland and both Germany and Italy intervened in Spain's bloody civil war, far overshadowed the threat to Far Eastern peace from Japanese imperialism.

The American response to European disturbances was to retreat into an isolation far more pronounced than that of the 1920's, and to seek through new neutrality legislation to insulate itself completely from Europe's quarrels. Possible hostilities in Asia were not specifically in mind when Congress adopted, in 1935-1937, its bans on munitions shipments, and the cash-and-carry provisions for all other trade with a belligerent nation. But the desire to keep out of war which they expressed reflected an attitude that was just as applicable to the Far East as to Europe. The American people did not wish to be drawn into any conflict, no matter what nations were involved nor what might be its causes. They were prepared to rely wholly upon the broad barriers of the Atlantic and the Pacific to safeguard their own peace.

As America thus drew within herself, war was rapidly developing in Asia. Ever since the occupation of Manchuria, the forces of national resistance within China had been gaining strength. The people themselves were determined to combat further Japanese aggression, and a new spirit of unity was created by a common danger. It found dramatic expression at the close of 1936 when after the most complicated political maneuvers, highlighted by the sensational kidnaping of Chiang Kai-shek and his subsequent unconditional release, a truce was concluded between the Nationalists and the Chinese Communists.

Civil strife had continued between these two political factions ever since the Communists' expulsion from the Kuomintang. In order to escape from the ever-tightening cordon which Chiang Kai-shek had drawn about the territory they controlled south of the Yangtze, the Communists had finally, in 1934 and 1935, made a spectacular retreat, ever since known as the "Long March," to a new area in the northern province of Shensi where they set up their capital at Yenan. Here they were once again hemmed in by Nationalist troops. The Communists, however, took the lead in urging that internal differences be set aside to offer united resistance against Japan, and the events centered about the kidnaping episode reflected the growing desire of the Chinese people to accept the Communist proposals. Chiang Kai-shek was recognized on all sides as the symbol of this new-found unity, and in preparing at long last to resist the further threat of Japanese imperialism, he was responding to a national demand to defend China's independence.

The Japanese militarists quickly recognized the force of this movement, and—impatient to carry through their program of conquest before it grew still more powerful—they prepared to strike once again at China. A minor skirmish between Chinese and Japanese troops at the Marco Polo bridge near Peking, on July 7, 1937, became the signal for what was to prove an all-out assault upon China. It was not this time to be halted, according to Japanese plans, short of the complete conquest of the entire country. Once again the militarists hoped that the confusion in which the rest of the world found itself in the face of Hitler's threatening demands would enable them to carry through their program without outside interference.

War was not formally declared by either Japan or China, but it was war in everything but name. China resisted bitterly every Japanese advance, and when unable to prevent the triumph of far superior enemy forces, her armies retreated to fight again whenever opportunity offered. In time the Japanese were to win full control of the Yangtze Valley, occupy virtually all China's seaports and large cities, and drive the government from Nanking to Chungking, but the Chinese scornfully repulsed all suggestions of surrender. "My armies may bend," Chiang Kai-shek declared, "but they will not break." Despite all her political weakness and shortcomings, China was destined in the coming years to give the whole world a magnificent example of stubborn refusal to acknowledge defeat even when virtually cut off from all outside aid and fighting a seemingly hopeless battle.

Upon the outbreak of hostilities, Secretary Hull issued a long statement outlining the fundamental bases of American policy and offering our good offices to both countries in seeking a solution of their quarrel. But there was no suggestion whatsoever of bringing any concerted pressure upon Japan to respect Chinese sovereignty. "The interest, although sympathetic," Madame Chiang Kai-shek was later to say in describing the American attitude in 1937, "was as detached as that of spectators at a college football game cheering from the safety of the stand while taking no personal risk in the game themselves."

While maintaining our neutrality, the provisions of the new legislation were not invoked. The official reason for this was that neither nation had declared war, but actually our stand was taken because of a belief that application of the ban on munitions shipments, and enforcement of the cash-and-carry rule, would benefit Japan rather than China. The former's control of the seas would have enabled her under such conditions to carry on her normal trade in everything except munitions, including such basic war materials as scrap iron and oil, while without any shipping of her own, China would have been cut off not only from military supplies, but from all other commodities as well.

The issue was nevertheless hotly debated in Congress and in the press. Although no move was made by the President to comply with the demand in some quarters that the law be applied, he nevertheless refused to commit himself definitely as to possible future action. In a statement issued on September 14, he declared that government vessels would not transport munitions to either belligerent, any other ships doing so proceeded at their own risk, and that the general question of neutrality remained *in statu quo*. Our policy, he concluded, was on a "twenty-four-hour basis."

In so far as the protection of our material interests in China were concerned, expediency also governed what Secretary Hull described as "a middle-of-the-road policy." While some additional marines were sent to Shanghai to safeguard the International Settlement, bringing our total force there to some 2,500 men, the ten thousand or so American nationals in China were at the same time warned that they remained in the country on their own responsibility.

This hands-off-eastern-Asia program was generally upheld by the American people. Indifference to the implications of the new Chinese-Japanese conflict was a natural consequence of our isolationist mood. Public opinion polls revealed that, although those persons interviewed who had any opinion on the issues at stake almost universally favored China, a majority did not feel that the United States was in any way concerned—and they were not even prepared to state where their sympathies lay. Moreover the withdrawal of all American troops in China was widely urged as a means to avoid the risks of becoming in any way involved in the actual fighting. "There is nothing in the Far Eastern situation," the *New Republic* stated emphatically, "that warrants the entanglement of this country."

Other factors also affected both our official and non-official attitude. The greater value of our commerce with Japan in comparison with trade with China, newly enhanced by the profitability of sales of scrap iron and oil, caused some persons to oppose any move that could be interpreted as one of hostility toward Tokyo. It was even urged that Japanese control in eastern Asia, enforcing a new measure of law and stability, would increase our trade with China and therefore be to the interests of the United States. There is no evidence that such considerations were a determining factor in the adoption of our policy. They sustained the decision to remain on the sidelines, but it was more largely due to fear of the possible political consequences of intervention. In the final analysis, our stand was the result of the feeling that the cause of collective security had so completely collapsed that any move on our part to support China might well lead to war rather than peace. The American people felt that Far Eastern interests no more justified our running any such risks—or justified them even less—than six years earlier. The isolationism fostered by impending war in Europe was reinforced by actual war in Asia.

China had appealed to Geneva, as she had in 1931, on the ground that Japan was openly violating her treaty commitments in making unprovoked and aggressive war. But the United States rejected any idea of taking joint action with the League of Nations. While Secretary Hull finally went so far as to inform the Japanese government that the United States "looked with disapproval on Japan's foreign policy and the methods of the military," there was nothing for Geneva's advocates of sanctions but a vague suggestion that we might consider possible "parallel action." As if rebuking Geneva for the failure to heed our more forthright gesture toward cooperation six years earlier, Hull declared that the United States had already gone further than any other nation in trying to uphold the principles of world peace, and that the time would appear to have come when other countries might well direct their efforts to catching up with us.

The League finally adopted a report of its Far Eastern Advisory Committee condemning Japan for aggression in her undeclared war and proposing a conference of the signatories of the Nine-Power Treaty, and other interested nations, to consider the whole situation. The United States duly accepted an invitation for this conference which was to meet at Brussels in November. From the outset it was realized, however, that both Europe's absorption in problems nearer home and American isolationism made the Brussels meeting a wholly futile gesture. Its declared purposes were "to provide a forum for constructive discussion . . . and to endeavor to bring the parties together through peaceful negotiation." The American representative, Norman H. Davis, was given instructions so general in scope that they meant little or nothing, and he was carefully warned "to observe closely the trend of public opinion in the United States and take full account thereof."

The popular attitude remained generally apathetic. On October 5—that is, while the League of Nations was still considering the issue—President Roosevelt had delivered his famous "quarantine speech" at Chicago calling for "positive measures to preserve peace" in a world in which the security of 90 per cent of the people was being jeopardized by an aggressive 10 per cent. "The peace-loving nations," the President declared, "must make a concerted effort in opposition to those violations of treaties and those ignorings of humane instincts which today are creating a state of international anarchy and instability from which there is no escape through mere isolation or neutrality. . . ." While he was thinking quite as much of Germany and Italy as he was of Japan, the immediate relevancy of his proposals to the latter nation was inescapable. But the public was not aroused to the need for positive action, and there was no shaking the general conviction that the United States should keep out of things in Asia quite as much as in Europe.

Former Secretary Stimson, for all the discouragement he had met in earlier official efforts along such lines, strongly urged that the United States place an embargo on the shipment of military supplies to Japan. His proposals won some support and were widely debated. But a poll taken in Congress showed a two-to-one majority lining up against sanctions in any form, and all samplings of public opinion confirmed this general attitude. The fact of the matter was that our policy of trying to check Japan had become wholly divorced from the realities of our military and naval program. We were not prepared to run the risks of war which sanctions implied or to uphold any Far Eastern commitment by force. President Roosevelt himself stated: "We are determined to keep out of war." And this contradictory attitude of trying to restrain Japan but being unwilling to accept the possible consequences of making such a policy effective was to be maintained until 1941.

Under such circumstances, the Brussels conference lived up to expectations—and accomplished nothing. Japan refused to take part in its deliberations, and there was in any event no chance of conciliating Japanese and Chinese views. After three weeks of wholly futile talk, during which the Russian envoy, Maxim Litvinov, alone urged effective measures to restrain Japan, the meetings were adjourned. Resolutions had been adopted upholding the Nine-Power Treaty and stating that a suspension of hostilities in the Far East would be in the interest of both Japan and China, but no real effort was made to enforce peace.

In many ways the developing situation in China, where Japanese troops were everywhere driving back the Chinese and the actual fighting had spread to the Yangtze Valley, threatened American interests far more directly than anything that had happened in 1931 and 1932. Yet our relations with Japan followed a much smoother course. Through the withdrawal of American citizens from the war zone, 4,500 having taken ship from Shanghai by the end of October, we were doing everything possible to avoid any provocative incidents. The friendly settlement of the *Panay* affair, when Japanese planes bombed and sank an American gunboat, together with three merchant vessels, on the Yangtze on December 12, was a striking instance of our desire, at almost any cost, to keep out of war. Moreover, with the general support of public opinion, the marine reinforcements that had been sent to Shanghai and the infantry troops stationed at Tientsin were soon recalled.

As 1937 gave way to 1938, however, there were increasing signs that popular apathy over what might happen in eastern Asia was giving way to a revival of sympathy for China. Bombings of the civilian population of Chinese cities, in a world not yet hardened to the brutality of mass air raids, awoke the national conscience when it was realized that the Japanese military were using planes and gasoline exported by the United States. Church organizations took the lead in demanding an end to the sale of aviation supplies, and vigorously denounced our supplying Japan with the means to wage "an aggressive and inexcusable war." Many newspapers that had shown little interest in former Secretary Stimson's original proposals for an economic boycott backed up such protests, and called for a national policy more in keeping with both humanitarian ideals and our traditional sympathy with the Chinese people. In comparison with the earlier public opinion polls that had shown so little concern over China, surveys conducted in July 1938 revealed that the American people had now become more exercised over Japanese aggression than either Axis intervention in Spain or Germany's seizure of Austria. A majority had actually swung over to favor some sort of official action to halt all Japanese munitions shipments.

The State Department also appeared to be moving slowly toward a more positive policy. While the idea of a complete ban on the export of war materials was rejected for fear of possible retaliatory action leading to war, a moral embargo was now placed upon the export of aircraft. This was soon extended to aircraft supplies, and to plans or information dealing with the production of high-quality aviation gasoline. A sterner note was also adopted in protesting against Japanese activities that threatened either the loss of American lives or destruction of American property in China. Secretary Hull was prepared to go much further than he had yet gone on any previous occasion in demanding explicit assurances from Japan that our treaty rights would be observed and the Open Door maintained in those parts of China that had fallen under Japanese control.

In a note dispatched to Tokyo in October 1938 it was pointed out that the United States had not imposed any trade restrictions upon Japan and consequently felt more than justified in insisting upon respect for its interests. Hull specifically called for an end to all discriminatory exchange controls in China, monopolistic practices favoring Japanese nationals and interference with American property rights. Tokyo's reply was a complete denial that any such discrimination existed, but it was couched in terms that showed little disposition to become unduly concerned over our attitude. Any attempt to apply "inapplicable ideas and the principles of the past" to the new conditions existing in China, the Japanese government declared, would neither "contribute toward the establishment of real peace in East Asia nor solve the immediate issue."

No reference to Chinese rights or Chinese interests had been made in the original protest, but Secretary Hull now emphatically reaffirmed the refusal of the United States to recognize any "new order" or "new situation" that had been brought about by force of arms. The United States was willing to consider any suggestions for the modification of existing treaties through peaceful negotiation. It would not give its assent to any impairment of its existing rights by the arbitrary action of any other government.

When such diplomatic action proved completely ineffective in halting Japan, the popular movement for an embargo gained further headway. An American Committee for Non-Participation in Japanese Aggression, headed by former Secretary Stimson, was calling for an immediate ban on the shipment of all war materials, including scrap iron and oil. Favorable votes for such a move were recorded early in 1939 at meetings of the Conference on the Cause and Cure of War, and of the General Assembly of the Presbyterian Church. Unofficial boycotts on the purchase of Japanese goods were also widely urged, and thousands of persons tried to give effective expression to their new sympathy for China by pledging themselves not to buy anything made in Japan. The refusal to wear silk stockings, even though it could hardly bring the Japanese war machine to a halt, became sign and symbol of the growing opposition to Tokyo's policy.

With neutrality legislation coming up for further debate, several resolutions favoring economic sanctions against Japan were introduced in Congress and gave every sign of commanding wide support. One proposed by Senator Pittman, chairman of the Senate Foreign Relations Committee, would have authorized the President to bar the shipment of all arms and war materials to any nation violating the Nine-Power Treaty; another, sponsored by Senator Schwellenbach, would have made such a move mandatory. While immediate action on these proposals was still opposed by the State Department, and also by the Navy, Secretary Hull soon showed that he was ready to pave the way for their possible adoption if Japan did not modify her policy. On July 26, 1939, he served official notice on the Tokyo government that on the expiration of the required six months' period, the United States would abrogate the existing Japanese-American commercial treaty.

The public greeted the announcement of this move with more enthusiasm than it had shown toward any step taken by the State Department since Japan had first launched her attack on China. It did not win unanimous approval. Some fears were expressed of the danger of unilateral opposition to Japan by the United States. Gallup poll investigators, however, reported that 80 per cent of those interviewed wholly supported denunciation of the trade pact, and about the same number favored an embargo on war materials as soon as the expiration period had elapsed.

A few months later, Ambassador Grew underscored the warning to Japan implicit in Secretary Hull's move by an extremely frank and candid exposition of the attitude of the United States before the American-Japan Society in Tokyo. American public opinion was almost unanimous in its condemnation of Japan's policy toward China, he declared, and it had become convinced that Tokyo's objective was to establish Japanese control over a large part of Asia and then to impose on such areas a closed economy. While his speech was a plea for better understanding between the peoples of America and Japan, he nonetheless made it clear that only a change in Japanese policy could provide the basis for the renewal of our old friendship.

As this situation in eastern Asia grew more and more tense, war broke out in Europe. Hitler's armies marched into Poland, and England and France accepted a challenge they no longer dared to meet by appeasement. Naturally these momentous developments had their repercussions in the Far East, and created new uncertainties as to Japanese policy. Already associated with Germany as a signatory of the anti-Comintern pact, Japan might be expected to make the most of the new opportunities afforded her by the European war and there was the further danger, soon to be realized, of her openly joining the Axis partnership. The United States had to reconsider the proposed embargo on Japanese trade in the light of its possible effects in a world where its democratic allies were already engaged in war.

Upon the expiration of the trade treaty in January 1940, it was nevertheless almost daily expected that the embargo resolutions before the Senate Foreign Relations Committee would be reported for favorable action. But the committee was apparently evenly divided on the issue. A situation was created where the influence of the administration became paramount, and at this critical juncture it was thrown strongly against any action that might provoke Japan to take retaliatory steps. Secretary Hull refused to appear at the Senate hearings and the embargo resolution, in spite of its original sponsorship by Senator Pittman, was never reported out by his committee. "We fired a few blank cartridges," Senator Connally declared, "and then fell back."

President Roosevelt was no more willing to apply sanctions against Japan in the spring of 1940 than President Hoover had been in the spring of 1932. Both men were convinced that an embargo would drive Japan to war. There was, however, this difference in their attitude. Hoover wished to avoid possible hostilities at all costs and therefore believed that the United States should under every circumstance limit its intervention in eastern Asia to moral pressure. Roosevelt also wished to avoid war, but he had come to question whether this was possible in the long run without a sacrifice of American interests that the country would not tolerate. His refusal to run the risk of imposing an economic boycott on Japan in January 1940 was apparently due to his conviction that the United States had to gain more time to prepare for the war that sanctions might precipitate. His policy was governed not so much by unwillingness to accept the challenge of Japanese imperialism as by a reluctance to force the issue until all possible alternatives had been fully explored and the United States was ready for every eventuality.

XVI

THE CHALLENGE OF JAPAN

THE sweep of Hitler's armies over western Europe and the fall of France changed the pattern of world affairs far more than had the outbreak of war itself. For the first time, the possibility of a Fascist victory was really brought directly home to the American people. They suddenly realized the dangerous position in which the United States might find itself should Great Britain—and the British fleet—fall victim to Nazi aggression. Under such circumstances, the protection of our western flank in the Pacific also took on a new significance. What happened in China and eastern Asia generally had an important bearing on the immediate issue of national security. Situated between two potential foes, the United States was confronted by the immediate necessity of strengthening its defenses in both the Atlantic and the Pacific against the possibility of finding itself engaged in a war on both its ocean fronts.

In instructions to Ambassador Grew in Japan, Secretary Hull nevertheless stated that developments in Europe did not alter the bases of our policy in the Far East. The United States was all the more determined in its opposition to any nation resorting to force to attain its international objectives. Moreover, in conversations with the British Ambassador in Washington, he declared that the United States was ready to exert strong economic pressure against Japan, had stationed its fleet in the Pacific and was doing everything possible—"short of a serious risk of actual hostilities"—to stabilize the situation. No agreement would be reached with Tokyo, the Secretary of State concluded, that involved the sacrifice of Chinese territory and interests, or the principles of international policy to which the United States was committed.

Confirmation of the dangers inherent in this situation,

together with warnings against the risk of any move that might serve to spread hostilities, was contained in a dispatch from Ambassador Grew on September 12, 1940. Our envoy in Tokyo reported that the Japanese militarists saw a "golden opportunity" in existing conditions to push still more aggressively their program of expansion. He felt the threat to American interests in Asia to be both real and immediate. If we continued to let things drift, a progressive deterioration in American-Japanese relations seemed unavoidable, but should we take such drastic action as an embargo on oil shipments, retaliation by the army or navy through some "sudden stroke" was highly possible. Grew advised a *firm* policy to maintain the status quo until England should have won the European war. Then Japan might be successfully called to account by "a show of force, coupled with determination that it will be used if necessary. . . ."

Almost immediately after receipt of this note, two further moves by Japan gave additional emphasis to Ambassador Grew's warnings. Tokyo had long since been exercising the strongest possible pressure to bring both the Dutch East Indies and French Indo-China within the Japanese "co-prosperity sphere." After the defeat of France, it was greatly intensified with respect to Indo-China. On September 22, an agreement was forced upon the helpless Vichy government of France that gave Japanese troops the right of transit in Indo-China, and soon led to the occupation of several key points in the northern parts of the colony. Less than a week later it was announced that Japan had definitely joined the Axis military alliance. The Tokyo militarists were not only trying to extend their New Order over all eastern Asia, but they had aligned themselves with our European enemy in a move that was clearly designed as a threat to block any American interference with their expansive plans.

There could no longer be any pretense of neutrality in the Japanese-Chinese War. We accepted Japan as a potential foe, and China as a prospective ally. The policy of the United States was driven to take on more precise shape and form. The restrictions that had already been imposed upon exports to Japan were gradually tightened up and our material aid to hard-pressed China was progressively expanded. Nevertheless, this policy was still to be carried out with a measure of caution which it was hoped would avoid for as long as possible American involvement in the immediate conflict. In an effort to protect our interests and uphold the principle of orderly processes in international relations, as President Roosevelt was later to state, the United States was ready to offer the greatest possible assistance to China, and yet would try to prevent war even though it meant shipping some supplies to Japan.

The decision to carry on what was in effect a delaying action against Japan was reached only after a careful weighing of all the factors involved. There were some differences of opinion among the President's advisers. Secretary Morgenthau, Secretary Ickes and Harry Hopkins were reported among those favoring a more positive policy in the belief that Japan was bluffing and that severe economic sanctions would bring her into line. Secretary Hull and Under Secretary Welles, on the other hand, apparently felt that the dangers in the general international situation dictated the more conservative course. There should be no abandonment of our position in the Far East nor desertion of China, according to their view, but the door should always be kept open to possible accommodation with Japan.

The paramount consideration governing our attitude, Under Secretary Welles has since stated, was the insistent demand on the part of the highest military and naval authorities that diplomacy prevent any hostilities with Japan until the last possible moment in order that the United States might not find itself confronted with a war in two oceans. "That was the compelling reason," he has written in *The Time for Decision*, "why the administration continued to permit until only three months prior to Pearl Harbor the exportation of certain grades of oil and scrap iron to Japan."*

The first steps in implementing our somewhat modified policy were taken almost at once. Under authority of the Export Control Act, passed in July, licenses were withheld for the further shipment to Japan of aviation gasoline and most types of machine tools. All export of iron and steel scrap (contrary to Under Secretary Welles' later statement) was also forbidden as a part of our general program to conserve supplies. Bluntly answering the immediate Japanese protest that these were unfriendly acts, Secretary Hull expressed his amazement that a government that had been so openly disregarding both American interests in China and its general treaty obligations could question our right to impose such an embargo. It was unheard of, he told the Japanese Ambassador on October 8, for a country engaged in aggressive war to turn to a third nation "and seriously insist that the latter would be guilty of an unfriendly act if it did not cheerfully provide some of the necessary implements of war to aid the aggressor nation in carrying out its invasion."

By the end of 1940, the list of exports subject to restrictions was still further expanded. In all, it included arms, ammunition, implements of war, aviation gasoline and many other petroleum products, machine tools, scrap iron, iron and steel manufactures, copper, lead, zinc and aluminum. The one most important commodity for the effective functioning of the Japanese military machine—oil—was still, however, free from all restrictions. And oil shipments were increasing. With all the new regulations in effect, the value of the principal American exports to Japan for the first quarter of 1941 (the last prewar period for which statistics are available) fell to $33,000,000, or less than half the total for the corresponding period in 1940. Nevertheless, the value of petroleum products slightly rose, to

* Revelations before the Congressional committee investigating Pearl Harbor have further confirmed the influence of military and naval authorities on a policy that sought to avoid war as long as possible.

almost $12,000,000, or some 40 per cent of the total for all commodities.

The other arm of our policy was to encourage Chinese resistance to Japan through increasing our direct aid in every possible way. The United States refused to recognize the puppet Nanking government established by the Japanese under Wang Ching-wei, and it protested strongly against British action in temporarily closing the Burma Road in the summer of 1940. With more concrete results, it extended generous financial credits to the Chinese government to enable it to obtain the foreign exchange for purchasing war materials. A first loan of $25,000,000, for non-military purposes, had been extended through the Export-Import Bank in December 1938, but additional advances during 1940 included loans of $20,000,000 and $25,000,000 in March and September respectively; and one of $100,000,000 in November, to be divided equally for the purchase of all types of supplies in the United States and establishment of a stabilization fund to support Chinese currency.

The political significance of these 1940 loans was emphasized by their timing. The first coincided with the establishment of the Nanking puppet government; the second was made on the eve of Japan's joining the Axis; and the third was announced on the very day of Tokyo's official recognition of the Wang Ching-wei regime. The United States was ready to extend direct financial assistance to China and also wished to give such moves all possible emphasis as an expression of both friendly feeling and confidence in the National government.

More important than any of these measures was the extension of Lend-Lease aid after passage of that significant legislation in March 1941. President Roosevelt was not only to include China among the nations whose defense was deemed vital to the defense of the United States, but in stating that we intended to support every democratic nation fighting against the tyranny of Fascist aggression, he paid an enthusiastic tribute to her stand against Japan. "China likewise expressed the magnificent will of millions of plain people to resist the dismemberment of their nation," he declared. "China, through the Generalissimo, Chiang Kai-shek, asks our help. America has said that China shall have our help."

The Chinese government immediately expressed its appreciation of this encouraging move. "The people of China," Chiang Kai-shek said in a note dispatched on March 18, 1941, "whether engaged in fighting the aggressor or toiling in the fields and workshops in the rear in support of the defenders, will be immeasurably heartened by your impressive reaffirmation of the will of the American people to assist them in their struggle for freedom from foreign domination, and in the resumption of their march towards democracy and social justice to all."

Within two months it was reported from Chungking that China had contracted for nearly $100,000,000 in Lend-Lease materials. Arrangements were made through the China Defense Supplies, Inc., headed by T. V. Soong, and shipments were at once commenced in such vitally important equipment as heavy-duty trucks, spare parts, gasoline, asphalt, road-building machinery and arsenal supplies.

The problem in carrying forward our program was the delivery of this equipment. With China virtually under blockade, the only available route was the long, tortuous Burma Road from Lashio to Kunming, which the Chinese had almost literally "scratched out of the mountains with their finger nails." Under the best of circumstances, only a very small amount of supplies could be transported by the handful of available trucks which dangerously negotiated its seven hundred miles of steep grades and hairpin turns. Every effort was made to improve road conditions, but inevitable congestion and frequent breakdowns created bottlenecks that seemingly could not be relieved. The average figure of transportation over the Burma Road was no more than 12,000 tons a month in 1941, with a peak of 20,000 about the time of Pearl Harbor. Moreover even such meager quantities of the supplies China so desperately needed did not always reach their rightful destinations. Graft and corruption among Chinese officials diverted war materials to local warlords, and precious gasoline was sometimes drained away from the motor trucks for black market sale.

Various technical missions were dispatched to afford other forms of assistance to China. In January 1941 a financial mission, consisting of Lauchlin Currie, administrative assistant to the President, and Emile Despres, an economist associated with the Federal Reserve System, visited Chungking. Five months later, Owen Lattimore was recommended by Roosevelt, and then appointed by Chiang Kai-shek, as a personal adviser to the Chinese leader. In August, a military mission, headed by Brigadier General John Magruder, undertook to help the National government in carrying out the general terms of the Lend-Lease agreement in order that the whole program might be made as efficient as possible.

These various measures, whether aimed at restricting Japanese purchases of war materials in the United States or facilitating their purchase by China, were fully approved by the American people. Sympathy for China had progressively increased, and the heightened danger to our whole position in the Far East further emphasized the importance of supporting her in every way possible. The public was once again prepared to go much further than the government. Ever since the startling events of the summer of 1940, it had appeared to be generally in favor of a complete embargo on all exports to Japan. The ban on scrap iron shipments had won almost universal approval, and by the spring of 1941 the demand for embargoing oil shipments as well had gathered renewed force. In August, a Gallup poll survey indicated that a majority of those interviewed were willing to run the risks of war in taking steps to prevent Japan from becoming more powerful.

The public found other ways of expressing its sympathy for China. A generous response was made to the appeals for funds issued by the United China Relief, with $1,250,000 contributed in 1940 and approximately twice this sum in 1941. Church organizations, women's clubs, civic associations and student societies competed in raising money for the Chinese Red Cross, child welfare and industrial cooperatives. A China Week was held in May 1941 with special tea sales and "bowl of rice" suppers. Orchestras gave special concerts, and theaters special matinees, for China relief. Al Smith made a nation-wide appeal for the adoption of Chinese war orphans through membership in the Esteemed Grandparents Club. When two giant pandas arrived in this country as a symbol of Madame Chiang Kai-shek's appreciation for our contributions to the relief funds, our sentimental affection for China found expres-sion in the popularity of children's toy pandas, taking the place of the teddy bears of an earlier day.

There was a warm response from China to both the official and unofficial steps taken to support the cause for which she was fighting. China's Ambassador in Washington, the noted scholar Hu Shih, reaffirmed on many occasions the feeling of gratitude for American help which Generalissimo Chiang Kai-shek had expressed when Lend-Lease aid was first extended. If there was still regret that such assistance had not come sooner, or could not be made more effective, it was not sug-gested in official comments. Moreover, many Chinese spokes-men declared that there was a growing feeling among their own people that the United States was at last prepared to make good the promise of its traditional friendship and would soon come even more directly to China's aid.

The most significant sign of our goodwill was final American recognition of China's right to recover complete control of her own affairs. In July 1940, Under Secretary Welles had stated that it was American policy to surrender as soon as practical all special privileges still retained under the unequal treaties. Ten months later, Secretary Hull repeated this pledge even more specifically. It went without saying, he informed the Chinese Minister for Foreign Affairs, that upon the reestablish-ment of peace, the United States intended "to move rapidly, by processes of orderly negotiation and agreement with the Chinese government, toward the relinquishment of the last of certain rights of a special character which this country, together with other countries, has long possessed in China by virtue of agreements providing for extraterritorial jurisdiction and related practices. . . ."

As the United States made these successive moves to bolster Chinese resistance, there were repeated warnings from Ambassador Grew of the increasing danger of possible retaliation by Japan. As early as January 27, 1941, he informed Secretary Hull that there were reports from many sources in Tokyo that the Japanese military planned a surprise mass attack on Pearl Harbor in case there should be further "trouble" with the United States. Without either minimizing the possibility of such a move, or allowing it to affect the policy that we were following, Hull continued to keep the way clear for a possible understanding with Tokyo. If war could be avoided by peaceful negotiation, so much the better. If it was indeed inevitable, diplomatic action might at least win more time for carrying out our defense program. When Admiral Nomura arrived in Washington during March as the new Japanese Ambassador, the Secretary of State consequently began a long series of secret conversations that were to last until December.

It is easy now to see that there was at no time any real chance that an accord could be reached. The Japanese and American positions were diametrically opposed. Neither nation was willing to make the concessions that could alone have afforded any real basis for peace. Japan was too deeply involved in her campaign to establish a New Order to back down, and the United States had no intention of accepting Japanese domination over all eastern Asia. The very fact that negotiations continued, in spite of every evidence of Japanese aggression, nevertheless tended to create a false sense of security among the American people. They hardly realized how increasingly critical the situation was becoming with each passing month.

The bases upon which Japan sought an agreement with the United States were outlined in proposals submitted by Admiral Nomura on May 12. Their core was the suggestion that this country at once request the Chiang Kai-shek regime to negotiate peace with Japan, and, should it refuse to do so, discontinue all further aid to China. Moreover, what Japan apparently intended by peace fell far short of meeting the fundamental premises of our policy. While the Tokyo government was theoretically prepared to respect Chinese sovereignty, it insisted upon the independence of Manchukuo and the right to maintain Japanese troops in China as a defense against Communism. There was no guarantee in these proposals of equality of trade in China, and, on the other hand, they called for American cooperation in allowing Japan to secure the raw materials she needed from southeastern Asia. Far from suggesting that under the terms of even such a one-sided settlement Japan would withdraw from the Axis alliance, Nomura sought to defend this pact as wholly defensive in nature.

Secretary Hull's reply was a comprehensive restatement of the position of the United States. Far more definite commitments as to Japan's intention to maintain peace were necessary, he said, if there was to be any American collaboration along the lines suggested by Tokyo. The United States could suggest to Chiang Kai-shek that he enter into peace negotiations only if Japan's terms were first communicated to this country, and fell within the framework of full respect for Chinese sovereignty, without annexations or indemnities: economic cooperation and non-discrimination, and the withdrawal of all Japanese troops from China. Over against Japan's obvious intention to dominate the Greater East Asia sphere, the United States emphatically restated the principle of Chinese integrity and equality of trade.

As these exchanges ever more clearly revealed the impassable gulf between American and Japanese policy, current events took on an even more ominous turn. When Hitler tore up the Russo-German non-aggression pact and threw the German armies into the invasion of the Soviet Union, Japan cynically ignored the peaceful protestations of her own diplomats and aggressively renewed her advance in southeastern Asia. With her northern flank apparently secured by Russia's absorption in the war in the west, southern Indo-China was promptly occupied by Japanese armies. Here was a new and even more immediate threat to the interests of both the United States and its democratic allies. Japan's advanced position directly menaced the Dutch East Indies, British possessions in Malaya and the Philippine Islands. It threatened our sources of tin and rubber; it threatened our communications in the whole area of the southwest Pacific.

The urgency of these dangers awoke the administration to the immense risk of following any longer a policy that, while it might postpone war, enabled Japan to build up her stockpiles of strategic materials. We were no longer merely allowing her to purchase supplies that could be used in conquering China, but exporting oil that might provide the motive power in attacks upon the United States. In a statement to the press, on July 24, 1941, Under Secretary Welles unequivocally stated that Japan was pursuing a policy of expansion by force, or the threat of force, which endangered our procurement of essential supplies of tin and rubber and threatened the safety of the Philippines. Then on July 26 the long-awaited action to cut off all further trade with Japan finally materialized. Acting in conjunction with Great Britain, President Roosevelt issued an executive order freezing all Japanese assets in the United States. It was a declaration of economic warfare against the Tokyo militarists.

Two days earlier, at the same time that Under Secretary Welles was in effect warning Japan of what was to come, the President had informally taken occasion to explain and justify the conciliatory policy that he was on the point of abandoning.

"It was very essential from our own selfish point of view of defense," Roosevelt said, "to prevent war from starting in the south Pacific. So our foreign policy was—trying to stop a war from breaking out down there.

"At the same time . . . we wanted to keep that line of supplies from Australia and New Zealand going to the Near East. . . .

So it was essential for Great Britain that we try to keep the peace down there in the south Pacific.

"All right, and now here is a nation called Japan. Whether they had at that time any aggressive purposes to enlarge their empire southward, they didn't have any oil of their own up in the north. Now, if we had the oil cut off, they probably would have gone down to the Dutch East Indies a year ago, and you would have had war.

"Therefore, there was, you might call it, a method in letting this oil go to Japan, with the hope—and it has worked for two years—of keeping war out of the south Pacific for our own good, for the good of the defense of Great Britain, and the freedom of the seas."

Japan's answer to the freezing of her credits was to hasten her occupation of all Indo-China and to transfer additional military and naval forces to southeast Asia. The United States countered by entering into defense negotiations with Great Britain, the Dutch East Indies and China. Active measures were taken to reinforce our positions in Hawaii, Guam and the Philippines, with General Douglas MacArthur placed in charge of the nationalized Filipino forces, and to withdraw all troops and gunboats still remaining in occupied China. In so far as possible, direct aid to Chungking was expanded. Americans were helping in the military training of Chinese troops, supervising basic engineering work on the Burma Road and serving as volunteers with the Chinese air force.

The public response to these dramatic developments was one of almost universal support for the measures taken against Japan. There should be no surrender under any circumstances, newspaper after newspaper stated, and the United States should not hesitate to resort to force if its interests were further threatened. Extremists called for an immediate declaration of war rather than to wait until Japan seized the initiative.

The gathering hostility toward Japan was paralleled by a heightened recognition of China's role in resisting aggression. "China is our ally," the *New Republic* declared, and the *Nation* joined with other periodicals in asserting that future peace in the Pacific depended "on a strong, independent China." An editorial in *Fortune* stated that any defense against Hitlerism would be frustrated if Japan were allowed to make a clean sweep of the Pacific, and the United States should come to China's aid with the full strength of its immense resources. *Time* hailed the action that had already been taken as throwing "our full weight, at last, on China's side, where it belongs."

Diplomatic negotiations with Japan were not broken off in spite of the seeming impossibility of reaching any agreement and the hurried preparations of both nations for war. While the United States rejected a proposal for a meeting between President Roosevelt and Prince Konoye, the Japanese Premier, Secretary Hull was still unwilling to let slip any more practical possibility, however remote, of reaching an accord. He also wished to gain the months, or even weeks, that would allow further reinforcement of our military position. When Admiral Nomura was joined, early in November, by Saburo Kurusu as a special envoy from the new Tojo ministry in Tokyo, a new series of conversations began. Ambassador Grew's dispatches from Tokyo apparently alternated between grave warnings that attack by Japan was an "imminent possibility" and war might come "with dangerous and dramatic suddenness," and contradictory interpretations of the more peaceful intentions of the new Japanese government. "It is premature," he wrote in his diary on October 20, "to stigmatize the Tojo government as a military dictatorship committed to the furtherance of policies which might be expected to bring about armed conflict with the United States."

On November 20, Japan submitted new proposals to the United States which, because of their insistence upon the extreme position of the Tokyo government, were later to be characterized by Secretary Hull as virtually amounting to an ultimatum. His answer, delivered on the twenty-sixth, was to prove to be the final statement of American policy. Japan's adherence to the Axis and her threatening penetration in southeastern Asia may have been largely responsible for the gradual stiffening of our attitude, but this note nevertheless demonstrated that the status of China remained the crux of the entire problem of peace or war in eastern Asia. An accord with Japan could in all probability have been reached at any time that the United States showed itself willing to abandon China. The Tokyo government might well have agreed to withdraw its troops from southeastern Asia, averting the immediate threat to the security of both our economic and political interests in that part of the world, had we canceled all aid to Chiang Kai-shek and agreed to recognize Japanese domination over China.

There was no idea of such appeasement in Secretary Hull's note. He made a forthright demand for immediate withdrawal of Japanese troops from both China and Indo-China, and unqualified recognition by Tokyo of Chinese sovereignty and the principle of trade equality. He specifically proposed that both the United States and Japan agree that they would support no other government in China than the National government with its capital at Chungking, and undertake to surrender all extraterritorial rights and special privileges that they might claim in China under existing treaties. On the basis of such commitments, and only with such commitments, the United States was prepared to reestablish trade relations with Japan and enter into further agreements for maintaining the peace of the Pacific.

A few days later Hull told the British Ambassador that "the diplomatic part of our relations with Japan was virtually over," and he gravely warned that she might "move suddenly and with every possible element of surprise" in meeting our challenge to her further territorial conquests.

Secretary Hull's final note was in direct line with the policy the United States had pursued for over a century in eastern Asia. The principles he laid down as governing our attitude were a reaffirmation of those embodied in Secretary Hay's Open Door notes, in the Nine-Power Treaty of the Washington Conference and in the non-recognition policy of Secretary Stimson.

But now in November 1941, for the first time in all its history, the United States was prepared to run the risks of war in upholding what had so often been said and never enforced. We were defending our own interests, but they were predicated upon respect for China's sovereignty as the only surety for peace in eastern Asia and the Pacific.

The account of Japan's response hardly needs retelling. The American proposals were summarily rejected. But before the Japanese envoys handed the official reply of their government to the Secretary of State, and before any word had been received from a final plea for peace made directly by President Roosevelt to the Japanese Emperor, a far more conclusive answer had been made by Japan. The issue of peace or war was entirely taken out of our hands by the devastating attack on Pearl Harbor on December 7. On the next day, President Roosevelt had no alternative other than to go before Congress and ask for recognition of the state of war that already existed through enemy assaults upon American territory.

XVII

WARTIME ALLIES

PEARL HARBOR was not only the signal for war between America and Japan. It led at once to British and Chinese declarations of war against Japan, and to German and Italian declarations of war against the United States. The separate wars raging in Europe and Asia merged as this country was drawn into what now became a truly global conflict. The United States and China had become allies in a common cause that embraced all those nations that had suffered attack by any one of the Axis powers.

The first step in creating this new world-wide alliance was the signature at Washington, on January 1, 1942, of the Declaration of the United Nations. Twenty-six countries, headed by the United States, Great Britain, Soviet Russia and China, pledged themselves to adhere to the principles of the Atlantic Charter, drawn up by Roosevelt and Churchill during the previous summer; to employ in close cooperation their full military and economic resources against those members of the Axis with which they were at war, and to make no separate peace or armistice with their enemies. The pact thus provided for the cooperation of the United States, Great Britain and Soviet Russia in Europe, while the United States and Great Britain joined forces with China in Asia. There was to be no peace with Japan until she had been driven out of the conquered territory in China and southeastern Asia, and her militaristic government had been wholly defeated by force of arms.

American and British entry into the war did not mean any immediate relief for the hard-pressed armies of China. They had been fighting Japan for four long and bitter years. Except for guerrilla areas behind the lines, over a quarter of Chinese territory, including the greater part of the eastern coast, the lower valley of the Yangtze and the onetime treaty ports, remained in enemy hands. Actual hostilities had resolved into an apparent stalemate. Japan seemed unable to extend her conquests any further, or was perhaps unwilling to take the risks of advancing upon the capital at Chungking, and China was still totally incapable of martialing the resources for any full-scale offensive action. The hope that at once flared up among the Chinese of American aid that would enable them to launch such an attack was doomed to bitter disappointment. Far from causing any quick turn in the fortunes of Far Eastern war, allied arms underwent the humiliating experience of those successive defeats which lost to enemy control all southeastern Asia. Hongkong, Malaya and Singapore, the Dutch East Indies, Burma and the Philippines were captured. Japanese armies spread inexorably over the Asiatic world with the United States and Great Britain unable to halt their victorious advance.

The loss of Burma cut off China's last tenuous link with the outside world, and she found herself deprived of even the feeble flow of supplies that had been brought in over the Burma Road. Already overwhelmed by seemingly insoluble economic problems reflected in soaring inflation, Chungking suffered a new crisis in morale marked by bitter discouragement and disillusionment.

The tide of Japanese conquests was finally stopped at the Battle of Midway, in June 1942, and a first step was taken on the long road back with our initial landings at Guadalcanal. Yet the recovery of the Solomon Islands and New Guinea, even the occupation of the Marshall Islands, the Carolines and, eventually, the Philippines, brought no relief to isolated China. There was a promise of ultimate victory in our unrelenting military and naval advance, but to the Chinese their day of liberation seemed to have been postponed rather than hastened when the first results of our entry into the war were Japan's seizure of new territories and new sources of supply. Moreover global strategy dictated a concentration of the major allied forces in Europe rather than in Asia. Berlin was to be taken on the road to Tokyo. Events were fully to demonstrate the wisdom of this decision, but in the desperate straits to which she had been reduced, China found it hard to accept. She could not help feeling that she was being deserted in her hour of greatest need.

Our Chinese policy during these critical years was directed toward doing everything possible, within the limitations imposed by military strategy, to bolster up the authority and prestige of the National government and thereby encourage continued resistance against Japan. Such aid as could be spared and could be made available was extended to Chungking, and every assurance given that the war against Japan would be carried through to complete victory. President Roosevelt repeatedly pledged this country to increase our direct assistance just as rapidly as circumstances permitted, declaring that ultimately China would realize "the security, the prosperity, and the dignity, which Japan has sought so ruthlessly to destroy."

Military reinforcement of China could hardly go beyond the token stage because of the Japanese conquest of Burma, but from the very outset of the war every effort was made to re-establish communications and provide new means of transporting Lend-Lease supplies to Chungking. General Joseph Stilwell, head of the American military mission in China, was designated both commander of all ground forces in the China-Burma-India theater and chief-of-staff to Generalissimo Chiang Kai-shek. After the unsuccessful campaign to defend Burma, he began at once upon the threefold task of training new Chinese divisions for the eventual reconquest of this territory, establishing an air transport to Chungking and building the Ledo Road—to become known as the Stilwell Road—as a branch line from northern Assam to that part of the Burma Road still in Chinese hands.

Few developments in the entire war were more spectacular than the gradual expansion of the supply service to China by

American planes flying over the massive hump of the Himalayas. It was initiated in April 1942 with what has been described as "a handful of antiquated crates," and for many months there were "almost no staff, almost no pilots, almost no spare parts, almost nothing in fact." But huge transport planes, flying blind through sleet and snow at 17,000-foot levels, were soon carrying in to China Lend-Lease material the equivalent in tonnage of that formerly transported over the Burma Road. By early 1945, with still more planes and pilots, the monthly total of all supplies flown to Chungking had miraculously risen to some 44,000 tons a month—still much too little to be truly effective but almost twice the peak figures of former overland transportation.

Further direct aid was provided by the United States Army Air Force stationed in China. The nucleus for this organization was the American Volunteer Group which had been organized before Pearl Harbor to defend the Burma Road. Its members had operated by special contract with the Chinese government (so much bounty for each enemy plane shot down) much as had the Ever Victorious Army during the Taiping Rebellion almost a century earlier. Under the command of Colonel—later General—Claire L. Chennault, the "Flying Tigers" performed miracles in combating the Japanese air forces, and for the first time since 1938 they relieved Chungking of the constant menace of bombing attacks. In all, they downed some 286 planes, although the total strength of the squadron never rose above 55. When reorganized as the Fourteenth Army Air Force, considerably greater assistance could be afforded Chinese ground troops, and steadily increasing raids were made against Japanese bases in eastern China.

Air operations, whether in the transport of supplies or in attacks upon the enemy, could not begin to meet the needs of the Chinese in building up their strength to counterattack the Japanese. Even with their further expansion in the closing period of the war, and the still greater availability of supplies after the completion of the Stilwell Road and the reconquest of Burma, China remained largely dependent on her own meager resources in carrying on her struggle. She could do little more than immobilize the Japanese troops holding so much of her territory. Effective relief for China was to be realized only with final victory in the great naval and military campaigns of the Pacific.

Important political moves in the meantime again demonstrated the goodwill of the United States and its desire to compensate in so far as it could for its inability to afford more immediate military aid. In February 1942, Congress passed without a dissenting voice a measure extending financial credits of $500,000,000. The speed and unanimity with which this bill was passed, as President Roosevelt was able to report to Generalissimo Chiang Kai-shek, testified "to our earnest desire and determination to be concretely helpful to our partners in the great battle for freedom." Six weeks later, a definite accord was reached for carrying out the declared purposes of this loan in strengthening Chinese currency, financing the production of additional war supplies and combating the dangerous rise in Chinese domestic prices. A new mutual aid agreement was also signed with the provision that final settlements in the exchange of war materials and supplies between the two governments would be left to the postwar period.

Definitive action was taken to carry out the pledges already made by both Under Secretary Welles and Secretary Hull for the abolition of extraterritorial rights and recognition of China's complete independence of all foreign controls. Negotiations on this age-old source of controversy were held in Washington in the fall of 1942, paralleling similar negotiations between the Chinese and British in Chungking, and they resulted in the signature of a new treaty on January 11, 1943. Consular jurisdiction and all other unilateral privileges written into earlier treaties were formally relinquished. The United States gave up the right to maintain troops or gunboats in China, undertook to cooperate with the National government in returning to Chinese control the legation quarter in Peiping and the international settlements at Amoy and Shanghai, and renounced all special rights in inland trade or navigation. A clean sweep was made of those unequal provisions in the earlier treaties between the United States and China which had so notably contributed to the bitter anti-foreign feeling in the 1920's, and a firm pledge given that there should be no further interference with Chinese sovereignty.

The American public accepted conclusion of this epochal accord as a reform long overdue and a move which was the very least the United States could do in assuring China of its good faith. It was, indeed, pointed out that we were surrendering something that had been largely swept away by Japan's conquests, and could hardly be reestablished after her ultimate defeat. The realities of the situation in eastern Asia compelled the surrender of extraterritoriality. Nevertheless the promise that there would be no attempt at the end of the war to reimpose upon China the semicolonial status to which she had for so long been subjected, had a far-reaching significance which was duly appreciated in Chungking.

The close of 1943 also saw final atonement for the injustice done China in barring her nationals from the United States. The repeal of the old exclusion laws and admission of Chinese on a quota basis, with rights of naturalization, were still opposed in some quarters. The animosities and prejudices that had been so powerful at the close of the nineteenth century had not wholly disappeared on the west coast. But for the country as a whole, the idea that the admission of some 105 Chinese a year could have any possible adverse effect upon American standards of living appeared to be fantastic, while the argument that we could hardly afford to discriminate against a friendly people who had become our wartime allies was unanswerable. When the new law was adopted by Congress in December, the public wholeheartedly upheld President Roosevelt's contention that the United States was big enough to recognize past mistakes and to correct them.

Even more significant than the abolition of extraterritoriality or the repeal of the exclusion laws was the further recognition of China's complete sovereignty implicit in the agreements reached at the Cairo Conference. Our policy of building up the authority and prestige of the National government as a means of strengthening the will of the Chinese people to continue the war had its most striking demonstration in this international acceptance of China, for the first time in all history, as a great power. Nothing could have more successfully dramatized her new place in the world than this meeting of Generalissimo Chiang Kai-shek with President Roosevelt and Prime Minister Churchill.

The agreement reached by these three statesmen, as announced on December 1, 1943, indicated an intention to return to political boundaries existing in eastern Asia a full half-century earlier. Japan was to be reduced to her status before the first Chinese-Japanese War in 1894; China was to be restored to a position that she had not held since her days of imperial glory. The United States, Great Britain and China declared it to be their purpose, in compelling the unconditional surrender of the enemy, that Japan should be stripped of the islands she had occupied in the Pacific and other conquests resulting from the war, and that "all the territories Japan had stolen from the Chinese, such as Manchuria, Formosa, and the Pescadores, shall be restored to the Republic of China."

The promise of Cairo was thus an entirely new division of power in which a free and independent China was to replace Japan as the leading nation in eastern Asia. It was made under the circumstances then prevailing in the Pacific war to reassure and encourage China as to allied peace aims, but it was based upon the fundamental conviction that a reconstituted China would eventually serve to stabilize political conditions in the Far East more effectively than any other possible development. Here was the best guarantee, it was believed, both for future peace and for further expansion of trade and commerce throughout the whole Pacific area.

Twenty years earlier, the Washington Conference had sought

to achieve a similar goal through adoption of a treaty guaranteeing Chinese sovereignty and the principle of trade equality. But it was built around compromises that tried to restrain rather than nullify Japanese imperialism, and that postponed rather than settled the issue of removing existing restrictions upon China's freedom of action. The Cairo Conference did not have to make any such concessions to either Japanese or western imperialism. Except for Hongkong, the United States and Great Britain had already agreed to surrender their special rights in China, and Japan was to be compelled to give up hers by force of arms.

Public opinion in the United States universally approved war aims which in pledging the creation of a strong, independent China so closely conformed with our traditional Far Eastern policy and thereby further promoted our own interests in eastern Asia. "We cannot half support China in her struggle for liberty," declared the *New York Times*, and other newspapers agreed with its conclusion that we could hardly do less than promise the return of her lost territories if we expected China to remain in the war.

The realization that Chinese armies—and the Chinese people—had withstood Japanese pressure for more than six years of continuing struggle, and through trading space for time had saved the United States from having to combat what would otherwise have been a far more powerful Japan, had by now given rise to unexampled admiration and sympathy for China. Our heightened feeling of friendship had, indeed, been vividly demonstrated earlier in the year by the fervent reception accorded Madame Chiang Kai-shek on a goodwill visit to the United States. Aided by her own sincerity of purpose, winning personality and gracious manner, this extraordinary and lovely woman had been hailed as the living symbol of a new and progressive China that had proved to be unconquerable for all the attacks of a ruthless and powerful military foe.

Madame Chiang Kai-shek had in the past had some very harsh things to say of the record of western imperialism in Asia and of the failure of the United States to come sooner to China's support against Japan. She was still critical of our policy of making Germany the number one enemy. But her primary purpose in 1943 was to win American allegiance to the National government and convince this country that it could count upon China to continue with her share in the war effort if given the aid and encouragement to which she was entitled. Madame Chiang was a guest at the White House. Her appearance before both the Senate and the House not only shattered all precedents (Queen Wilhelmina of Holland being the only other woman accorded such honors), but aroused tremendous enthusiasm. Among other public meetings, she addressed a great rally at New York's Madison Square Garden. Some 17,000 persons paid a warm tribute to her charm, her dignity and her flawless eloquence as she thanked all Americans "for what you have done and what you are doing."

There was a strongly sentimental flavor to the popular reaction to Madame Chiang Kai-shek's appeals. Americans were ready to accept on faith everything that was said about China's heroic war effort. Admiration for her people's refusal to give in to Japan stilled any possible questioning of the more recent course of developments in Chungking. Chinese unity and Chinese democracy were accepted uncritically under the spell of her magnetic personality. Even her gentle implication that the Allies might do more for China awoke a wide response. On the basis of public opinion polls, the public appeared to be swinging over to the belief that Japan rather than Germany was our principal enemy, and that China should consequently be afforded more direct support as part of a reinvigorated Pacific war.

Government officials felt obliged to assert that everything feasible was being done and that there was no idea of minimizing our responsibilities in Asia. "We intend to give China as much aid as can possibly be sent to her," Edward R. Stettinius, Jr., then administrator of Lend-Lease, declared. President Roosevelt reaffirmed our determination to uphold China's cause and prosecute the war against Japan with the utmost vigor.

Actual conditions in China, however, were quite different from the optimistic picture of them drawn by Madame Chiang Kai-shek. At the very time that she was speaking so eloquently of her country's role in the world struggle, and other Chinese spokesmen in the United States were almost equally persuasive in building up the prestige of the National government, various factors had combined to reduce China's war effort to the lowest level since 1937. The Chinese people had become increasingly weary and discouraged. They could not easily recover from their disillusionment over the failure of allied aid to materialize after Pearl Harbor. There was deep resentment at the decision to concentrate on the European war rather than the war against Japan. And in so far as military operations were concerned, Chungking newspapers demanded bitterly that more attention be paid to China's ideas on general strategy because of her vital role in Asia. Lend-Lease aid was said to have been needlessly diverted from the China-India-Burma theater, and air reinforcements delayed beyond all reason, because of American failure to understand China's needs.

While such perfectly natural discouragement, and understandable if not wholly justified resentments, seriously affected public morale, economic and political conditions were also a heavy drag upon the popular will to continue what so often seemed a hopeless struggle. Prices continued to skyrocket as commodities of all sorts became increasingly scarce, and this uncontrolled inflation led to a creeping paralysis in manufacturing and business activity. It fostered profiteering and speculation, and with these twin evils a wave of corruption spread through official circles. Energies that should have been directed toward national goals were dissipated in making money and protecting special privilege.

Far from becoming more democratic as envisaged by Sun Yat-sen, the National government had also fallen under increasingly conservative and even reactionary influences. The interests of the Chinese masses were often subordinated to those of the landlord class. Peasants and workers had no voice in government, and the country's intellectual leaders found themselves almost wholly deprived of political rights in the strict party dictatorship maintained by the Kuomintang. There was no real freedom of speech, and a rigid censorship was imposed upon both the Chinese press and all foreign correspondents.

Among other liberal Chinese, Dr. Sun Fo, the son of Sun Yat-sen, bore witness to these demoralizing conditions. "The number of our party members is less than one per cent of the total population of the country," he declared in frank discussion of the Kuomintang dictatorship. ". . . But we have come to regard ourselves as if we were the sovereign power in the state, entitled to the enjoyment of a special position and to suppress all criticism against us. The whole civilized world is fighting dictatorship and tyranny, which breed fascism and aggression. People of the whole world who stand for progress and the reign of law and order, both internally and externally, are pouring out their blood in a sacrifice to destroy these two pernicious evils. For these reasons we should revise our own psychological approach to internal problems and correct our own attitude of intolerance."

An even more immediate danger than such reactionary tendencies was the renewal of the old strife between the Nationalists and the Communists. The truce that had been made before the outbreak of war had almost entirely broken down. Although both groups were fighting Japan, there was no longer any cooperation between their forces. Charges and counter-charges flew back and forth between Chungking and the Communist capital at Yenan. Each claimed that the other was sabotaging the war, more concerned over building up its own political power than in fighting the common enemy. Generalissimo Chiang Kai-shek was accused of employing perhaps as many as 500,000 troops that might have been engaging Japanese forces in maintaining a blockade of the Communist-controlled areas.

Upon the conclusion of the 1937 truce, the Communists had at least temporarily set aside their revolutionary aims. Their immediate program became one of radical agrarian reform rather than Marxist socialism, and they received no direct support from Moscow. When foreign visitors were later allowed to penetrate the blockade maintained by the National government, they asserted that "Communist" was actually a misnomer for these Chinese whose primary concern was introducing land reform and democratic rule in the territory they controlled. Their government was said to be fully representative of all political groups, and able to command the wholehearted support of its adherents, while its guerrilla troops were credited with some of the most effective fighting of the entire war against Japan.

The Communists maintained that the Nationalists had broken the agreement which was to create a united front against Japan. They demanded the abolition of the Kuomintang dictatorship and the formation of a democratic government for all China in which they would have adequate representation. Until such a regime was fully assured, they refused to place their own armies under Chungking's control. The Nationalists insisted in turn that it was the Communists who had violated the commitments made in 1937. They charged that in refusing to obey the orders of the National government the Yenan regime was maintaining a state within a state in defiance of all established authority. The placing of all Communist armies under Chiang Kai-shek's command was asserted to be a necessary preliminary to any political accord.

The American public was largely ignorant of these developments and of the clashing views of Nationalists and Communists until a truer picture of conditions in China gradually emerged in 1944 from behind the veil of official censorship. There had been some earlier warnings that not all was well. In an article in *Life* in May 1943 Pearl Buck had drawn attention to Chungking's suppression of civil liberties and to the friction between Nationalists and Communists; Hanson W.

Baldwin, the military expert of the *New York Times*, wrote a critical article in the *Reader's Digest* under the title "Too Much Wishful Thinking About China"; and T. A. Bisson went so far in the *Far Eastern Survey* as to characterize the Nationalist regime as "feudal China" and the Communist-controlled area as "democratic China." These articles did not make very much impression on the American public, however, in the face of the great desire to believe the best of China and of her National government.

Official Washington also awoke very slowly to the situation. Nevertheless as early as 1942, Under Secretary Welles had intimated that the United States had a great interest in the maintenance of Chinese political solidarity, and there were suggestions at the time of the Cairo Conference that President Roosevelt had urged upon Generalissimo Chiang Kai-shek the importance of settling the dispute with the Communists. Without at any time withdrawing support from Chungking, the United States began to exercise an increasing pressure upon the National government to come to grips with the country's economic and political problems, and to take such steps as would recreate the united front so necessary for successful prosecution of the war.

A first direct move reflecting our heightened anxiety over developments in China was the visit of an American military mission to Yenan in July 1944. But even more important were the trips to Chungking that same summer of Vice President Wallace and Donald Nelson, Chairman of the War Production Board. It was clearly indicated by these two special emissaries that continuance of American Lend-Lease aid, and of such other assistance as we were able to extend to China, demanded full assurance that the National government was doing everything in its power to cope with both economic problems and internal political dissensions.

Vice President Wallace showed himself to be particularly concerned with the danger of civil war leading to friction between the National government and Soviet Russia, and a consequent cleavage in American and Russian policies, because of the sympathy Moscow might be expected to have for the Chinese Communists. The importance of a strong, unified China was repeatedly stressed in all his public comments, and he also emphasized the need for renewed assurances of future peace, both internal and foreign, if China was to obtain the postwar aid which she expected from the United States in modernizing her industries and building up her economic plant.

"Cognizance was taken of the cornerstone position of China in Asia and of the importance of China in any structure of peace in the Pacific area," declared a joint statement issued by Wallace and Chiang Kai-shek on June 25, 1944. "It was assumed as axiomatic that essential to such a peace structure would be continuation of the ties of friendship that have characterized Chinese-American relations for over a century, and the maintenance of relations on a basis of mutual understanding between China and Soviet Russia—China's nearest great neighbor—as well as between China and her other neighbors. No balance-of-power arrangement would serve the ends of peace."

Donald Nelson's visit was concerned with assisting China in the establishment of a Chinese War Production Board to provide for more effective utilization of her economic resources. He was accompanied by Major General Patrick Hurley, who sought to give comparable assistance along military lines in view of the possible landing of American troops in eastern China. There was no question, however, but that both these men also impressed upon Generalissimo Chiang Kai-shek the American view of the necessity of Chinese unity.

The interest of the public in this issue had by now been fully aroused, and a marked reaction developed from the somewhat sentimental ideas in regard to China which had been so prevalent during Madame Chiang Kai-shek's visit a year earlier. There appeared to be some danger, as Raymond Gram Swing said in a broadcast, of our basic sympathy for China being undermined by heated controversy over whether Nationalists or Communists were more deserving of our support. Swing urged the State Department to impress upon Chungking that China's future relationship with the United States depended upon the earliest possible extension of democracy, and in the meantime stanch resistance to extreme one-party despotism. An editorial in *Life* was more outspoken. Stating that a fascistic, repressive government would be all too likely to get in trouble with Russia, while one which stood for freedom, reform and international cooperation would not, it warned Chungking that the United States would have no sympathy for a regime which followed the former course. "Under no circumstances would the American people," *Life* declared, "ever wish to be embroiled with the Soviet Union in a struggle in which they would feel politically on the wrong side."

Possibly as a consequence of such mounting pressure from the United States as well as from inside China, negotiations were held intermittently during the summer of 1944 between the Nationalists and the Communists. But no real progress was made, and by September they had broken down. Soon thereafter the grave implications of this embittered tug-of-war in China's internal politics were dramatically stressed by the unexpected announcement that upon Generalissimo Chiang Kai-shek's request, General Stilwell had been recalled. The incident was cloaked in mystery. No official details were given out as to just what had happened, but it provided startling evidence that all was not well in Chinese-American relations.

Chiang Kai-shek had quite clearly stiffened in his opposition to our pressure for those measures which Washington held to be essential for the successful conduct of the war. There could be no other reason for insisting upon the withdrawal of a man who had served China so well and who was just bringing to completion the Ledo Road, with its promise of new communications between Chungking and the outside world. It was reliably reported that General Stilwell had demanded three things of Chiang Kai-shek in the name of his government:

thorough military reorganization with establishment of American command over all forces in China; control by the United States of the distribution of Lend-Lease aid; and the incorporation of the Chinese Communist armies in the National forces. The Generalissimo had refused to meet these demands and requested General Stilwell's recall because he pressed them so insistently. President Roosevelt complied rather than risk a complete break with the National government.

This incident, underscored by the almost simultaneous resignation of Ambassador Gauss, created an immediate sensation. There was widespread criticism, in the light of the recent revelations of Chungking's policies, of what was termed our surrender to the conservative interests within China and abandonment of the more liberal elements. The United States had thrown away what influence it might have exerted toward promoting national unity, it was said, and encouraged the Chungking reactionaries to postpone all internal reforms. It soon developed, however, that while President Roosevelt had been unwilling to force the issue, he remained deeply concerned over the attitude of Chiang Kai-shek. The pressure for reform was not relaxed. Our efforts to induce the Kuomintang to reconcile its differences with the Communists were by no means given up.

Major General Wedemeyer was appointed to take General Stilwell's place, and Major General Hurley became the new Ambassador to Chungking. Donald Nelson also returned to carry through his program for organizing the Chinese War Production Board. All three men continued to work for Chinese unity, and they clearly expressed themselves as considering it basic for carrying on the war and laying the foundations for peace. After a visit by the new Ambassador to Yenan, negotiations between the Nationalists and the Communists were renewed and Chungking also showed itself to be more responsive to our desires in other political developments. Internal shifts within the National government, eventually leading to the appointment of T. V. Soong first as acting and then as permanent President of the Executive Yuan, and a certain measure of military reorganization were interpreted as at least pointing toward the reforms upon which the United States had been insisting. Ambassador Hurley declared that these moves were responsible "for putting the National government, the United States military mission and this embassy in one team."

In spite of these developments Under Secretary of State Grew did not hesitate to express again the grave apprehension of the United States over the situation and its hope for a Kuomintang-Communist agreement. "We earnestly desire the development of a strong and united China," he told correspondents on January 23, 1945. "To that end this government has been lending its best efforts to be of service in appropriate ways, such as through the exercise of friendly good offices when requested by the Chinese, through direct military assistance in the prosecution of the war against Japan, and through assisting China's economy to survive the strain of war."

There was, indeed, no question but that our entire political policy, as well as military strategy, was firmly predicated, as had so often been declared, upon the creation of a strong China. We had done everything possible to sustain her international prestige, welcoming her at Cairo as a great power even though both her military and industrial resources hardly gave her such a status. It was clearly to our national interest, from the point of view of both future peace and future trade in eastern Asia, that China should be strengthened and sustained. But the basic issue remained: what kind of China?

Could the United States afford to back up the National government to the extent of supporting it in possible civil war against the Communists? Should it disregard Chungking in insisting that the Communists deserved American aid and assistance because they too were fighting Japan? We were so deeply involved in the Chinese situation that whatever we did, it could not fail to affect directly, and perhaps decisively, the course of future developments. There could be no question of withdrawing. The United States was caught on the horns of as difficult a dilemma as it had ever faced in the long history of its relations with China.

In reporting a conversation with Roosevelt soon after the Yalta Conference in February 1945, Edgar Snow wrote that the President was very much disturbed over the entire situation and unwilling to back up the Nationalists to the extent of depriving the Communists of all aid. "I've been working with two governments there," Snow reported Roosevelt as saying, "and I intend to go on doing so until we can get them together."

Our policy of cooperating with Chungking and yet trying to induce it to come to terms with Yenan nevertheless leaned more and more toward outright support of the Nationalists in the following months. Ambassador Hurley, who had at first made a gesture of trying to bring the two parties into some agreement, stated in April that all American aid for China was being given to the National government and none whatsoever to the Communists. Moreover, this return to a more completely pro-Chungking policy was reflected in the attitude of the Nationalists themselves. American cooperation, Generalissimo Chiang Kai-shek was quoted as saying in July 1945, was more satisfactory than at any time in the diplomatic history of the two countries.

Criticism of our apparent willingness to back up Chungking, whatever its attitude toward the Communists, now flared up once again and liberals renewed their vigorous attacks upon what they interpreted as a reversal of the Stilwell-Gauss policy of insisting upon national unity in favor of Ambassador Hurley's completely pro-Nationalist tactics. They declared that we could not afford to ignore the rights of any group fighting Japan, and that the Communists were entitled to our assistance. Even so conservative a newspaper as the *New York Herald Tribune* proposed that no matter what the National government might say, United States troops should be sent into the Communist-controlled areas to strengthen still further their resistance to Japan. It was reiterated that the Communists were maintaining a far more democratic regime than the Nationalists, and that if we continued to support a reactionary Chungking, we might find ourselves in an impossible situation should civil warfare actually break out. Without suggesting that we sever relations with the National government, critics of our policy strongly urged that we also cooperate actively with Yenan. Our role in China was so important, according to this thesis, that it had to be one of impartiality rather than exclusive support for any single faction in Chinese political life.

The war was rushing toward its dramatic climax while these uncertainties in regard both to China's internal situation and our possible role in the event of a direct clash between Nationalists and Communists troubled the Far Eastern scene in the summer of 1945. Had military strategy called for American landings in China, a crisis might possibly have been precipitated. But the problem was to be postponed for peacetime rather than wartime solution when Japan suddenly and unexpectedly surrendered to allied arms.

The abrupt end to hostilities was the result of a combination of factors in which the atomic bomb played the most spectacular but not the only part. The combined sea and air blockade had steadily weakened Japanese powers of resistance as the constant threat of invasion hung over the almost prostrate country, and Russia's entry into the war finally destroyed whatever lingering hopes the Japanese leaders may have had of allied disunity. The victory was complete even though it had been consummated without the expected land operations in either China or Japan itself. Whether it would also pave the way for settlement of the problems inherent in the potentially dangerous situation still existing in China remained to be answered.

XVIII

CHINA AND THE PEACE

JAPAN'S surrender for a time gave every sign of bringing the deepening conflict between Chinese Nationalists and Communists to a head. The sudden removal of the war's pressure for unity at once intensified factional rivalry. Both Nationalists and Communists sought to strengthen their political and military positions through their own troops' reoccupation of Japanese-held territory and seizure of the arms and ammunition of the defeated enemy. China knew neither peace nor war. If immediate fears of a large-scale outbreak of hostilities were not realized, neither were immediate hopes of an end to internal dissensions. The situation was both confused and fast-changing. While the United States steadfastly maintained its policy of dealing only with the National government, its role in China's domestic affairs became one of increasing difficulty.

One highly favorable development, however, took place simultaneously with the end of the war against Japan. China and Soviet Russia concluded an "alliance of good neighborliness." While Moscow had remained scrupulously correct throughout the war in maintaining relations only with Chungking, and did not extend any assistance to the Chinese Communists, the possibility could not be wholly ignored that in pursuit of her own aims in eastern Asia, Russia might decide to support the Yenan regime in a postwar struggle for political power within China. A move bringing Russian and American policy toward China in closer alignment in support of the National government was consequently of immense importance in relieving immediate fears of new international crises in eastern Asia.

The terms of the Chinese-Russian treaty and its supplementary agreements, to remain in force for thirty years, were not announced until twelve days after they had been signed; that is, on August 26, 1945. It was then revealed that China had granted Russia joint ownership and operation of the Manchurian railways in which she had formerly had an interest, established Port Arthur as a joint naval base and opened Dairen as a free port. In return, the Soviet Union fully recognized Chinese sovereignty in Manchuria, pledged itself not to interfere in China's internal affairs and declared that whatever support or material assistance it gave China would be "given fully to the National government as the central government of China." The concessions China had made were important and far-reaching. They did not, however, involve the sacrifice of sovereignty (except possibly in an undertaking to recognize the independence of Outer Mongolia) which had characterized those exacted by either Czarist Russia or Imperial Japan in earlier periods. The treaty as a whole was a further guarantee of China's political and territorial integrity.*

Reaffirmation by both the United States and Soviet Russia of their support for the National government did not in either case solve the problem of how far such support would be carried in the event civil war should break out with the Chinese Communists. Only if such strife were somehow averted could there be any surety of escaping future international complications. While the United States was fully prepared to carry out its wartime commitments to aid the National government in taking over the territory formerly controlled by the Japanese, it consequently undertook once again to use its influence in behalf of a friendly agreement between Chungking and Yenan for the restoration of Chinese unity. Ambassador Hurley urged Chiang Kai-shek to send repeated invitations to the Communist Mao Tse-tung to come to Chungking for direct personal talks, and he flew to Yenan, on Mao's invitation

* The concessions involved in this treaty were pledged to Soviet Russia, as subsequently revealed on February 11, 1946, by the Yalta accord concluded by President Roosevelt, Prime Minister Churchill and Marshal Stalin on February 11, 1945.

and with the full approval of the Generalissimo, to promote the Communists' acceptance of the National government's proposal.

"I am happy to be returning to Yenan," Hurley announced on August 27. "We have worked continually for more than a year to help the Nationalist government remove the possibility of civil war in China. In this controversy there have been so many conflicting elements that it is a source of gratification to us that we have been able to maintain the respect and confidence of leaders of both parties."

Both the stand previously taken by Ambassador Hurley and later developments cast more than a little doubt on the extent to which he had the confidence of the Communists. For a time, however, the negotiations he finally succeeded in initiating seemed to hold out greater promise of success than any previously held. By early October, the parties had reached what could at least be described as "an agreement to agree." Nationalists and Communists promised to submit their differences to a Political Consultative Council under the chairmanship of Chiang Kai-shek. It was to be composed, according to announcement from Chungking, of representatives from the Kuomintang, the Communists and other groups in Chinese political life, and its decisions were to be made binding. Both Nationalist and Communist leaders reiterated their desire to avoid civil strife, and to achieve under the aegis of Chiang Kai-shek the national unity which had so long evaded them.

Chiang Kai-shek also revealed a more conciliatory attitude toward other phases of China's internal problems. On September 3, he definitely stated his intention to institute the domestic reforms for which the United States had been so long pressing in order to give China's government a more democratic character. He pledged himself to legalize all political parties within the country, to convoke the national assembly in order to set up a constitutional regime patterned more nearly after those of the United States and Great Britain, and to remove all restrictions on free speech and freedom of person. Economic reforms, relating both to land tenure and industrial monopolies, were further promised as Chiang called upon his countrymen to make China "a model democratic state in the Far East."

The promise of these encouraging moves toward peace and unity was not at once borne out by events. Negotiations dragged on at Chungking, but both Nationalists and Communists showed themselves to be far more concerned over establishing themselves in former Japanese-occupied territory than in reaching an accord. As each faction jockeyed for position, both military and political, fighting broke out on a score of fronts, there was a mad scramble between opposing forces to win strategic control of Manchuria, and by late October civil war was again threatened on a broad scale.

The United States found itself in a highly ambiguous position. Although Ambassador Hurley had promoted the negotiations between Nationalists and Communists, he now appeared to revert to the attitude that he had assumed in the closing days of the war. Unqualified aid for Chungking replaced mediation in support of national unity. In carrying out our pledge to aid in disarming the Japanese, American troops played an increasingly important role in protecting communications and railways for the Nationalists, in providing them sea and air transportation and in seeing to it by every means short of active hostilities that enemy-held territory was surrendered to them rather than to the Communists.

The cry was at once raised that the United States was directly intervening in China's internal affairs and that instead of using our influence in behalf of peace, we were encouraging Chiang Kai-shek in his efforts to suppress the Communists by force. Hurley was roundly criticized by liberals for following a policy which he himself was said to have described as "pulling the rug out from under the Communists," rather than holding Chiang Kai-shek to fulfillment of his own democratic pledges. While the American people as a whole hardly understood the issues at stake, the spectacle of our military forces apparently taking sides in an incipient civil war, through support of a regime which was notoriously anti-democratic, aroused growing dissatisfaction.

What was the real American policy? In previous periods of internal strife in China, we had always upheld the existing government or supported the more conservative faction in order to promote the stability that we felt would best safeguard our own trade and investments. The United States had favored the Imperial Government rather than the Taipings in the middle of the nineteenth century, withheld recognition from the Republic proclaimed in 1912 until the complete collapse of the Manchu dynasty left us no alternative, and in the 1920's hesitated long before entering into relations with the Nationalists. Were we once again trying to back up a highly conservative government with which we thought we could most advantageously do business and using our influence to block the advance of the more progressive forces in Chinese life? No one seemed to know the answer, nor was such confusion in any way lightened when Ambassador Hurley, who had returned to this country, suddenly resigned, charging that not he but certain members of the State Department were seeking to undermine the basic principles which had been adopted to govern our attitude in China.

This dramatic move, and the subsequent hearing before the Senate Foreign Relations Committee in which the Ambassador's charges were refuted by Secretary Byrnes, had more important repercussions than the airing of an intradepartmental squabble. President Truman at last acted vigorously to clarify the situation. Having appointed General George C. Marshall as a special envoy to China immediately upon Hurley's resignation, he issued, on December 15, a clear-cut statement of just what constituted our Chinese policy.

There was nothing new in this statement. The President reaffirmed our belief in the importance for the peace of the world, and specifically for the success of the United Nations Organization, of the creation of a strong, united and democratic China. He declared it to be the determination of the United States not to intervene in China's internal affairs and to continue to recognize the National government with which it had been allied throughout the war. But with greater precision than the American government had ever before used, he bluntly stated that the United States believed it to be essential that a cessation of hostilities be arranged between the armies of the National government and the Chinese Communists, and that a national conference of representatives of the major political parties be held to solve the problem of internal strife and bring about national unification. Nor did President Truman hesitate to characterize the Chungking regime as a "one-party government" and clearly to imply that unless China moved toward peace and unity by broadening the basis of representation, she had no warrant to count upon our aid in her political and economic reconstruction.

Some two weeks later, this policy received added confirmation in new evidence of the underlying unity in the views of the United States and Soviet Russia, as well as Great Britain, growing out of the Moscow conference of their foreign ministers. For in a final communique on the results of this meeting, the foreign ministers declared themselves to be in full agreement on the need for a unified and democratic China under the National government, restated their policy of noninterference in China's internal affairs and emphasized the desirability of withdrawing all foreign troops in China as soon as they had fulfilled their obligations in assisting the Chinese to disarm and evacuate Japanese forces.

How successfully General Marshall could implement American policy, and what its effect might be upon the internal situation in China, were vital questions at the opening of 1946. The position of the National government had been greatly strengthened through the successful reoccupation of the greater part of north China and Manchuria by its military forces. Even though the Communists still controlled large areas of the country, they were not in so strong a position to challenge Chungking as they had perhaps hoped to be on conclusion of the war. They could still block complete Chinese unity, as they had for almost two decades, but the prestige and power of the National government were unquestionably enhanced as a result of postwar developments. Retention of its newly won power nevertheless remained dependent, in the view of most observers, on its success in maintaining the allegiance of the Chinese masses. And not only the Communists but other democratic elements, both within and without the Kuomintang, were insistently demanding a broadening of the bases of government and an end to one-party rule. This more general phase of the Chinese problem was, indeed, far more important than was generally realized because of the highly dramatic aspects of the open strife between Nationalists and Communists.

Could the democratic forces within China prevail over the reactionary tendencies of the Kuomintang? It had now been made clear, this time it was hoped beyond dispute, that continued American support for the National government was definitely predicated upon its undertaking to stabilize a situation that concerned not only China but the peace of all eastern Asia. Our insistence upon measures that would actually lead to the creation of a more liberal government, commanding nationwide popular support, might be expected to convince Chiang Kai-shek that he could retain American friendship only by reasonable concessions to the political parties opposing the Kuomintang, and also to encourage such parties, including the Communists, to believe that they could win the right to participate in government without a resort to force. On such grounds, there was new hope that China might actually achieve stability.

Further developments appeared to substantiate these hopes. By mid-January a truce had been concluded between Nationalists and Communists through the mediation of General Marshall, and the projected Political Consultative Council began its deliberations with China enjoying at least temporary peace

for the first time in several decades. At the close of the
month, it was possible for Chungking to announce that an
agreement had been reached to form a coalition government
which was to remain in office until the adoption of a new
democratic constitution.

Whatever the immediate course of events in eastern Asia,
the end of the Pacific war had basic consequences of immense
significance when set against the background of the whole
history of Chinese-American relations and the general evolution of Far Eastern politics. China had attained a new international status. The abandonment of extraterritorial rights
by the United States and Great Britain, the unreserved recognition of Chinese sovereignty by Soviet Russia, and Japan's
forced relinquishment of the special privileges once enjoyed
in Manchuria and Shantung, as well as of all territories seized
by war, were progressive steps toward complete freedom and
independence. It was true that England still retained her
colony at Hongkong, but otherwise China had finally shaken
off the last vestiges of the foreign control to which she had
been subjected throughout the nineteenth century. Moreover,
as the Cairo conference had first demonstrated, the West
was prepared to act upon the principle that China was a
great power. She was recognized as one of the Big Five in
world affairs, and on such a basis attended the various con-
ferences which set up the United Nations Organization and
prepared to negotiate the future peace treaties. President
Truman's statement as to the American belief that a strong,
united and democratic China was essential for the success of
the UNO was in itself a striking demonstration of how her
potential role in international affairs was being viewed.

None of this meant weakening of the old ties between China
and America. On the contrary, what was happening was the
final realization of the traditional objectives of our Far Eastern
policy in the full establishment of China's political and territorial integrity. In the future as in the past, our interest would

be in helping China to sustain her independence, and China could be expected to look to the United States for a continuation of American support. Moreover, there was little question that in matters of more general policy, involving the maintenance of international peace, the United States and China retained a common viewpoint. Their interests were alike in seeking to encourage the development of a peaceful Japan; in maintaining full understanding with Soviet Russia; and in strengthening the bonds of international friendship throughout the Pacific as the best way to uphold their own national security.

It still remained true that for China to realize her potentialities as a force for peace and order in eastern Asia she needed extensive foreign aid in developing her economic resources and building up her national industries. If the first requisites for the development of a strong China were internal peace and basic economic reform, help from abroad was also essential.

This situation, too, conformed to the pattern of our earlier relations. Once again China's need appeared to be America's opportunity. As China succeeded in carrying forward a program of modernization and industrialization in her internal economy, she would be opening up new horizons for American trade and investment. Her great market had not lost the hold it had traditionally exercised upon popular imagination. It was perhaps more clearly realized than ever before that the economic backwardness which had so long restrained her industrial progress would have to be overcome, and that the standard of living of her people would have to be materially raised if her economic potentialities were to be translated into realities, but still the old dream persisted of our own expansive opportunities in helping China to help herself.

Donald Nelson had reaffirmed this century-old view of America's role in eastern Asia upon returning to this country after his visit to Chungking in November 1944. In his report to President Roosevelt at that time, he optimistically forecast the future expansion of our Far Eastern trade in terms reminiscent of the prophecies of the nineteenth century.

"The success of China's venture in planned war production," Nelson wrote, "if properly followed up by the American government and business channels, will make for close postwar economic relations between China and the United States. China has the capacity and the desire to develop herself industrially with American aid. If that aid is realistically planned, and if financial arrangements are put on a sound business basis, China should soon after the war begin to replace Japan as the leading industrial nation of the Orient. In that event, a market of enormous size should progressively open up for American export industries. I believe, too, that with American guidance China's development can be turned into peaceful and democratic channels, eliminating much of the fear of war which has for so long shaped the political attitudes in the Orient and the South Pacific."

Vice President Wallace also envisaged the emergence of China in the postwar world both as the leading power in eastern Asia and as a tremendous market for American goods. Stating that our trade with the Far East had risen progressively until that area provided some 30 per cent of our total imports, and accounted for approximately 15 per cent of our total exports, he foresaw a future commerce valued in several billion dollars. Both to strengthen the security of the Pacific world and to promote this trade, Wallace called for an American policy that would help to sustain the full independence of China and other nations in eastern Asia, avoid interference in the internal affairs of such countries and fully cooperate with them "in minding the world community's common business." Echoing the words of William H. Seward almost a hundred years earlier, and of Senator Beveridge at the opening of the present century, he expressed the conviction that the world was "entering what might be called 'The Era of the Pacific.'"

The vision of a China freed of foreign domination, drawn

together in a new spirit of unity and progressing toward a fuller realization of Sun Yat-sen's Three Principles of Nationalism, Democracy and the People's Livelihood, also awoke an American interest and sympathy which went deeper than matters of trade and commerce. Those idealistic elements in the historic friendship between the two nations which had grown out of the role of American missionaries and educators in helping China to align herself with the advanced technology and progressive thought of western civilization were reinforced by the consequences of the common victory over Japan. The very difficulties in which we found ourselves enmeshed in trying to carry out our policy in the immediate aftermath of war helped to create a new sense of responsibility as to our national role in China.

Even though there undoubtedly would be grave difficulties in the future, and disappointments might be expected as China struggled to work out her domestic problems, any long-term view of policy in eastern Asia thus clearly demanded that the United States continue to act in close collaboration with China. Moreover, the record of the past, in spite of occasions when we had taken advantage of China's helplessness in insisting upon special rights and privileges, provided a solid foundation for carrying forward such a program. The common interests of the two nations, as history had clearly demonstrated, were a compelling reason for strengthening still further the bonds of what, despite all vicissitudes, had proved to be an enduring friendship.

BIBLIOGRAPHY

Abend, Hallet, *Treaty Ports*, New York, 1944.
Alden, C. S., *Lawrence Kearny*, Princeton, 1936.
Alsop, Joseph, and Robert Kintner, *American White Paper*, New York, 1940.

Bailey, Thomas A., *A Diplomatic History of the American People*, New York, 1940.
Baker, R. S., *Woodrow Wilson and World Settlement*, 3 vols., Garden City, 1922.
Barnes, Joseph, (and others), *Empire in the East*, New York, 1934.
Bau, M. J., *The Open Door Doctrine*, New York, 1923.
Beard, Charles A., *The Idea of National Interest*, New York, 1934.
Bemis, S. F., *The American Secretaries of State and Their Diplomacy*, 10 vols., New York, 1927-29.
———, *A Diplomatic History of the United States*, New York, 1936.
Biggerstaff, Knight, "The Official Chinese Attitude Toward the Burlingame Mission," *American Historical Review*, XLI, 1936.
Bisson, T. A., *America's Far Eastern Policy*, New York, 1945.
Buell, Raymond L., *The Washington Conference*, New York, 1922.

Cahill, Holger, *A Yankee Adventurer*, New York, 1930.
Cameron, Meribeth E., "American Recognition Policy Toward the Republic of China, 1912-1913," *Pacific Historical Review*, II, 1933.
Carnegie Endowment for International Peace, *Treaties and Agreements with and Concerning China, 1919-1929*, Washington, 1929.
Christy, Arthur E., *The Asian Legacy and American Life*, New York, 1945.
———, *The Orient in American Transcendentalism*, New York, 1932.
Clark, Arthur H., *The Clipper Ship Era*, New York, 1910.
Clark, Grover, *Economic Rivalries in China*, New Haven, 1932.
———, *The Great Wall Crumbles*, New York, 1935.
Cleland, R. G., "Asiatic Trade and the American Occupation of the Pacific Coast," *American Historical Association Reports*, 1, 1914.
Clement, P. H., *The Boxer Rebellion*, New York, 1915.
Clyde, P. H., "The Open Door Policy of John Hay," *Historical Outlook*, XXII, 1931.
———, *United States Policy Toward China*, Durham, N.C., 1940.
Conant, Charles A., *The United States in the Orient*, Boston, 1901.
Coolidge, M. R., *Chinese Immigration*, New York, 1909.
Council on Foreign Relations, *Survey of American Foreign Relations*, 4 vols., New Haven, 1928-1931.
———, *The United States in World Affairs*, 10 vols., New York, 1932-1942.
Croly, Herbert, *Willard Straight*, New York, 1924.

Dennett, Tyler, *Americans in Eastern Asia*, New York, 1922.
———, *John Hay*, New York, 1933.

BIBLIOGRAPHY

Dennett, Tyler, "The Open Door Policy as Intervention," *American Academy of Political and Social Science Annals*, CLXVIII, 1933.

———, *Roosevelt and the Russo-Japanese War*, New York, 1925.

———, "Seward's Far Eastern Policy," *American Historical Review*, XXVIII, 1932.

Dennis, A. L. P., *Adventures in American Diplomacy, 1896-1906*, New York, 1928.

Dodsworth, W., *Our Industrial Position and Our Policy in the Orient*, New York, 1898.

Dulles, Foster Rhea, *America in the Pacific*, Boston, 1932.

———, *Forty Years of American-Japanese Relations*, New York, 1937.

———, *The Old China Trade*, Boston, 1930.

Etherton, Percy T., *The Crisis in China*, Boston, 1927.

Farley, Miriam S., *America's Stake in the Far East*, Institute of Pacific Relations, New York, 1936.

Field, F. V., *American Participation in the China Consortiums*, Chicago, 1931.

———, (editor), *Handbook of the Pacific Area*, Garden City, 1934.

Finch, G. A., "American Diplomacy and the Financing of China," *American Journal of International Law*, XVI, 1922.

Forbes, Robert B., *Remarks on China and the China Trade*, Boston, 1844.

Forman, H., *Report from Red China*, New York, 1945.

Foster, John W., *American Diplomacy in the Orient*, New York, 1903.

Fuess, Claude M., *The Life of Caleb Cushing*, 2 vols., New York, 1923.

Garis, Roy I., *Immigration Restriction*, New York, 1927.

Grew, Joseph C., *Ten Years in Japan*, New York, 1944.

Griffin, Eldon, *Clippers and Consuls*, Ann Arbor, 1938.

Griswold, A. Whitney, *The Far Eastern Policy of the United States*, New York, 1938.

Hail, William J., *Tseng Kuo-fan and the Taiping Rebellion*, New Haven, 1927.

Hinton, H. B., *Cordell Hull*, New York, 1942.

Holcombe, Arthur N., *The Chinese Revolution*, Cambridge, 1930.

Hornbeck, Stanley K., *Contemporary Politics in the Far East*, New York, 1916.

———, *Principles of American Policy in Relation to the Far East*, Washington, 1934.

———, *United States and the Far East*, Boston, 1942.

Howard, H. P., *America's Role in Asia*, New York, 1943.

Howland, C. P., *see* Council on Foreign Relations.

Hunter, William C., *The 'Fan Kwae' at Canton*, London, 1882.

Ichihashi, Yamato, *The Washington Conference and After*, Stanford, 1928.

Institute of Pacific Relations, *Our Far Eastern Record*, 2 pamphlets, New York, 1940, 1942.

BIBLIOGRAPHY

Jessup, Philip C., *Elihu Root*, 2 vols., New York, 1938.
Johnstone, William C., *The Shanghai Problem*, Stanford, 1937.
——, *The United States and Japan's New Order*, New York, 1941.

Kennan, George, E. H. *Harriman's Far Eastern Policy*, New York, 1917.
Kuo, P. C., "Caleb Cushing and the Treaty of Wanghia, 1844," *Journal of Modern History*, v, 1933.

La Fargue, T. E., *China and the World War*, Stanford, 1937.
——, *China's First Hundred*, Pullman, 1943.
Lansing, Robert, *War Memoirs*, Indianapolis, 1935.
Latourette, K. S., *A History of Christian Missions in China*, New York, 1929.
——, "The History of Early Relations Between the United States and China, 1784-1844," *Transactions of the Connecticut Academy of Arts and Sciences*, xxviii, 1927.
Lattimore, Owen, *Solution in Asia*, Boston, 1945.
Lattimore, Owen and Eleanor, *The Making of Modern China*, New York, 1944.
League of Nations, *Report on the Commission of Enquiry*, Document C. 663. M 320, 1932, vii, Geneva, 1932.
Lippmann, Walter, *U.S. Foreign Policy*, Boston, 1943.
——, *U.S. War Aims*, Boston, 1944.

McKenzie, R. D., *Oriental Exclusion*, New York, 1927.
MacMurray, J. V. A., *Treaties and Agreements with and Concerning China, 1894-1919*, 2 vols., New York, 1921.
Mahan, A. T., *The Problem of Asia*, Boston, 1900.
Masland, John W., "Missionary Influence upon American Far Eastern Policy," *Pacific Historical Review*, x, 1941.
Miller, D. H., *The Drafting of the Covenant*, 2 vols., New York, 1928.
Morison, Samuel Eliot, *Maritime History of Massachusetts*, Boston, 1925.
Morse, H. B., and H. F. McNair, *Far Eastern International Relations*, Boston, 1931.

National Foreign Trade Council, *American Trade Prospects in the Orient*, New York, 1935.
Norton, H. K., *China and the Powers*, New York, 1927.

Paullin, C. O., "Early Voyages of American Naval Vessels to the Orient," *Proceedings of the United States Naval Institute*, xxxvi, Annapolis, 1910.
Peffer, Nathaniel, *Basis for Peace in the Far East*, New York, 1942.
——, *China: the Collapse of a Civilization*, New York, 1930.
——, *Must We Fight In Asia?* New York, 1935.
Pettigrew, R. F., *The Course of Empire*, New York, 1920.
Pollard, R. T., *China's Foreign Relations, 1917-31*, New York, 1933.
Pratt, J. W., *Expansionists of 1898*, Baltimore, 1936.
Pringle, Henry F., *Theodore Roosevelt*, New York, 1931.

BIBLIOGRAPHY

Quigley, H. S., *Chinese Politics and the Foreign Powers*, New York, 1927.
——, *Far Eastern War, 1937-41*, Boston, 1942.
Quigley, H. S., and J. H. Blakeslee, *The Far East*, Boston, 1938.

Reid, J. G., *The Manchu Abdication and the Powers, 1908-1912*, Berkeley, 1935.
Reid, Whitelaw, *Problems of Expansion*, New York, 1900.
Reinsch, Paul S., *An American Diplomat in China*, New York, 1922.
Remer, C. F., *Foreign Investments in China*, New York, 1933.
Roosevelt, F. D., *Public Papers and Addresses*, 9 vols., New York, 1938-1941.
Rosinger, Lawrence K., *China's Crisis*, New York, 1945.
——, *China's Wartime Politics*, Princeton, 1944.
Rowe, D. N., *China Among the Powers*, New York, 1945.

Scroggs, W. O., *see* Council on Foreign Relations.
Seward, F. W., *Seward at Washington as Senator and Secretary of State*, New York, 1891.
Seymour, Charles, *The Intimate Papers of Colonel House*, 4 vols., Boston, 1926-1928.
Shaw, Major Samuel, *The Journals of, edited and with a Life of the Author by Josiah Quincy*, Boston, 1847.
Simonds, F. H., *American Foreign Policy in the Postwar Years*, Baltimore, 1935.
Smith, Robert Aura, *Our Future in Asia*, New York, 1940.
Snow, Edgar, *People on Our Side*, New York, 1945.
——, *Red Star Over China*, New York, 1938.
Steiger, G. N., *China and the Occident*, New Haven, 1927.
Stimson, Henry L., *The Far Eastern Crisis*, New York, 1936.
Sullivan, Mark, *The Great Adventure at Washington*, New York, 1922.
——, *Our Times: the Turn of the Century*, New York, 1926.

Taylor, George E., *America in the New Pacific*, New York, 1942.
Tupper, E. and G. E. McReynolds, *Japan in American Public Opinion*, New York, 1937.

United States, *Congressional Record*, 55th Congress, 3rd Session; 67th Congress, 1st Session; 74th Congress, 1st Session.
United States, Department of State, *Bulletin*, 1939-1945.
United States, Department of State, *Japan, 1931-1941*, 2 vols., Washington, 1943.
United States, Department of State, *Papers Relating to the Foreign Relations of the United States*, Washington, 1861–.
United States, Department of State, *Peace and War. United States Foreign Policy, 1931-1941*, Washington, 1942.
United States, Department of State, *Press Releases*, 1929-1939.
United States, *House Executive Document*, 33rd Congress, 1st Session, Number 123 (Marshall correspondence).

BIBLIOGRAPHY

United States, *Senate Executive Documents*:

28th Congress, 2nd Session, Numbers 58, 67, and 138 (Cushing correspondence);

35th Congress, 2nd Session, Number 22 (McLane and Parker correspondence);

36th Congress, 1st Session, Number 30 (Reed and Ward correspondence);

50th Congress, 1st Session, Number 273 (Treaty of 1888);

57th Congress, 1st Session, Number 67 (Rockhill correspondence);

67th Congress, 1st Session, Number 126 (Conference on Limitation of Armaments);

72nd Congress, 1st Session, Number 55 (Conditions in Manchuria).

Van Dorn, Archer, *Twenty Years of the Chinese Republic*, New York, 1932.

Viton, Albert, *American Empire in Asia?*, New York, 1943.

Wallace, Henry A., *Our Job in the Pacific*, New York, 1944.

Whyte, Sir Frederick, *China and the Foreign Powers*, London, 1928.

Wilbur, R. L., and A. M. Hyde, *The Hoover Policies*, New York, 1937.

Williams, E. T., *China: Yesterday and Today*, New York, 1923.

Williams, F. W., *Anson Burlingame*, New York, 1912.

Williams, S. Wells, "Establishment of American Trade at Canton," *China Review*, v, 1876.

———, *The Middle Kingdom*, 2 vols., New York, 1901.

Willoughby, W. W., *China at the Conference*, Baltimore, 1922.

———, *Foreign Rights and Interests in China*, 2 vols., Boston, 1927.

———, *The Sino-Japanese Controversy and the League of Nations*, Baltimore, 1935.

Wood, W. W., *Sketches of China*, Philadelphia, 1830.

World Peace Foundation, *Documents on American Foreign Relations, 1938-1944*, 6 vols., Boston, 1939-1945.

Yen, En-tsung, *The Open Door Policy*, Boston, 1923.

Young, C. W., *The International Relations of Manchuria*, Chicago, 1929.

INDEX

INDEX

East India Company, 14, 15, 19, 21
Education, American support for in China, 182-83
Eliot, Captain Charles, 20
Embargo, on shipments to Japan, proposed during Manchurian incident, 194, 197; rejected by Secretary Hull, 202; popular attitude toward between 1937-1941, 208-09, 210, 212-20 *passim*, 223; adopted, 227-28
Emerson, Ralph Waldo, quoted, 40
Emily, 14, 15
Empress of China, 1-3, 36
Ever Victorious Army, 61, 64
Experiment, 3, 6-7
Extraterritoriality, established by Treaty of Wanghia, 30-31; in Shanghai, 48, 54-55; expanded, 96; and League of Nations, 149; at Washington Conference, 158-60; movement for abolition of, 163-70, 174-76; abolition of, 224-25, 230, 236-37, 239, 258

Feng Yu-hsiang, 181
Fifteen Passenger Bill, 86, 88
Five Power Treaty, 154, 204
Floyd, Representative John, 33
"Flying Tigers," 235
Forbes, John M., 35
Forbes, Robert B., 22
Formosa, 57, 98, 238
Fortune, quoted, 229
Foster, John W., 92n
Four Power Treaty, 154-55, 158
France, in war against China (1858), 57-62 *passim*, and cooperative policy, 66; in Boxer Rebellion, 118; encroachments upon China, 97-98, 99, 101; joins consortium, 132, 185; at Washington Conference, 154; protests Nanking incident, 171; and Manchurian incident, 196; in Second World War, 215, 217, 218
Fukien, 121

Garfield, President, 87, 88
Gauss, Ambassador, 247, 249
Germany, seizes Chinese territory, 98; and Philippine Islands, 104; policy toward Open Door, 107; joins consortium, 132; loses Shantung, 140; surrenders extraterritoriality, 164; and Second World War, 205, 210, 215, 217, 232, 240
Gordon, Major Charles G., 61
Grand Turk, 3, 7
Grant, President, 97
Gray, Captain Robert, 8, 9, 10
Great Britain, early trade at Canton, 5; embassy to Peking, 13; and Opium War, 18-24 *passim*, 45; signs Treaty of Nanking, 20-21, 29; and Anglo-French war, 57-62 *passim*; seizes Chinese territory, 97, 99, 101; accepts Open Door policy, 111; role during Boxer Rebellion, 118; joins consortium, 132, 185; and Washington Conference, 152, 154, 161; protests Nanking incident, 171; and Manchurian incident, 195, 196, 199; and Second World War, 215, 217, 228; surrenders extraterritoriality, 231, 239; postwar policy toward China, 256
Green, Captain John, 1, 2
Grew, Joseph C., reports from Tokyo, 204, 218, 225, 229; on American policy toward Japan, 214-15; on situation in China, 248
Guadalcanal, 233
Guam, 155, 161, 228

Hanna, Mark, 103
Harding, President, 150, 153
Harriman, E. H., 130
Harrison, President, 92
Harte, Bret, quoted, 84
Hawaiian Islands, 10, 63, 102, 228
Hawthorne, Nathaniel, 40
Hay, John, proposes Open Door policy, 107-13, 121-22, 124; policy during Boxer Rebellion, 115-16,

INDEX